CRACKING CREATIVITY

THE SECRETS OF CREATIVE GENIUS

CRACKING CREATIVITY
THE SECRETS OF CREATIVE GENIUS

Michael Michalko

Ten Speed Press
Berkeley, California

Ten Speed Press
P.O. Box 7123
Berkeley, California 94707
www.tenspeed.com

Distributed in Australia by Simon and Schuster Australia, in Canada by Ten Speed Press Canada, in New Zealand by Southern Publishers Group, in South Africa by Real Books, in Southeast Asia by Berkeley Books, and in the United Kingdom and Europe by Airlift Books.

Cover design by Brent Beck, Fifth Street Design
Interior design by Timothy Horn Design

Library of Congress Cataloging-in-Publication Data

Michalko, Michael, 1940-
Cracking Creativity : the secrets of creative genius / Michael Michalko.
        p. cm.
ISBN 0-89815-913-X (cloth)
1. Creative thinking. 2. Creative ability. I Title.
BF408.M484 1998
153.3'5--dc21   97-39273
                                                      CIP

First printing, 1998
Printed in the United States of America

2 3 4 5 6 7 8 9 10 - 02 01 00 99

Dedicated with love to my mother,
Frances Busten Michalko,
who is the rose in the garden of my life.

CONTENTS

ACKNOWLEDGMENTS

It's an author's practice to acknowledge the many people who have assisted with the development of the book. And many people have helped me. However, this time around, I would like to acknowledge, in print, the one person who has helped me most, not only with this book, but in life as well. I would like to thank Pat Lehman of Marco Island, Florida, for her wit, wisdom, and faith, who, among many other things, taught me that my reach should exceed my grasp for, as Pat puts it, what else is heaven for?

How do geniuses come up with ideas? What is common to the thinking style that produced *Mona Lisa* and the one that spawned the theory of relativity? What characterizes the thinking strategies of the Einsteins, Edisons, da Vincis, Darwins, Picassos, Michelangelos, Galileos, Freuds, and Mozarts of history? What can we learn from them? The goal of this book is to describe these thinking strategies and show how we can apply them to become more creative in our work and personal life.

For years, scholars and researchers have tried to study genius by giving its vital statistics, as if piles of data somehow illuminated genius. In his 1904 study, Havelock Ellis noted that most geniuses are fathered by men older than thirty, had mothers younger than twenty-five, and were usually sickly as children. Other scholars reported that many were celibate (Descartes, Galileo, Newton) and that others were fatherless (Dickens) or motherless (Darwin, Marie Curie). In the end, the piles of data illuminated nothing.

Academics also tried to measure the links between intelligence and genius. But intelligence is not enough. Marilyn vos Savant, whose IQ of 228 is the highest ever recorded, has not contributed much to science or art. She is, instead, a question-and-answer columnist for *Parade* magazine. Run-of-the-mill physicists have IQs much higher than Nobel Prize-winner Richard Feynman, whom many acknowledge to be the last great American genius (his IQ was a merely respectable 122).

Genius is not about scoring 1600 on the SATs, mastering ten languages at the age of seven, finishing the *New York Times* crossword in record time, having an extraordinarily high IQ, or even about being smart. After a considerable debate in the sixties, initiated by J. P. Guilford, a leading psychologist who called for a scientific focus on creativity, psychologists reached the conclusion that creativity is not the same as intelligence. An individual can be far more creative than he or she is intelligent, or far more intelligent than creative.

Most people of average intelligence, given data or some problem, can figure out the expected conventional response to the problem. For example, when asked, "What is one-half of thirteen?" most of us immediately answer six and one-half. You probably reached the answer in a few seconds and then turned your attention back to the text.

Typically, we think reproductively, on the basis of similar problems encountered in the past. When confronted with problems, we fixate on something in our past that has worked before. We ask, "What have I been taught in my life, education, or work that will solve this problem?" Then we analytically select the most promising approach based on past experiences, excluding all other approaches, and work in a clearly defined direction toward the solution of the problem. Because of the apparent soundness of the steps based on past experiences, we become arrogantly certain of the correctness of our conclusion.

In contrast, geniuses think productively, not reproductively. When confronted with a problem, they ask themselves how many different ways they can look the problem, how they can rethink it, and how many different ways they can solve it, instead of asking how they have been taught to solve it. They tend to come up with many different responses, some of which are unconventional, and possibly, unique. In response to the earlier question, a productive thinker would say that there are many different ways to express "thirteen" and many different ways to halve something. Following are some examples.

Examples of 13 Being Halved
6.5
Six and one-half
Thir and teen = 4 (4 Letters on Each Side)
13 = 1, 3
XIII = 11, 2
XIII = 8, 8 (Halving Horizontally Gives Us 8 on Top and 8 on the Bottom)

With productive thinking, one generates as many alternative approaches as one can, considering the least as well as the most likely approaches. It is the willingness to explore all approaches that is important, even after one has found a promising one. Einstein was once asked what the difference was between him and the average person. He said that if you asked the average person to find a needle in a haystack, the person would stop when he or she found a needle. He, on the other hand, would tear through the entire haystack looking for all the possible needles.

Most people see this pattern as a square composed of smaller squares or circles, or as alternate rows of squares and circles. It isn't easily seen as columns of alternate squares and circles.

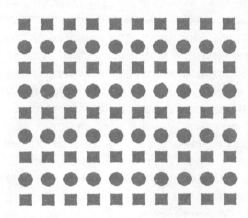

Once it's pointed out that it can also be viewed as columns of alternate squares and circles, we, of course, see it. We have become habituated to passively organize similar items together in our minds. Geniuses, on the other hand, subvert habituation by actively looking for alternative ways to look at and think about things.

Richard Feynman proposed teaching productive thinking in our educational institutions in lieu of reproductive thinking. He believed that the successful user of mathematics is an inventor of new ways of thinking in given situations. Even if the old ways are well known, he thought it is usually better to invent your own way or a new way than it is to look up an old solution and apply what you've looked up.

For example, 29 + 3 is considered a third-grade problem, because it requires the advanced technique of carrying; yet Feynman pointed out that a first grader could handle it by thinking 30, 31, 32. Or a child could mark numbers on a line and count off the spaces—a method that becomes useful in understanding measurements and fractions. One can write larger numbers in columns and carry sums larger than 10, or use fingers or algebra (2 times what plus 3 is 7?). He encouraged teaching people how to think about problems many different ways, using trial and error.

In contrast, reproductive thinking fosters rigidity of thought, which is why we so often fail when confronted with a new problem that is superficially similar to past experiences, but is different from previously encountered problems in its deep structure. Interpreting such a problem through the lens of past experience will, by definition, lead the thinker astray. Reproductive thinking leads us to the usual ideas and not to original ones. If you always think the way you've always thought, you'll always get what you've always got—the same old, same old ideas.

In 1968 the Swiss dominated the watch industry. The Swiss themselves invented the electronic watch movement at their research institute in Neuchtel, Switzerland. It was rejected, however, by every Swiss watch manufacturer. Based on their experience in the industry, they believed the electronic watch couldn't possibly be the watch of the future. After all, it was battery powered, did not have bearings or a mainspring, and had almost no gears. Seiko took one look at this invention that the Swiss manufacturers rejected at the World Watch Congress that year and took over the world watch market. When Univac invented the computer, they refused to talk to business people who inquired about it, because they said the computer was invented for scientists and had no business applications. Then along came IBM. IBM, itself, once said that according to their past experiences in the computer market, there was virtually no market for the personal computer. In fact, they said they were absolutely certain there were no more than five or six people in the entire world who needed a personal computer. Then along came Apple.

We need to vary our ideas in order to succeed. In nature, a gene pool that is totally lacking in variation would be totally unable to adapt to changing circumstances. In time, the genetically encoded wisdom would convert to foolishness, with consequences that would be fatal to the species' survival. A comparable process operates within us as individuals. We all have a rich repertoire of ideas and concepts based on past experiences that enable us to survive and prosper. But without any provision for the variation of ideas, our usual ideas become stagnate and lose their advantages, and in the end, we are defeated in our competition with our rivals.

Consider the following:

• In 1899 Charles Duell, the director of the U.S. Patent Office, suggested that the government close the office because everything that could be invented had been invented.

• In 1923 Robert Millikan, noted physicist and winner of the Nobel Prize, said that there was absolutely no likelihood that man could harness the power of the atom.

• Phillip Reiss, a German, invented a machine that could transmit music in 1861. He was days away from inventing the telephone. Every communication expert in Germany persuaded him there was no market for such a device, as the telegraph was good enough. Fifteen years later, Alexander Graham Bell invented the telephone and became a multimillionaire, with Germany as his first most enthusiastic customer.

• Chester Carlson invented xerography in 1938. Virtually every major corporation, including IBM and Kodak, scoffed at his idea and turned him down. They claimed that since carbon paper was cheap and plentiful, no one in their right mind would buy an expensive copier.

• Fred Smith, while a student at Yale, came up with the concept of Federal Express, a national overnight delivery service. The U.S. Postal Service, UPS, his own business professor, and virtually every delivery expert in the United States predicted his enterprise would fail. Based on their experiences in the industry, no one, they said, would pay a fancy price for speed and reliability.

Once we have an idea we think works, it becomes hard for us to consider alternative ideas. We tend to develop narrow ideas about what will work or what can be done and stick with it until proven wrong. Genius, on the other hand, operates more in accordance with the laws of biological evolution.

I have always been impressed by Darwin's theory of evolution by natural selection and am fascinated with scholastic attempts to apply Darwinian ideas to creativity and genius. My own outlook about genius has roots in Donald Campbell's blind-variation and selective-retention model of creative thought. Campbell was not the first to see the analogy between Darwinian ideas on evolution and creativity. As early as 1880, the great American philosopher, William James, in his essay "Great Men, Great Thoughts, and the Environment," made the connection between Darwinian ideas and genius. Campbell's work has since been elaborated on by Dean Keith Simonton and Sarnoff Mednick.

Their work suggests that genius operates similarly to Darwin's theory of biological evolution. Nature is extraordinarily productive. Nature creates many possibilities through blind "trial and error" and then lets the process of natural selection decide which species survive. In nature, 95 percent of new species fail and die within a short period of time.

Genius is analogous to biological evolution in that it requires the unpredictable generation of a rich diversity of alternatives and conjectures. From this variety of alternatives and conjectures, the intellect retains the best ideas for further development and communication. An important aspect of this theory is that you need some means of producing variation in your ideas and that for this variation to be truly effective it must be "blind." Blind variation implies a departure from reproductive (retained) knowledge.

How do creative geniuses generate so many alternatives and conjectures? Why are so many of their ideas so rich and varied? How do they produce the "blind" variations that lead to the original and novel? A growing number of scholars are offering evidence that one can characterize the way geniuses think. By studying the notebooks, correspondence, conversations, and ideas of the world's greatest thinkers, they have teased out particular common thinking strategies that enabled geniuses to generate a prodigious variety of novel and original ideas, creating a very clear picture of the nature of creativity. The strategies are not a set of piecemeal formulas. In harmony, they provide a timeless, timely, and solid framework for creative thought.

This book presents the thinking strategies of creative giants from the sciences, arts, and industry. They most notably include Einstein, Darwin, da Vinci, Freud, Picasso, Edison, Mozart, Richard Feynman, Louis Pasteur, Galileo, Walt Whitman, Niels Bohr, Alexander Graham Bell, Aristotle, Alexander Fleming, Michelangelo, Bach, George Westinghouse, Nikola Tesla, Walt Disney, Martha Graham, T. S. Eliot, Paul Cézanne, Newton, David Bohm, Stravinsky, Tennyson, Edgar Allan Poe, Jonas Salk, and Bertrand Russell, among others.

The creative-thinking techniques will show you how to generate the ideas and creative solutions you need in your business and personal life. Each technique contains specific instructions and an explanation of why and how it works—including anecdotes, stories, and examples of how geniuses implemented the strategy to produce their breakthrough ideas. When you use the techniques, you will rethink the way you see things and will look at the world in a different way.

This may seem simple, but you cannot will yourself to look at things differently, no matter how determined you are to do so. To illustrate, following are two rows of parallel dots that are equal in length. Try to will yourself to see the rows of dots as unequal in length. Try to will one row longer than the other. No matter how hard you concentrate and how long you look at the dots, the two rows remain equal.

• • • • • • •

• • • • • • •

However, if you combine the dots with two convergent straight lines, your perception of the dots changes: The top row appears longer than the bottom.

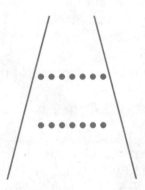

The rows are still equal (go ahead and measure them), yet you are now seeing something different. Combining the dots with straight lines changed your focus and caught your brain's processing routines by surprise, changing your perception of the pattern and allowing you to see something that you could not otherwise see. Similarly, the techniques in this book change the way you think by focusing your attention in different ways and giving you different ways to interpret what you focus on. The techniques will allow you to look at the same information as everyone else and see something different.

It is not enough to understand the strategies. To create original ideas and creative solutions, you must use the techniques. Try to explain the thrill of climbing mountains to a nomad who has never left the Sahara. You can show him some crampons and other climbing equipment and a picture of mountains, and perhaps get some of the idea across. However, to fully realize the thrill and challenge of mountain climbing, our nomad must put on the crampons and head up a mountain. If you merely read these strategies, you will have no more than a suggestion of how to get ideas. You'll be like the nomad standing in the desert, staring at a pair of crampons and a photo of Mt. Everest, with a small notion of what mountain climbing might be like.

If you organize your thinking around these strategies, you will learn to see what no one else is seeing and how to think what no one else is thinking. The book is organized into two parts. Part I, "Seeing What No One Else Is Seeing," presents strategies of geniuses who look at problems differently from the conventional ways we have been taught. You will learn how to look at your problem in many different ways. Part II, "Thinking What No One Else Is Thinking," is the heart of the book and presents seven creative-thinking strategies that geniuses use to generate their breakthrough ideas and creative solutions. These are the strategies that are common to the thinking styles of geniuses in science, art, and industry throughout history. These strategies will show you how to multiply your ideas and how to get ideas you cannot get using your usual way of thinking.

Following are thumbnail descriptions of the strategies:

Part I: Seeing What No One Else Is Seeing

Part I, "Seeing What No One Else Is Seeing," incorporates two strategies: "Knowing How to See" and "Making Your Thought Visible." These strategies demonstrate how geniuses generate a rich variety of perspectives and conjectures by representing their problem in many different ways, including diagrammatically.

1. *Knowing How to See.* Genius often comes from finding a new perspective that no one else has taken. Leonardo da Vinci believed that to gain knowledge about the form of problems, you begin by learning how to restructure it in many different ways. He felt the first way he looked at a problem was too biased toward his usual way of seeing things. He would restructure his problem by looking at it from one perspective and move to another perspective and still another. With each move, his understanding would deepen, and he would begin to understand the essence of the problem. Einstein's theory of relativity is, in essence, a description of the interaction between different perspectives. Freud's analytical methods were designed to find details that did not fit with traditional perspectives in order to find a completely new point of view.

Perhaps most telling about geniuses is that they do not approach problems reproductively, that is, on the basis of similar problems encountered in the past. Interpreting problems through past experience will, by definition, lead the thinker astray. In order to creatively solve a problem, the thinker must abandon the initial approach that stems from past experience and reconceptualize the problem. By not settling with one perspective, geniuses do not merely solve existing problems, like discovering a cure for cancer. They identify new ones. It does not take a genius to analyze dreams; it required Freud to ask in the first place what meaning dreams carry from the psyche.

2. *Making Your Thought Visible.* The explosion of creativity in the Renaissance was intimately tied to the recording and conveying of a vast knowledge in a parallel language; a language of drawings, graphs, and diagrams–as, for instance, in the renowned diagrams of da Vinci and Galileo. Galileo revolutionized science by making his thought visible with diagrams, maps, and drawings while his contemporaries used conventional mathematical and verbal approaches.

Once geniuses obtain a certain minimal verbal facility, they seem to develop a skill in visual and spatial abilities that gives them the flexibility to display information in different ways. When Einstein had thought through a problem, he always found it necessary to formulate his subject in as many different ways as possible, including diagrammatically. He had a very visual mind. He thought in terms of visual and spatial forms, rather than thinking along purely mathematical or verbal lines of reasoning. In fact, he believed that words and numbers, as they are written or spoken, did not play a significant role in his thinking process.

Part II: Thinking What No One Else Is Thinking

The first strategy, "Thinking Fluently," presents a set of timeless and solid principles on how to produce a quantity of ideas. In addition to producing many ideas, an important aspect of genius is the means to produce original and novel variations in ideas, and for this variation to be truly effective, it must be "blind." The next five strategies, "Making Novel Combinations," "Connecting the Unconnected," "Looking at the Other Side," "Looking in Other Worlds," and "Finding What You're Not Looking For," demonstrate how geniuses get novel and original ideas by incorporating chance or randomness into the creative process in order to destabilize their existing patterns of thinking and reorganize their thoughts in new ways. The last strategy, "Awakening the Collaborative Spirit," presents the conditions for effective group brainstorming and a collection of world-class brainstorming techniques.

1. *Thinking Fluently*. A distinguishing characteristic of genius is immense productivity. Thomas Edison held 1,093 patents, still the record. He guaranteed productivity by giving himself and his assistants idea quotas. His own personal quota was one minor invention every ten days and a major invention every six months. Bach wrote a cantata every week, even when he was sick or exhausted. Mozart produced more than six hundred pieces of music. Einstein is best known for his paper on relativity, but he published 248 other papers. T. S. Eliot's numerous drafts of "The Waste Land" constitute a jumble of good and bad passages that eventually was turned into a masterpiece.

Nature creates many possibilities and then lets the process of natural selection decide which species survive. Most do not survive; in fact, 95 percent of new species fail and die in a short period of time. In a study of 2,036 scientists throughout history, Dean Keith Simonton found that the most respected produced not only more great works, but also more "bad" ones. Out of their massive quantity of work came quality. Geniuses produce. Period.

2. *Making Novel Combinations*. In his 1988 book, *Scientific Genius*, Dean Keith Simonton of the University of California, Davis, suggests that geniuses are geniuses because they form more novel combinations than the merely talented. His theory has etymology behind it: *Cogito*–"I think"–originally connoted "shake

together." *Intelligo,* the root of *intelligence,* means to "select among." This is a clear early intuition about the utility of permitting ideas and thoughts to randomly combine with each other and the utility of selecting from the many the few to retain. Like the highly intelligent child with a pail of Legos, a genius is constantly combining and recombining ideas, images, and thoughts into different combinations in their conscious and subconscious minds. Consider Einstein's equation, $E=mc^2$. Einstein did not invent the concepts of energy, mass, or speed of light. Rather, by combining these concepts in a novel way, he was able to look at the same world as everyone else and see something different. Einstein vaguely referred to the way he thought as "combinatory play." In fact, combinatory play seemed to be the essential feature in his productive thought.

3. *Connecting the Unconnected.* If one particular style of thought stands out for creative geniuses, it is the ability to make juxtapositions that elude mere mortals. Call it a facility to connect the unconnected by forcing relationships that enable them to see things to which others are blind. Leonardo da Vinci forced a relationship between the sound of a bell and a stone hitting water. This enabled him to make the connection that sound travels in waves. In 1865 F. A. Kekule intuited the shape of the ringlike benzene molecule by forcing a relationship with a dream of a snake biting its tail. Samuel Morse was stumped while trying to figure out how to produce a signal strong enough to be received coast to coast. One day he saw horses being exchanged at a relay station and forced a connection between relay stations for horses and strong signals. The solution was to give the traveling signal periodic boosts of power. Nikola Tesla forced a connection between the setting sun and a motor that made the AC motor possible by having the motor's magnetic field rotate inside the motor just as the sun (from our perspective) rotates around the earth.

4. *Looking at the Other Side.* Physicist and philosopher David Bohm believed geniuses were able to think different thoughts because they could tolerate ambivalence between opposite or incompatible subjects. Dr. Albert Rothenberg, a noted researcher on the creative process, identified this ability in a wide variety of geniuses, including Einstein, Mozart, Edison, Pasteur, Joseph

Conrad, Picasso, and Niels Bohr. Bohr believed that if you held opposites together, then you suspend your thought and your mind moves to a new level. The suspension of thought allows an intelligence beyond thought to act and create a new form. The swirling of opposites creates the conditions for a new point of view to bubble freely from your mind. Bohr's ability to imagine light as both a particle and a wave led to his conception of the principle of complementarity.

5. *Looking in Other Worlds.* Aristotle considered metaphor a sign of genius, believing that the individual who had the capacity to perceive resemblances between two separate areas of existence was a person of special gifts. If unlike things are really alike in some ways, perhaps they are so in others. Alexander Graham Bell observed the comparison between the inner workings of the ear and the movement of a stout piece of membrane to move steel and conceived the telephone. Thomas Edison invented the phonograph, in one day, after developing an analogy between a toy funnel and the motions of a paper man and sound vibrations. Underwater construction was made possible by observing how shipworms tunnel into timber by first constructing tubes. Einstein derived and explained many of his abstract principles by drawing analogies with everyday occurrences such as rowing a boat or standing on a platform while a train passed.

6. *Finding What You Are Not Looking For.* Whenever we attempt something and fail, we end up doing something else. As simplistic as this statement may seem, it is the first principle of creative accident. We may ask ourselves why we have failed to do what we intended—and this is the reasonable, expected thing to do—but the creative accident provokes a different question: What have we done?

Answering that question in a novel, unexpected way is an essential creative act. It is not luck, but creative insight of the highest order. Alexander Fleming was not the first physician to notice the mold that formed on an exposed culture while studying deadly bacteria. A less gifted physician would have trashed this seemingly irrelevant event, but Fleming noted it as "interesting" and wondered if it had potential. This "interesting" observation led to penicillin, which has saved millions of lives.

Thomas Edison, while pondering how to make a carbon filament, was mindlessly toying with a piece of putty, turning and twisting it in his fingers, when he looked down at his hands and the answer hit him between the eyes: Twist the carbon like rope.

B. F. Skinner emphasized a first principle of scientific methodologists: When you find something interesting, drop everything else and study it. Too many fail to answer opportunity's knock at the door because they have to finish some preconceived plan. Creative geniuses do not wait for the gifts of chance; instead, they actively seek the accidental discovery.

7. *Awakening the Collaborative Spirit.* The notion that the collective intelligence of a group is larger than the intelligence of an individual can be traced back to primitive times when hunter-gatherer bands would meet to discuss and solve common problems. It is a commonly understood and accepted practice. What's difficult is for a group to come together in a collegial atmosphere that will allow thinking to grow through open and honest collaboration. This section presents the principles and conditions for participants to retain their individuality while combining their efforts and talents in a group in ways that are vital to creating a cooperative synthesis.

Summary

Creative geniuses are geniuses because they know "how" to think instead of "what" to think. Sociologist Harriet Zuckerman published an interesting study of the Nobel Prize winners who were living in the United States in 1977. She discovered that six of Enrico Fermi's students won the prize. Ernest Lawrence and Niels Bohr each had four students who won them. J. J. Thomson and Ernest Rutherford between them trained seventeen Nobel laureates. This was no accident. It is obvious that these Nobel laureates were not only creative in their own right, but were also able to teach others how to think. Zuckerman's subjects testified that their influential masters taught them different thinking styles and strategies, rather than what to think.

If you have the intention of becoming more creative in your work and personal life and apply the thinking strategies in this book, you will become more creative. You may not become another da Vinci or Einstein, but you will become much more creative than someone without the intention or knowledge. There is no way of knowing how far these things can take you. We live in a world that offers no guarantees, only opportunities.

PART I
SEEING WHAT NO ONE ELSE IS SEEING

The French artist Paul Cézanne brought forth a new consciousness of the multiplicity of perspectives inherent in viewing the world. His exploration started with a rather simple fact: If one approached a visual surface first with one eye open and then closed that eye and looked at the same area with the other eye, the view changed. Similarly, if one changed position, the view was altered again. Cézanne's genius was to recognize the creative possibilities these differences of perception offered the artist in viewing the world, and he changed the nature of art.

Count up the number of *O*s in the following diagram.

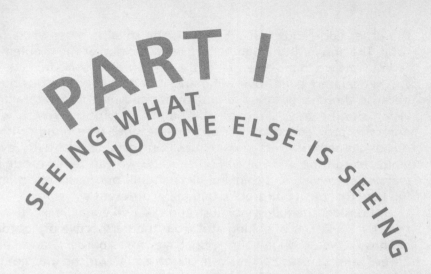

```
XOOOOO
XXOOOO
OOOOOX
OOOOXO
OOXXOO
OOOOOO
```

The usual way to solve this puzzle is to count the *O*s one by one. However, it is much easier and quicker if you change your perspective and count the *X*s. You can find the number of *O*s by multiplying the number of *X*s and *O*s along one edge of the diagram by the number along the other edge and then subtracting the small number of *X*s from this total. The answer is the number of *O*s. By looking at the problem in a different way, we found an easier and quicker way to solve it.

A cataract builds over time and its effects become obvious slowly, because the change goes almost unnoticed until the cataract reduces vision significantly. Likewise, the habits and routines with which we approach problems gradually accumulate until they significantly reduce our awareness of other possibilities. Our original creativity eventually yields to routine and habit. Fortunately, we can remove our habitual ways of perceiving and thinking by changing our perspectives and learning how to look at our problems in many different ways.

Consider the following illustration of two equal lines. We recognize that 1 + 1 = 2. This is looking at it from the perspective of "borders" and "edges." If you change your perspective from "borders" and "edges" to "area" and "surface," you can count equal widths and count three widths (one of them being negative). Now 1 + 1 = 3. Furthermore, of the two strips, if you cross the one horizontally over the other, you can create four arms or extensions and 1 + 1 = 4. You can also, with imagination, see four rectangles, four triangles, and four squares. By shifting centers and angles, arms and the in-between figures become unequal. Altogether, one line plus one line results in many meanings.

$$| + | = ||$$

$$\times \;\; \mathsf{X} \;\; \mathsf{+} \;\; +$$

Looking at the two lines in different ways illustrates that any particular way of looking at things is only one from among many possible ways. When you look at a problem using several perspectives instead of one stabilized view, you bring forth a new understanding of the possibilities. This is why geniuses cultivate more perspectives than is typical. Aristotle, for instance, sought several different types of "causes" in his analyses. Leonardo da Vinci systematically used several different perspectives when entertaining ideas, and Einstein formulated problems many ways, including visually.

The strategies in Part I demonstrate how creative geniuses generate a rich variety of different perspectives by representing a problem in different ways. They include the following:

• Restating a problem many different ways
• Diagramming, mapping, and drawing a problem

Imagine you had a bag of black gum balls and just one white gum ball. The chances of picking the white gum ball would be low. If you added five more white gum balls to the bag, your chances of picking a white one would increase. If you added ten more white gum balls, your chances would increase even more. Looking at a problem in different ways is as definite a procedure as putting more white balls into the bag. Each time you look at a problem in a different way, you increase your probability of discovering the unique perspective or insight that will lead to the breakthrough idea.

STRATEGY ONE: KNOWING HOW TO SEE

19

Leonardo da Vinci believed that to gain knowledge about the form of a problem, you began by learning how to restructure it to see it in many different ways. He felt the first way he looked at a problem was too biased toward his usual way of seeing things. He would look at his problem from one perspective and move to another perspective and still another. With each move, his understanding would deepen, and he would begin to understand the essence of the problem. Leonardo called this thinking strategy *saper vedere* or "knowing how to see."

Genius often comes from finding a new perspective. Einstein's theory of relativity is, in essence, a description of the interaction between different perspectives. Freud would "reframe" something to transform its meaning by putting it into a different context from how it has previously been perceived. For example, by reframing the unconscious as a part of the mind that was "infantile," Freud began to help his patients change the way they thought about and reacted to their own behavior.

One of the many ways our minds attempt to make life easier is to create a first impression of a problem. Like our first impressions of people, our initial perspectives on problems and situations are apt to be narrow and superficial. We see no more than we've been conditioned to see—and stereotyped notions block clear vision and crowd out imagination. This happens without any alarms sounding, so we never realize it's occurring.

Once we have settled on a perspective, we close off all but one line of thought. Certain kinds of ideas occur to us, but only those kinds and no others. What if the paralyzed man who invented the motorized cart had defined his problem as "How can I occupy my time while lying in bed?" rather than "How can I get out of bed and move around the house?"

Have you ever looked closely at the wheels on a railroad train? They are flanged. That is, they have a lip on the inside to prevent the train from sliding off the track. Originally train wheels were not flanged. Instead, the railroad tracks were. The problem of railroad safety had been expressed "How can the tracks be made safer for trains to ride on?" Hundreds of thousands of miles of track were manufactured with an unnecessary steel lip. Only when the problem was redefined–"How can the wheels be made to stay on the track more securely?"–was the flanged wheel invented.

To start with, it's helpful to phrase problems in a particular way. Write the problem you want to solve as a definite question. Use the phrase "In what ways might I. . . ?" to start a problem statement. This is sometimes known as the invitational stem and helps keep you from settling on a problem statement that may reflect only one perception of the problem. For example, in the series of letters below, cross out six letters to make a common word.

C S R I E X L E A T T T E R E S

If you state the problem as "How can I cross out six letters to form a common word?" you'll find it difficult to solve. If, instead, you framed it "In what ways might I cross out six letters to form a common word?" you will likely find yourself inspired to think of many alternative possible solutions, including the solution which is to literally cross out the letters *S, I, X, L, E, T, T*, and so on, leaving the word "CREATE."

A number of experiments have shown the significance of language for problem solving. Adults who write out or verbalize problems perform far better than those who silently go about the job. Consider the following problem. Four cards are laid out with their faces displaying, respectively, an *E*, a *K*, a four and a seven. You are told that each card has a letter on one side and a number on the other. You are then given a rule, whose truth you are expected to evaluate. The rule is "If a card has a vowel on one side, then it has an even number on the other." You are then allowed to turn over two, but only two, cards in order to detemine whether the rule is correct as stated.

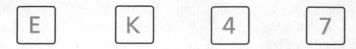

If you worked this problem silently, you will almost certainly miss the answer, as have over 90 percent of the people to whom it has been presented. Most people realize that there is no need to select the card bearing the consonant, since it is irrelevant to the rule; they also understand that it is essential to turn over the card with the vowel, for an odd number opposite would prove the rule incorrect. Most people make the fatal error of picking the card with the even number, because the even number is mentioned in the rule. But, in fact, it is irrelevant whether there is a vowel or a consonant on the other side, since the rule does not state what must be opposite to even numbers. On the other hand, it is essential to pick the card with the odd number on it. If that card has a consonant on it, the result is irrelevant. If, however, the card has a vowel on it, the rule in question has been proved incorrect, for the card must (according to the rule) have an even (and not an odd) number on it.

The fact that this problem proves hard (even though, once explained, it seems evident enough) should make one consider how a problem is stated. The content of this specific problem determined how we proceeded and how we screwed up on an apparently simple reasoning task. Subjects who framed the challenge as "In what ways might I evaluate the statement as given?" and looked at it from different angles were more likely to solve it.

Genius often comes from finding a new perspective on a problem by restructuring it in some way. When Richard Feynman, the Nobel laureate physicist, was "stuck" with a problem, he would look at it in a different way. If one way didn't work, he would switch to another. Whatever came up, he would always find another way to look at it. Feynman would do something in ten minutes that would take the average physicist a year because he had a lot of ways to represent his problem.

The important thing is not to persist with one way of looking at a problem. Consider the following interesting twist, again using four cards. This time, however, each card has a city on one side and a mode of transportation on the other. The cards have printed on them the legends, respectively, "Los Angeles," "New York," "airplane," and "car"; and the rule is "Every time I go to Los Angeles, I travel by airplane."

While this rule is identical to the number-letter version, it poses little difficulty for individuals. In fact, now 80 percent of subjects immediately realize the need to turn over the card with "car" on it. Apparently, one realizes that if the card with "car" on it has the name "Los Angeles" on the back, the rule has been proved incorrect; whereas it is immaterial what it says on the back of the "airplane" since, as far as the rule is concerned, one can go to New York any way one wants.

Why is it that 80 percent of subjects get this problem right, whereas only 10 percent know which cards to turn over in the vowel-number version? By changing the content (cities and modes of transportation substituted for letters and numbers), we restructured the problem, which dramatically changed our reasoning. The structure of a problem colors our perspective and the way we think.

Add up the following numbers in your head as quickly as you can without using pencil and paper.

$$
\begin{array}{r}
1000 \\
40 \\
1000 \\
30 \\
1000 \\
20 \\
1000 \\
\underline{10}
\end{array}
$$

For some reason, our brains have trouble processing these numbers in this particular arrangement, especially for those of us who have been taught to add using a base-ten number system. Many of us come up with 5,000 as the answer. This is incorrect. The correct answer is 4,100. It seems that even the structure of a simple arithmetic problem can confuse our brains and lead us astray.

As a boy, Einstein had a favorite uncle, Jakob, who taught him mathematics by changing the content of the exercises. For example, he would present algebra as a game about hunting a small mystery animal (X). When you bag your game (solve the problem), you pounce on it and give it its right name. By changing the content and converting math into a game, he taught Einstein to approach problems as play rather than work. Consequently, Einstein focused on his studies with the intensity that most people reserved for play.

Consider the letter-string FFMMTT. You'd probably describe this as three pairs of letters. If you're given KLMMNOTUV, you'd probably see it as three letter triplets. In each case, the letters MM are perceived differently: as one chunk or as parts of two different chunks. If you were given MM alone, you'd have no reason for seeing it as either and now would see it as a simple pair of letters. It's the context of the information that inclines you to describe an input in a certain way and perhaps to abandon an initial description for another.

The more times you state a problem in a different way, the more likely it is that your perspective will change and deepen. When Einstein thought about a problem, he always found it necessary to formulate his subject in as many different ways as possible. He was once asked what he would do if he was told that a huge comet would hit and totally destroy the earth in one hour. Einstein said he would spend fifty-five minutes figuring out how to formulate the question and five minutes solving it. What Freud says about the subconscious sounds like a new science, but in fact, it is just a means of representing the subject in a new way. What a Copernicus or Darwin really achieved was not the discovery of a new theory, but a fertile new point of view.

Before you brainstorm any problem, restate the problem at least five to ten times to generate multiple perspectives. The emphasis is not so much on the right problem definition but on alternative problem definitions. Sooner or later, you'll find one that you are comfortable with. Following are several different ways to restructure your problem:

- Make it more global and specific.
- Separate the parts from the whole.
- Change the words in some fashion.
- Make positive action statements.
- Switch perspective.
- Use multiple perspectives.
- Use questions.

Global and Specific Abstractions

One can always look at anything from different levels of abstraction. A very detailed description of a beach would include every position of every grain of sand. Viewed from a higher vantage point, the details become smeared together, the grains become a smooth expanse of brown. At this level of description, different qualities emerge: the shape of the coastline, the height of the dunes, and so on.

Abstraction is a basic principle in restructuring a problem. For instance, the standard procedure in physical science is to make observations or to collect systematic data and to derive principles and theories therefrom. Einstein despaired of creating new knowledge from already existing knowledge. How, he thought, can the conclusion go beyond the premises? So he reversed this procedure and worked at a higher level of abstraction. This bold stance enabled him to creatively examine first principles (for example, the constancy of the speed of light independent of relative motion). Einstein took as his starting premise and simply reasoned from the abstractions what others were not willing to accept because the abstractions could not be demonstrated by experimentation.

Even Galileo used thought experiments to imagine a possible world in which a vacuum existed. In this way he could propose the astounding hypothesis that all objects fall through a vacuum with the same acceleration regardless of their weight. No laboratory vacuums large enough to demonstrate this spectacular idea existed until years after Galileo's death. Today, this demonstration is standard fare in many science museums, where there are two evacuated columns in which a brick and feather released at the same moment fall side by side and hit the floor together.

It's important to spend time rephrasing problems in both more global and more specific ways. More specific problem statements lead to quicker solutions but less conceptual creativity than general statements. Think of the difference between cleaning up the oil spilled on your drive-way and the problem of environmental pollution, or the difference between developing a new computer keyboard and developing a new niche in the global information business.

Look for the appropriate level of abstraction, the best viewpoint from which to gather ideas. In the 1950s, experts believed that the oceangoing freighter was dying. Costs were rising, and it took longer and longer to get merchandise delivered. The shipping industry experts downsized the crew and built faster ships that required less fuel. Costs still kept going up, but the industry kept focusing its efforts on reducing specific costs related to ships while at sea and while working.

A ship is capital equipment and the biggest cost for capital equipment is the cost of not working, because interest has to be paid without income being generated to pay for it. Finally, an outside consultant globalized the challenge to "In what ways might the shipping industry reduce costs?"

This allowed the shipping companies to consider all aspects of shipping, including loading and stowing. The innovation that saved the industry was to separate loading from stowing, by doing the loading on land, before the ship is in port. It is much quicker to put on and take off preloaded freight. The answers were the roll-on/roll-off ship and the container ship. Port time has been reduced by three-quarters, and with it, congestion and theft. Freighter traffic has increased fivefold in the last thirty years, and costs are down by 60 percent.

Widening the problem by making it more abstract made it possible for the shipping companies to challenge assumptions, generate new perspectives, and uncover a new approach to the problem. According to his autobiographical study, Freud believed that one of the keys to his genius was his ability to widen problems and make them more abstract and complex. When he widened his problem space and made it more abstract, he would identify what he called his "missing links" (gaps of information). Once he identified the "missing links," he utilized his imagination, using what he called "free creation," to interpret the meaning of these missing links. These interpretations would sometimes lead to a new approach to a problem.

Perceiving your problem from different levels of abstraction changes the implications of the problem. To find the appropriate level of abstraction, ask "Why?" four or five times, until you find the level where you're comfortable. Suppose your challenge is "In what ways might I sell more Chevrolet Luminas?"

Step One: Why do you want to sell more Luminas?

   "Because my car sales are down."

Step Two: Why do you want to sell more cars?

   "To improve my overall sales."

Step Three: Why do you want to improve overall sales?

   "To improve my business."

Step Four: Why do you want to improve your business?

   "To increase my personal wealth."

Step Five: Why do you want to improve your personal wealth?

   "To lead the good life."

Now you shape your challenge in a variety of ways:

In what ways might I sell more Luminas?
In what ways might I sell more cars?
In what ways might I improve overall sales?
In what ways might I improve my business?
In what ways might I improve my personal wealth?
In what ways might I lead the good life?

Look for the level of abstraction where you're comfortable. You may choose to stick with the original challenge of selling more Luminas, or you may choose a more global challenge of improving your personal wealth. By phrasing the problems as improving your personal wealth, you are free to embrace more opportunities. You could negotiate a higher commission return for each vehicle sold, go into another business, make investments, sell other products, and so on.

If you find it difficult to think about the whole problem, take a less global approach. Try focusing on one part at a time. Identify each part as a subproblem. This makes your challenge easier to handle. Imagine trying to find an address, knowing that it was somewhere in Montreal. If you knew it was west of Old Montreal, it would be easier to find. If someone told you it was within walking distance of the Hotel Bonaventure, it would be still easier to find. So it is with challenges. The more specifically you define your challenge, the easier it is to generate ideas. Ask who, what, where, when, why, and how.

Who helps you identify individuals and groups who might be involved in your challenge, have special strengths or resources or access to useful information, and who might gain from a resolution of the problem.

What helps identify all the things involved in the situation: the requirements, difficulties involved, rewards, and advantages and disadvantages of formulating a resolution.

Where considers the places, locations, and focal points of the problems.

When probes the schedules, dates, and timeliness of the situation.

Why helps you reach an understanding of your basic objective.

How helps you recognize how the situation developed, actions that

Defining your problem as specifically as you can helps you identify the most important part or parts of the problem and their boundaries.

Separate the Parts from the Whole

Seeing is one of the most comprehensive operations possible: Your vision encompasses an infinity of forms and objects, yet it fixes on but one object at a time. Similarly, when Leonardo da Vinci embraced a subject, he would see the whole but would move from one detail to another, seeking the origin or cause of each detail. He believed you gained knowledge by separating the parts from the whole and examining all the relationships and key factors that may influence a given situation.

Fishbone Diagrams

Professor Kaoru Ishikawa of the University of Tokyo incorporated this strategy in his Ishikawa diagram, which is commonly known as the "fishbone" diagram because of its unique shape. The fishbone diagram is a way to visually organize and examine all the factors that may influence a given situation by identifying all the possible causes that produce an effect. An effect is a desirable or undesirable result produced by a series of causes. In teaching this tool, the Japanese often use as an effect a "perfect plate of rice." In a typical diagram, minor causes are clustered around four major cause categories. For example, common major cause categories in the manufacturing process might be "materials," "people," "methods," and "machinery," and major cause categories in public education might be "teachers," "methods," "environment," "students," and "policies."

Suppose we want to improve creativity in our organization. Following are guidelines for fishboning the situation:

1. Our effect would be "perfect organizational creativity." We would write this in the box on the right (the fish's head). A straight line is drawn to the left to resemble the backbone of the fish.

2. The next step is to brainstorm the major cause categories. What

are the major causes that would produce perfect organizational creativity? You can have as many major causes as are warranted. There are typically three to six. We decide that the four major categories for organizational creativity are "People," "Environment," "Materials," and "Policies." The major cause categories become the ribs of the fish.

3. Minor causes are then grouped around the major causes as fish bones. "Train to be creative" would be a bone attached to the "People" rib, and "stimulating" would be a bone attached to the "Environment" rib.

4. For each minor cause, ask, "How can we make this happen?" Then post the response as branches off the bones. "Hire an outside expert to conduct the training" would be a branch off the "Train" bone.

To fishbone an existing problem, you write the problem in the fish's head, identify the major cause categories of the problem, and group minor causes around the ribs. Then for each minor cause, ask, "Why does this happen?" Post the responses as branches off the appropriate bone. In the example on page 30, a company's new product had poor sales. By fishboning the effect, they discovered that the causes were many, including a poorly designed product that came out too late, a sales staff that was too small and poorly trained, lack of advertising money because the head of marketing did not buy in, and the failure to find the right distribution channels because the target market was not clearly defined.

Once all the causes are identified and grouped around the appropriate category, brainstorm for solutions and place the solutions on the right side of the rib.

In a group brainstorming session, write the problem in the fish's head on a large sheet of paper taped to the wall. (Use a large sheet or sheets to give participants plenty of room to diagram.) Once the ribs (major causes) are drawn, the group brainstorms causes and diagrams them on the left side of the ribs. For each cause, ask, "Why does this happen?" Then post the responses.

Once all the causes have been identified, possible solutions and ideas (usually two or three per cause) are generated and placed on the right side of the rib. Use a different color Post-it note for each. This technique realizes its fullest potential when the group brainstorms the

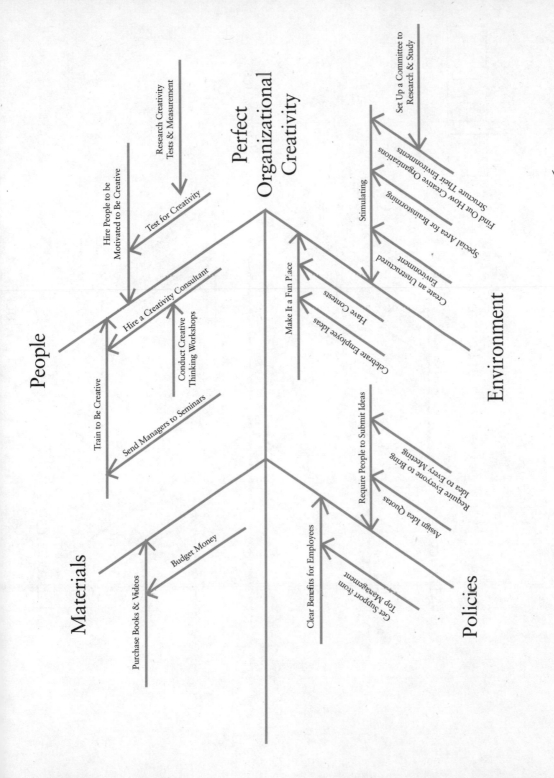

Perfect Organizational Creativity

People

- Research Creativity Tests & Measurement
- Hire People to be Motivated to Be Creative
- Test for Creativity
- Hire a Creativity Consultant
- Conduct Creative Thinking Workshops
- Train to Be Creative
- Send Managers to Seminars

Environment

- Set Up a Committee to Research & Study
- Find Out How Creative Organizations Structure Their Environments
- Special Area for Brainstorming
- Stimulating
- Create an Unstructured Environment
- Make It a Fun Place
- Have Contests
- Celebrate Employee Ideas

Materials

- Purchase Books & Videos
- Budget Money

Policies

- Require People to Submit Ideas
- Require Everyone to Bring Idea to Every Meeting
- Assign Idea Quotas
- Clear Benefits for Employees
- Get Support from Top Management

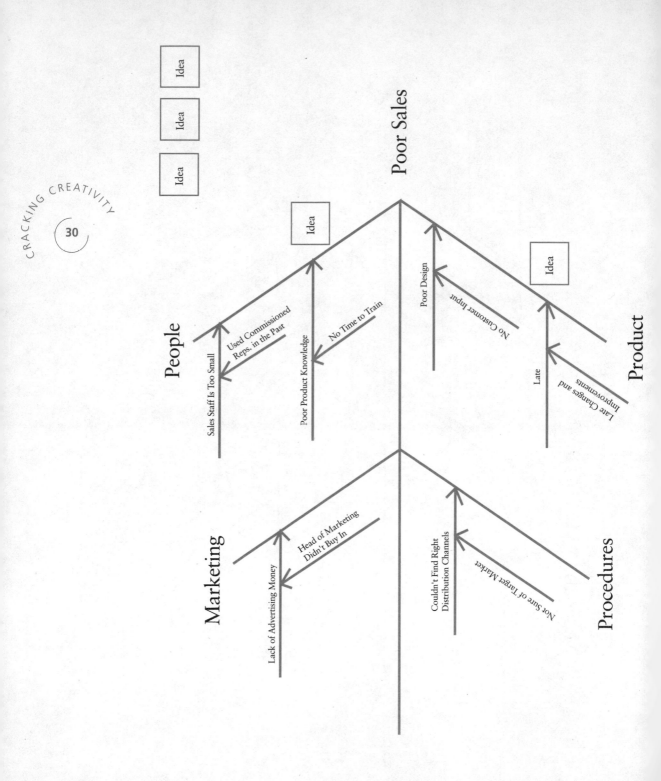

diagram over more than one session.

Fishboning allows you to see the relationships between causes and effects, allows you to consider all the different parts of a situation, and allows you to identify those areas where you need more data or information. It also triggers your subconscious. Ishikawa described the process as one in which you fishbone your problem and let it cook overnight. When you come back to it, you'll be amazed at the new thoughts and ideas that your subconscious has cooked up.

Words and Word Chains

While it seems clear that Aristotle was responsible for producing some of the greatest advances in human thought, modern society and education have focused more on the discoveries than on the mental processes and strategies through which the discoveries were made. In his book *On Interpretation* Aristotle described how words and chains of words were powerful tools for thought that both reflected and shaped his thinking. Aristotle believed that the words and chains of words that we use in framing a problem play a significant role in the way we approach problems.

Consider the following problem: Patches of water lilies double in area every twenty-four hours. On the first day of summer, there is one water lily on the lake. Sixty days later, the lake is completely covered with water lilies. On which day is the lake half covered?

The words "double," "twenty-four," "one," "on which day," and "sixty" coax most people to divide the sixty days by two and propose the thirtieth day as the solution, but since the lilies increase in area geometrically, this answer is incorrect. The lilies cover half the pond on the next-to-last day. The wording of the problem influences us to come up with the incorrect answer.

Thought is fluid. When you frame a problem in words, you crystallize your thoughts. Words give articulation and precision to vague images and hazy intuitions. But a crystal is no longer fluid and committing yourself to the first words that come to mind may disrupt your thought process.

Rephrase the Problem

Richard Feynman once reviewed his children's schoolbooks. One book began with pictures of a mechanical windup dog, a real dog, and a motorcycle, and for each the same question: "What makes it move?" The proposed answer–"Energy makes it move"–enraged him.

That was a tautology, he argued–an empty definition. Feynman, having made a career of understanding the deep abstractions of energy, said it would be better to begin a science course by taking apart a toy dog, revealing the cleverness of the gears and ratchets. To tell a first-grader that "energy makes it move" would be no more helpful, he said, than saying "God makes it move" or "movability" makes it move.

He proposed teaching students how to rephrase what they learn in their own language, without using definitions. For instance, without using the word "energy," tell me what you know now about the dog's motion.

Other standard explanations were just as hollow to Feynman. When someone told him that friction makes shoe leather wear out, his response was "Shoe leather wears out because it rubs against the side-walk, and the little notches and bumps on the sidewalk grab pieces and pull them off." That is knowledge. To simply say, "It is because of friction," is meaningless, an empty definition.

Always try to rephrase a problem in your own words, without using definitions. In another famous Feynman example, he was working with NASA engineers on a serious problem, and they kept defining the problem as a "pressure-induced vorticity oscillatory wa-wa or something." After considerable time and discussion had passed, a confused Feynman finally asked them if they were trying to describe a whistle. To his amazement, they were. The problem they were trying to communicate to him exhibited the characteristics of a simple whistle. Once he understood what they were trying to do, he solved the problem instantly.

This figure is a square defined by four dots. A square is a rectangle with four equal sides and four ninety-degree angles. Move two dots and create a square twice as big as the one defined by the dots as they are presently arranged. (sixty-second time limit)

Solution: The trick is the word "square." The definition of the word "square" biases your thinking and diminishes your capacity to see the right answer. Most people try to solve this problem by keeping the sides of the larger square parallel with the smaller one. That won't work. But if you rephrase the problem and rethink the illustration, you might figure out that a diamond is a "square on a point." Then by connecting one diagonal and then moving the two other dots to make the remainder of the points, you've got a square twice as large as the original one.

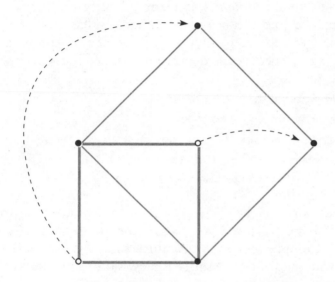

Change the Words

For every word a person uses, psychologists say there is a mediating response that provides the meaning of that concept for that individual. Thus, our response to the word "square" in the above problem was to think of constructing a larger square parallel to the smaller one. When we defined a square as a diamond, the problem was easily solved. Just what the mediating responses are for all words is not known. Many times they may not be responses in the usual sense, but all provide meaning for individuals. When you change the words in your problem statement, you initiate an unobservable process in your mind that may lead to a new thought or idea.

A few years back, Toyota asked employees for ideas on how they could become more productive. They received few suggestions. They reworded the question to "How can you make your job easier?" They were inundated with ideas. Even tiny changes can lead to unpredictable, cataclysmic results. In a sentence, one can randomly change a single letter and alter the way every other word is used. "The kids are flying planes" becomes "The lids are flying planes."

A simple change of words or the order of words in a problem statement will stimulate your imagination by adding new dimensions of meaning. Consider the statement "Two hundred were killed out of six hundred," as compared to "Four hundred were spared out of six hundred."

Examine your problem statement, identify the key words, and change them five to ten times to see what results. One of the easiest words to change is the verb. Suppose you want to increase sales. Look at the changing perspectives as the verb is changed in the following:

In what ways might I increase sales?
In what ways might I attract sales?
In what ways might I develop sales?
In what ways might I extend sales?
In what ways might I repeat sales?

In what ways might I keep sales? Magnify sales? Restore sales? Target sales? Inspire sales? Cycle sales? Encourage sales? Grow sales? Copy sales? Complement sales? Acquire sales? Vary sales? Spotlight sales? Motivate sales? Prepare sales? Renew sales? Force sales? Organize sales? And so on.

Play with Verbs and Nouns

Playing with verbs and nouns encourages you to think of perspectives that you would probably not think of spontaneously. Try changing the nouns into verbs and verbs into nouns in your problem statement. For example, a problem might be "How can I sell more bottles?" Changing the verbs into nouns and nouns into verbs makes this into "How can I bottle more sales?" Bottling sales now suggests looking for ways to close sales, instead of ways to sell more bottles.

The problem "How can I improve customer relations?" becomes "How can I customize related improvements?" This new perspective leads one to consider customizing products and services for customers, customizing all relevant aspects of the customer relations department, or other customizations.

Another way to change your perspective is to substitute an antonym for the noun. If your problem is "How can I increase sales?," convert sales to its antonym, "expenditures." The new line of speculation now becomes one of spending more to get more: Should we budget more money in our sales budget? Should we sell higher quality products? Should we buy more advertising? And so on.

Transpose the Words

One of Aristotle's favorite ways to test a premise was what he called "convertibility." He felt that if a premise were true, then the reverse premise should be convertible. For example, if every pleasure is good, some good must be pleasure. By simply transposing words, you achieved a different perspective. Sometimes changing the order of words in a problem statement will create a verbal-conceptual chain that may trigger a different perspective.

In the following illustration, words were arranged in two different series, A and B, and subjects were asked to solve certain situations. When "skyscraper" was listed first, subjects tended to come up with architectural concepts, and when "prayer" was transposed with "skyscraper" and listed first, it increased the likelihood of a religious direction.

Series A	Series B
Skyscraper	Prayer
Prayer	Skyscraper
Temple	Temple
Cathedral	Cathedral

Transpose the words in your problem. Following are some examples:

In what ways might I get a promotion?
In what ways might I promote myself?
In what ways might I advertise my T-shirts?
In what ways might I use my T-shirts to advertise?
In what ways might I learn how to use the Internet?
In what ways might I use the Internet to learn more?

A very simple change in the way something is stated can have a profound effect. One of the most effective medical discoveries of all time came about when Edward Jenner transposed his problem from why people got smallpox to why dairy workers apparently did not. From the discovery that harmless cowpox gave protection against deadly smallpox came vaccination and the end of smallpox as a scourge in the Western world.

One-Word Technique

According to Aristotle, words are sounds that become symbols of mental experience through the process of association. The most striking characteristic of the poetry of Shakespeare and Milton is the words they chose to build up a chain of associations in the reader's mind. The effect of their masterpieces was produced not so much by what they expressed, as by what they suggested, not so much by the ideas they conveyed, as by other ideas that were remotely connected with them.

Try using the following technique to build up a chain of associations in your mind about your subject.

1. Write down your problem in one sentence. Reduce it to one word.
2. What other words might be used? Look for synonyms in a thesaurus. Choose one.
3. What do you mean by that word? Fully describe the personal meaning of the word.
4. What is the dictionary definition of the word? Does this add any new dimensions?
5. Within your description of the dictionary definition, is there another word that better describes the essence of your problem or intrigues you?
6. If so, repeat the process with the new word.
7. If not, did any of the explorations give you a new way of looking at the problem?

Word Chain

In an atomic pile, a chain reaction comes about when a particle splits off from one atom nucleus and then collides with another atom nucleus and dislodges a second particle, which in turn, collides with another nucleus. If the mass of material is large enough, the chain reaction becomes an explosion. So it is with words. One new word can set off a reaction when it collides with another, and a sort of creative chain reaction follows.

1. Ask yourself what the theme of your problem is right now. What one word describes the current problem or situation you're dealing with?

2. Write down the key word at the top of a page of paper.

3. Then make a list of words that pop into your mind in connection with this word. Don't think about it. Let the words flow spontaneously. Let one word trigger another, and so on. Continue this for a few minutes.

4. Read over your word chain and write down your reactions and comments.

5. Look for a particular theme or issue that keeps recurring. These themes are worth exploring for significance to the problem. If a particular word evokes a strong emotional reaction, it's worth exploring.

Suppose my problem is how to improve the morale of employees. My key word is "enrichment." My word chain would include words such as "need," "interdependence," union," "the one and the many," "coming together," "fear," "loss of self," "communication," "bond," "weakness," "touching," "courage," "involvement," "trust," and so on. The phrase "loss of self" provokes a strong emotion that leads me to contemplate ways to improve morale that do not include ways to diminish individuation.

Positive Statements

In the *Universe Within*, Morton Hunt details experiments conducted by Herbert Clark at Stanford University that demonstrate how thinking positively facilitates and speeds up thinking. In the figure below, are the statements true or false?

The star is above the plus.	★ +
The star is above the plus.	+ ★

Notice how much longer it takes to reply to the false statement than to the true one. We instinctively assume statements are true. If they are, we think no further and move on. If they are not true, we step back and revise our assumption, thus answering more slowly. It takes approximately a half second more, or longer, to verify denials than affirmations. We are programmed to think more easily about what is than what is not.

Read the following sentences, pausing briefly between them.

Should we allow gays to serve in the military?
Should we not allow gays to serve in the military?

Did you feel your mind slowing down to interpret the second statement? Negatives make us pause and slow down our thinking processes. Suppose you misplaced your watch somewhere in your house. If you search for it and keep searching, you will eventually find it. This is a different perspective from "Did I misplace my watch in the house or did I misplace it somewhere else?" The belief that the watch is in the house, a positive, active statement speeds up your thinking and keeps you focused on your goal. Try framing your problem statement as a positive action statement. A positive action statement has four parts:

1. The Action: The thing you want to do.
2. The Object: A thing or person you want to change.
3. The Qualifeer: The kind of action change you want.
4. The End Result: The result you expect to follow.

Example: In what ways might I package (action) my book (object) more attractively (qualifier) so people will buy more (end result)?

Next, rate the action statement on a scale of one to ten. This serves as a benchmark to assess the probability of achieving workable solutions.

Shifting Perspective

In the illustration below, the cockroach is on the outside of the cube. If you focus on it in a different way, you can place the cockroach inside the cube on the floor. Stare at the intersection of the lines inside the box and after a few moments, the cube will flip inside out and place the cockroach inside on the floor. Shifting your perspective by looking at the image in a slightly different way creates a totally different image.

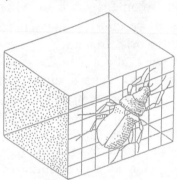

Our perceptual positions determine how we view things. Imagine that you are on the way to a Broadway play with a pair of tickets that cost one hundred dollars and discover you have lost the tickets. Would you pay another one hundred dollars? Now imagine you are on your way to the theater to buy these tickets. Upon arrival, you realize you have lost one hundred dollars in cash. Would you now buy tickets to the play? Clearly, on an objective basis, the two situations are identical–in both you are one hundred dollars in the hole. Nevertheless, most people report that they would be more likely to buy new tickets if they had lost the money than if they had lost the tickets. The same loss is seen differently from two different perspectives. The loss of the cash has comparatively little effect on whether one buys new tickets. On the other hand, the cost of the lost tickets is viewed as "attending the theater" and one is loath to accept the doubling of the cost of the play.

Because our perceptual positions determine how we view things, it's important to learn how to shift perspective and look at a subject in different ways. Walt Disney's ability to identify with the characters in

his animated films, as well as with his audience, is a good example of this skill. Freud's model and treatment of transference acknowledged the importance of assuming different perceptual positions. Leonardo acknowledged the pitfall of being stuck in one's own perceptual position and specified several ways to shift perspective (such as using a mirror and changing his internal state to look at his work as if it was someone else's) in order to evaluate one's work. Einstein imagined riding on a light beam or in the reality of a two-dimensional being. Tesla, by imagining himself living in the future, essentially took up a perceptual position in the future, creating new realities from which to view the world.

Switching Gender

The way men and women relate provides one of the primary metaphors around which we construct our perceptions of how things work in business and the world. Imagine, for a moment, that you would like a different point of view about a business situation (sales meetings, performance reviews, business lunches, etc.). Instead of trying to will a change in perspective, try the following exercise:

1. Close your eyes and relax.
2. Imagine yourself in the following situations, one at a time, but imagine (physically, emotionally, mentally) you are of the opposite sex.
  A. Walking down a street and running into a friend of the same sex you are imagining yourself as being
  B. Walking down a street and running into a friend of the opposite sex you are imagining yourself as being
  C. Being on a public beach, wearing a bathing suit
  D. Being at work and dealing with members of the opposite sex
  E. Being at a party, flirting and dancing
  F. Being out on a date with a special friend
  G. Being at home, after you and your spouse have had a hard day

3. Open your eyes and now examine the business situation from the viewpoint of the opposite sex. Ask yourself, "How would I view the situation if I were of the opposite sex?" Write down everything that comes to mind.

Does taking the role of the other sex lead you to notice things you normally would not? What, for instance, do you find yourself noticing and thinking about as a member of the opposite sex? What are the differences? The similarities? Do you find yourself approaching the situation differently? Has your viewpoint changed? In what ways?

As you switch genders, notice how your attention and thoughts change. You might find yourself, for instance, first thinking of competition as the spice of life and then shifting to regarding cooperation as the highest value. Or you might change your value system from one that is predicated on the past to one that emphasizes the values of the future. By turning things around in your mind, you are breaking expectations in a variety of ways, which will generate new ways of looking at things.

Taking on the role of the opposite sex can also be both entertaining and emotionally enriching. You will expand your empathic abilities and your flexibility in how you think of yourself. This sort of self-observation while taking on a new mental role is especially helpful for developing empathy for other people.

Suppose, for example, that you are always arguing with a member of the opposite sex about company policies and procedures. Instead of arguing your points to prove you are right and the other person is wrong, try playing this mental game and switch genders. You'll find your perspective changes from one of immediately trying to tear down the other person's position to one of looking for something positive that you can genuinely agree with or can use as a place to start for generating better ideas.

Friends and Enemies

Imagine yourself in one of two scenarios. First, imagine you're the same sex as the other person. The two of you are friends, and you're leisurely walking side by side. You have a certain belief about your subject, and you want your friend to believe it too. With these thoughts in mind, imagine you turn to your friend. What do you say? How do you say it? Jot the answers to those questions down on paper. Do they spark any new insights?

In the second scenario, imagine you're the same sex, only this time the other person is not your friend. You're in a crowded, noisy restaurant. You know that the other person does not share your beliefs about your subject, and you feel that it's important for the company that this person adopt these beliefs. Once again, what do you say? How do you say it? Jot down the answers and see if they spark any new ideas.

The ideas stemming from the first scenario should feel highly personalized and warm. Perhaps your ideas will include words or images that the other person can connect with and understand. The ideas stemming from the second scenario will probably be more bottom-line oriented and impersonal. Perhaps they will include an objective idea that the other person can readily understand and accept.

Da Vinci's Multiple Perspectives

Leonardo da Vinci equated comprehension of the deeper structure of his subject with having multiple perspectives, specifically, from at least three different points of view. This seems to be a very fundamental and key part of Leonardo's strategy—multiple points of view are synthesized together. Leonardo believed that until one perceived something from a minimum of three different perspectives, one did not yet have a basis for understanding it. A true and complete knowledge comes from the synthesizing of these views. For example, when he designed the first bicycle, he looked at this new form of transportation from the viewpoint of the inventor, investors who would sponsor prototypes and production, the bicycle rider or consumer, and the municipalities where bicycles would be used, and then he synthesized the views.

Just as the difference in point of view between your eyes allows you to perceive depth, multiple perspectives about your subject deepen your understanding. Educational psychologists have conducted many experiments illustrating how a multiplicity of perspectives opens awareness and creativity. In one study of beginning piano students, two groups were introduced to a simple C-major scale. One group was told to learn the scale by responding to multiple perspectives, including thoughts and feelings; the other group was told to practice the scale by the traditional memorization through repetition. When the groups were evaluated, the psychologists found the playing of the first group to be much more competent and creative.

In other experiments, researchers assigned chapters about particular subjects (e.g., the passage of the Kansas-Nebraska Act) to two groups. One group was asked to read the passage from multiple perspectives: its own, as well as that of the participants, wondering what they must have felt or thought at the time. The other group was told simply to learn the passage. Invariably, when the groups were tested, the group that studied using "multiple" perspectives outperformed the other group that used "traditional" learning methods, in terms of information retained, the content of the essays they wrote, and creative solutions proposed.

Look at your problem using multiple perspectives.

1. First, write the problem from your point of view.
2. Next, write the statement from the perspectives of at least two other people who are close to or involved in the problem.
3. Synthesize the different perspectives into one all-inclusive problem statement.

For instance, if you are starting a new business, write out your statement as you see it, then from the point of view of your potential customers, your potential employees, your potential competitions, and last, from the point of view of your banker. Synthesize these various perspectives together into one all-inclusive statement.

In physics Einstein suggested that even the distinction between matter and energy might depend upon a point of view. What was wave from one point of view was particle in another, what was a field in one experiment was a trajectory in another. The multiplication of different perspectives multiplies the possibilities. Consider how Paul Cézanne brought forth a new visual consciousness in art with his multiple versions of Mont Saint-Victoire and the multiple versions of apples on his tablecloth.

In the illustration below, you can look at it passively as a simple pattern of four dots that are equidistant from each other, or you can look at it creatively from different perspectives, and group them into more complex structures. The dots could represent the four arms of a cross, or four corners of a square, the points of a diamond, the bases on a baseball diamond, the points on a compass, and so on. Looking at something from different perspectives is not just a passive registering of data, but an active and creative process. When you look at a problem using a multiplicity of perspectives instead of one stabilized view, you bring forth a new creative consciousness and an expansion of the possibilities.

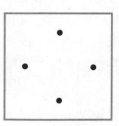

An easy way to generate a multiplicity of perspectives when working in a small group is to first give each participant five cards and ask him or her to write five different problem statements (one statement per card). Collect the cards and shuffle them. Then,

1. Randomly distribute three cards to each participant, taking care that no one gets his or her own cards. Ask everyone to arrange them in order of personal preference. While participants are doing this, spread the leftover cards on a table.
2. Ask participants to exchange cards they don't like with those on the table.
3. Ask participants to exchange cards with each other. Every participant should exchange at least one card and may exchange any number.
4. Form the group into three teams. Ask the teams to select three cards and discard the rest. Then, ask the team to synthesize the remaining three cards into one problem statement.
5. Ask each team to present its problem statement to the group. Now, ask the entire group to synthesize the three problem statements into one.

Take on a Different Role

Soren Kierkegaard, the nineteenth-century Danish philosopher, called it the "rotation method." He was thinking of crops. You can't grow corn indefinitely on the same field; at some point, to refresh the soil, you must plant hay. Similarly, to grow a different perspective, you will find it helpful to adopt a different role. Sigmund Freud once compared his method of listening to his patients "free associate" to adopting the perspective of the window of a moving train.

Try taking on a different role to get a different perspective. First, write your problem statement from your point of view. Then write your statement in two of the following ways:

How would a leader in your field write it?
How would a college professor write it?
How would a precocious child write it?
How would a risk-taking entrepreneur write it?
How would an evangelist write it?
How would a politician write it?

How would a physicist write it?
How would a psychologist write it?
How would an explorer write it?
How would a judge write it?
How would an investigative reporter write it?

As you write your statements, contemplate how each character would approach the problem. What would they do? What are the differences? The similarities? Synthesize the three statements. Can you merge them into one all-inclusive statement? Has your original perspective of the problem changed?

Imagine You Are the Problem

A cornerstone of Freud's strategy was to have his patients take a subject and transform its meaning by putting it into a different framework or context. By getting the patient to do this, he was able to change the way the patient thought.

In the illustration below, by restructuring the pattern and putting the content into another context, we change the meaning of the pattern. We change the letter pattern A, B, and C to the number pattern 12, 13, and 14.

$$12$$

$$A \quad 13 \quad C$$

$$14$$

Similarly, if you put the content of your problem into another context, you will change the way you think about it. One way to do this is to imagine that you are the problem or some aspect of it. This is a favorite technique of T.A. Rich, a famous inventor at GE, who often develops a unique perspective toward problems by imagining he is in the middle of the problem or is some aspect of the problem. For example, he would try to think like an electron or he would imagine himself as a light beam whose refraction is being measured. Einstein imagined he was riding a beam of light hurtling through space, which led him to the theory of relativity. By becoming part of the problem, you can discover new and original thoughts.

Try to imagine yourself as some part of the problem and try to see the situation from its perspective. Imagine that you are trying to design a new clock. Ask yourself what it would be like to be the minute hand on a clock. Can you imagine yourself as a unit of time? How would an hour feel? A minute? A second? What would it say to me if our positions were reversed? What would it say to me if it could think and talk the way I can?

Identify with an object or process and try to see the problem from the perspective of the object or process. Merge with the problem by asking yourself questions:

How would I feel if I were . . . ?
What would it say to me if it were me?
How would I feel if I were the idea I am developing?
What recommendation would it make?

The managers at a utility company wanted to dramatically reduce capital equipment costs. They spent three months imagining themselves as a kilowatt traveling through the company's various fossil fuel and nuclear power systems. As they imagined themselves traveling through each stage, they began to understand the complexity and diversity of the systems and saw ways to improve them. Their imaginary travels led to a redesigned maintenance plan that reduced the cost of maintenance ten times by replacing key parts instead of whole systems.

Questions

Certainly, a key characteristic of all geniuses is their intense child-like curiosity and a high degree of inquiry. Leonardo da Vinci wrote many questions to himself in his notebooks, seeking, like Aristotle, to find first principles. Einstein spent his life asking questions about objects and why objects behave the way they do and what would happened if rules were altered. Tesla created whole new worlds in his imagination and then wondered how to make them manifest. It does not take a genius to analyze dreams; it required Freud to ask in the first place what messages they carry from the psyche. In fact, genius comes more from asking bold questions than finding "right" answers.

Isolate the challenge you want to think about and dissect it in as many different ways as you can with the following questions:

- Why is it necessary to solve the problem?
- What is the unknown? How much of the unknown can you determine?
- What is it you don't yet understand?
- What is the information you have? Is the information sufficient? Or is it insufficient? Or redundant? Or contradictory?
- Can you derive something useful from the information you have? Have you used all the information?
- Can you draw a diagram of the problem? A figure?
- What are the boundaries of the problem?
- Can you separate the various parts of the problem? Can you write them down? What are the relationships of the parts of the problem?
- Have you seen this problem before? Have you seen this problem in a slightly different form? Do you know a related problem?
- Suppose you find a problem related to yours that has already been solved. Can you use that solution? Can you use its method?
- What are the best, worst, and most probable scenarios you can imagine?

Think Like a Child

Noam Chomsky of MIT, whose theory of the "deep structure" of language created modern linguistics, believes his insights come from the willingness to ask obvious questions, as children notoriously do. Einstein, too, was like a wonder-filled child, always asking the obvious questions about space, time, and God. Einstein once said that the ordinary person could learn all the physics he or she will ever need to learn if the person could learn to understand the mind of a child.

Get in touch with the child inside you. Close your eyes and imagine yourself when you were at your most inquisitive age. Suppose you imagine yourself at twelve years of age. Reconstruct the details of that age as much as possible. Experience again the Christmases, Fourths of

July, birthdays, vacations, friends, teachers, and the school days that you experienced. Deepen the experiences as much as you can. Remember "being in school" instead of "remembering being in school." Remember "being with your best friend" instead of "remembering being with your best friend." Now look at your problem as a twelve-year-old would look at it. What questions would a twelve-year-old ask?

Playful Questions

Ask playful questions to put yourself or a brainstorming group into a childlike, playfully aware state:

- Try seeing and thinking about your problem as a living creature. What would it look like? Draw a picture of it. For example, the problem of selling more houses might appear as a helpless, strange-looking creature.
- Think of the past and future reincarnations of your problem. What would they be?
- See your problem as edible. What would it taste like?
- Can you imagine the past and likely future of your problem?
- Look at the problem as the top of something and imagine what the underground portion looks like. Can you describe it?
- View the world from the perspective of the problem. What do you look like to the problem?
- Search the problem for something that is beautiful or aesthetically interesting. Can you find something?
- Imagine the personal life of the problem. What are its politics? Its religion? What would its love life be like? Where was the problem born? Does it have siblings? If so, are they friendly with each other? What is the problem afraid of?
- If you were the problem's psychotherapist, what would the problem confide to you?

Color Questions

Trigger your spirit of inquiry by using "color" questioning, a particular application of the work of Jerry Rhodes, who did extensive research with managers at Phillips. At the core of this technique are types of questions that one might ask. The questions are identified with colors as follows:

> **Green**: Think of the color green as fertile and creative. Green is the color of imagination and ingenuity. Ask, "What if?" or "Suppose we?"
>
> **Yellow**: Think of the color yellow as neutral and objective. Yellow is the color for description of fact. Ask, "What is?"
>
> **Blue**: Think of the color blue as hopeful and positive. Blue is the color for judgments and opinions of value and need. Ask, "What can we do?" or "What should we do?"
>
> **Red**: Think of the color red as negative. Red is the color of limitations and constraints. Ask, "What can't be done?" or "What's not possible?"

Many of us have a tendency to favor one or two of these types of questions, and some of us do so in such disproportion that we are unable to entertain questions outside of our predilections. Sometimes we'll get so hung up on a particular line of questioning that we're prevented from moving forward.

Color questioning prompts you to think of questions from each of the core categories. Label four separate sheets of paper: "green," "yellow," "blue," and "red." Think of as many "green," "yellow," and "blue" questions as you can and write them on the appropriate sheets. Whenever you have a negative question, write it on the sheet labeled "red." At a later stage, review the red questions, and try to look for ways to overcome them. You can post your questions in columns on a large sheet of paper. You can also write them on index cards and tape them to the wall under the appropriately colored card, or you can use colored markers and flip charts. After listing as many questions as you can for each color, prioritize the questions decide which questions you should address first.

If you're working with a group, simply have the participants brainstorm as many questions as they can about a specific topic. Afterward, organize the questions according to colors and post them on flip charts. Prompt the group to extend each category by asking questions, such as "What green questions might unlock our imaginations?" "Do we need more blue questions?" and "Have we exhausted the possible yellow question possibilities?" After the group has listed as many questions as they can for each category, have the group prioritize the questions and then decide which are the most important to address first.

STRATEGY TWO: MAKING YOUR THOUGHT VISIBLE

The explosion of creativity in the Renaissance was intimately tied to the recording and conveying of a vast body of knowledge in a parallel language: a language of drawings, diagrams, and graphs–as, for instance, in the renowned diagrams and sketches of Galileo. Galileo revolutionized science by making his thought visible with diagrams and drawings, while his contemporaries used conventional verbal and algebraic approaches. His diagrams of celestial bodies unfolded a deeply visual logic that produced insights far beyond those achieved by his peers and changed the history of science.

Leonardo da Vinci also used drawings, diagrams, and graphs as a way to capture information, a way to formulate problems, and the means of solving problems. In Leonardo's notebooks, the diagrams and drawings are the focal points, not the words. That is, his pictures were not intended simply as "illustrations" of his notes; rather, the notes were intended as comments on the pictures. Language took such a secondary role for Leonardo da Vinci that he viewed it as a way to name or describe discoveries, not to make them.

Language predisposes our mind to a certain way of thinking. Consider a rose. Using words, one might say a "rose" is a red, pink, or white flower one gives to a beautiful woman, a pleasant hostess, or to a deceased friend. Notice how the tagging of a complex flower with a simple verbal description detours human curiosity by predisposing us along certain avenues of thought. It's as if the language we use draws a magic circle around us, a circle from which there is no escape save by stepping out of the circle (language) into another. Consider the difficulties

of physicists, such as Ernest Rutherford, in the early days of atomic physics. The word "atom" meant "indivisible" in Greek. The notion that the atom was indivisible was a fixed one, and it was only when physicists stepped out of their verbal-mathematical language circle of thinking and into the visual circle of thinking were they able to demonstrate graphically that the atom was a divisible unit of matter.

In his essay, "On Truth and Lies," Friedrich Nietzsche made a brilliant argument that a verbal description of reality was rendered impossible by the structure of language itself. It's no wonder that many geniuses, such as the physicist, Richard Feynman, preferred to think visually. Richard Feynman put quantum electrodynamics on center stage in physics by describing it visually, with diagrams, rather than writing down formulae as other physicists were doing. This led to the famous Feynman diagrams that everybody uses now for any kind of calculation in field theory. What Feynman did was look at all the collected information, rearrange it into diagrams, and find the idea that had been lying dormant. His diagrams made it possible for physicists to look at a world that was previously unimaginable.

When Einstein thought through a problem, he thought in terms of visual and spatial forms rather than thinking along purely mathematical or verbal lines of reasoning. In fact, he believed that words and numbers, as they are written or spoken, did not play a significant role in his thinking process. One of the most complete descriptions of Einstein's philosophy of science was found in a letter to his friend, Maurice Solovine. In the letter, Einstein explained the difficulty of attempting to use words to explain his philosophy of science, because as he said, he thought about such things schematically. The letter started with a simple drawing consisting of (1) a straight line representing E, experiences, which are given to us, and (2) A, axioms, which are situated above the line but are not directly linked to the line.

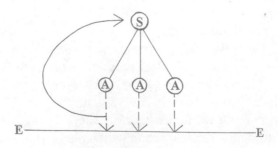

(This is an approximation. Einstein's original sketch is in the Albert Einstein Archives at the Hebrew University of Jerusalem, Israel.)

Einstein explained that, psychologically, *A* rests upon the *E*. However, no logical path exists from *E* to *A*, only an intuitive connection, which is always subject to revocation. From axioms, one can make certain deductions (*S*), which deductions may lay claim to being correct. In essence, Einstein was saying that the theory determines what we observe. Einstein argued that scientific thinking is speculative, and only in its end product does it lead to a system that is characterized as "logical simplicity." Unable to satisfactorily describe his thoughts in words, Einstein made his thought visible by diagramming his philosophy's main features and characteristics.

Diagram Your Thinking

The notebooks of Einstein, Martha Graham, da Vinci, Edison, and Darwin suggest that one of the primary reasons they achieved greatness was their ability to represent their subjects visually by diagramming and mapping. In Darwin's notebooks there is a frequently occurring diagrammatic representation of nature as an irregularly branching tree. His tree diagrams helped him capture his thoughts about evolutionary change by allowing him to reach out in many directions at once and pull seemingly unrelated information together. Each diagram was densely packed with potential meaning. Darwin drew a number of these diagrams, both to perfect the diagrams and to use them to comprehend what is known and to guide in the search for what was not yet known.

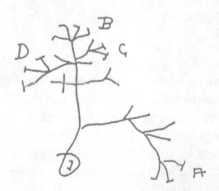

Darwin's diagrams were pivotal factors in the thinking process that led to his theory of evolution. He used them to work through many points: as a way of classifying the relation of different species to each other, as a way to represent the accident of life, the irregularity of nature, the explosiveness of growth, and of the necessity to keep the number of species constant. Within fifteen months after drawing his first tree diagram, Darwin had solved the major problems of his theory of evolution.

Try looking at your problem diagrammatically, as well as verbally. First, write your problem statement as completely as you can. Then diagram it by printing the problem in the center of a piece of paper and drawing a box around it. Ask yourself, "What are the main features and characteristics of the problem?" Print all potential answers above straight lines that emanate from the box. The following is a simple diagram on improving an organization's productivity. The main features branch out from the problem.

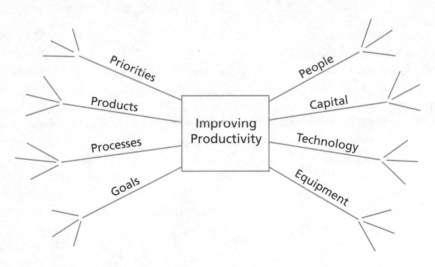

You can extend your thinking by mapping the answers to the question. In other words, if X is the answer to the first question–"What are the main features and characteristics of the problem?"–then you can ask, "What are the main features and characteristics of X?" (What are the main features and characteristics of people, capital, technology, and so on?) By drawing circles around related answers and linking them up in a contrasting color, you start to give texture to your understanding of the problem. Arranging information in this way invites you to look for relationships and connections among the answers. When you finish, ask,

- Did the diagram add to my understanding of the problem?
- Did I find out anything about the approach of the problem?
- What's missing?
- What areas are foggy?
- What am I now seeing?
- What should I be thinking about?

Everyone who thinks at all has noticed that language is practically useless for describing anything that goes on in the brain. Pure thinking is a dynamic, shifting, active thing. It is condensed and telegrammatic, and only when it is expanded in form and made communicable to others does it lose its active, volatile, and creative character. A way to capture your thought before it loses its active nature is to mind map it.

Mind Mapping

Mind mapping was formalized as a technique in the early 1970s by Tony Buzan, a British brain researcher, as a whole-brain alternative to linear thinking. Mind mapping makes it easier to access the tremendous potential of your brain by representing your thoughts using key words. It's an organized brainstorming method to find out what you know by writing a central theme and then depicting thoughts and associations as vines growing in all directions from the central theme.

Mind mapping does not select information by categories, but sees whatever is in the mind. In the illustration below, I start with the word "yellow" as the central theme and then print the first thoughts that come to mind. My first thoughts are "bus," "green," "orange," "daffodil," and "banana." A quick spray of associations comes from each thought as "bus" leads to "truck" to "ambulance" to "fire engine" to "fire" to "ambulance" to "hospital" and "green." Other thoughts lead to fruits and flowers and school. The associations are potentially infinite as each association triggers new ones.

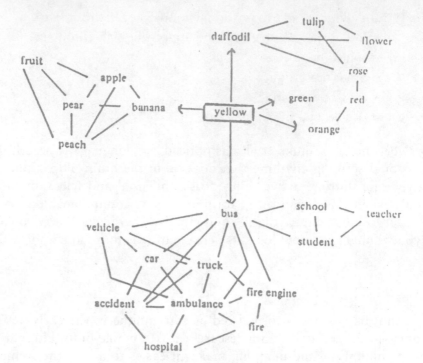

A mind map reaches out in all directions and catches thoughts from any angle. Once the human brain realizes that it can associate anything with anything else, it will instantaneously find associations. After you map your thoughts, you can then look for unifying patterns and connections that might link seemingly different thoughts or themes into a new idea or creative solution to a problem.

A major characteristic of creative geniuses is the tendency to extend their associative horizon widely and unusually. The rest of us tend to constrain our associative horizons, in the spirit of linear and explanatory thinking, and to minimize imaginative connections, which are seen as carelessness and lack of discipline. Yet associations and imaginative connections are essential elements of creativity; they distinguish ideas that are truly original and innovative from those that are logical but inconsequential.

A mind map is a tool to help us deliberately and consciously extend our associations so we can make imaginative connections and unleash our creative powers. Following is an example of a mind map about mind-mapping guidelines.

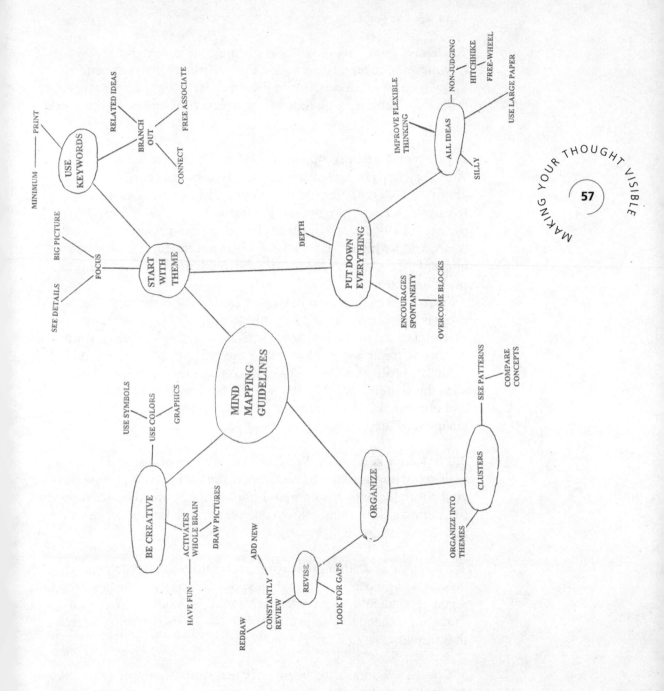

MIND MAPPING GUIDELINES

START WITH THEME
- USE KEYWORDS
  - MINIMUM — PRINT
  - BRANCH OUT
    - RELATED IDEAS
    - CONNECT
    - FREE ASSOCIATE
- FOCUS
  - BIG PICTURE
  - SEE DETAILS

PUT DOWN EVERYTHING
- DEPTH
- ALL IDEAS
  - IMPROVE FLEXIBLE THINKING
  - NON-JUDGING
  - HITCHHIKE
  - FREE-WHEEL
  - USE LARGE PAPER
  - SILLY
- ENCOURAGES SPONTANEITY
- OVERCOME BLOCKS

BE CREATIVE
- USE SYMBOLS
- USE COLORS
- GRAPHICS
- ACTIVATES WHOLE BRAIN
  - HAVE FUN
  - DRAW PICTURES

ORGANIZE
- REVISE
  - ADD NEW
  - REDRAW
  - CONSTANTLY REVIEW
  - LOOK FOR GAPS
- CLUSTERS
  - SEE PATTERNS
  - COMPARE CONCEPTS
  - ORGANIZE INTO THEMES

Here are the guidelines:

1. **Theme.** Print a word or short phrase that describes the essence of your subject on a large sheet of paper (the bigger, the better). Draw a circle around it. If you prefer, draw a picture that represents your subject. A picture will enhance your ability to think creatively.

2. **Key words and prompts.** Alfred, Lord Tennyson's fellow poet Arthur Henry Hallam observed that Tennyson's genius was the ability to collect fragments of thought and use them as themes from which his writing would spring. Tennyson would explore a theme, usually a word or short phrase that had popped into his mind, and let it trigger associated ideas and images. This process allowed a stream of ideas to gush forth where only a trickle previously had been found.

   Key words enable us to draw out related ideas through the process of association. It's possible to draw out complex patterns of association from a few key words. For example, from a drop of water one might associate out into the gushing Niagara or the vast Atlantic. Write down as quickly as you can thoughts associated with the center word. Use key words. Ignore all irrelevant words and phrases and concentrate only on expressing the essentials and what these "associations" excite in your mind.

3. **Print your key words.** Printing makes more of a visual image in your mind and is easier to remember than handwriting. Express your thoughts with a minimum number of key words. You want to minimize clutter and allow yourself the freedom to make creative associations.

4. **Put down everything that comes to mind.** Fill out the page as quickly as you can by printing all spontaneous associations even if they seem ridiculous or irrelevant. If you get stuck, pick out any thought on the map and print the first association you make from that thought.

5. **Connect.** Connect the key words with lines radiating from the center. By linking words, you show clearly how one thought relates to another and you will begin to see relationships that will

help you gather and organize your ideas into clusters. Add additional words if necessary.

Our brains are wired to see order and we invent elaborate architectures to do so. Psychologists have found that if you put people in a room with a contraption of lightbulbs wired to blink on and off at random, they will quickly discern what they believe are patterns, theories for predicting which bulb will be next to blink. Once a person becomes immersed in thinking about a subject, he or she will find it difficult not to see patterns and make connections.

6. **Use graphics**. Colors, pictures, and symbols can be used to highlight important thoughts and to show relationships between different areas on the map. You might color code the main points: red for most important, green for secondary points, and so on. Or you could use asterisks, numbers, letters, or geometric symbols as tools to help organize your thoughts. Pictures and abstract symbols can be used to stimulate your creativity by triggering your right brain.

7. **Cluster**. Organize the major clusters into themes. A mind map is a creation on paper that comes close to the way your mind clusters concepts in your brain. Because of this, the brain more readily accepts the information contained on a map. It can be pictured in the mind's eye. Once your ideas are clustered, you can move from the viewpoint of the creator to the viewpoint of the critic who is seeing the ideas for the first time. As a critic, you can test your associations, missing information, and areas where you need more and better ideas. Mind mapping is an idea generator. It is not the supplier of raw material, so your map may show areas where you need to collect more information.

8. **Revise**. Darwin's first tree diagram was primitive and fragmentary. As he progressed in his work, his diagrams become more elaborate and detailed. Similarly, Vincent van Gogh's artistic genius followed a similar process of revision. He would move from his original vision to completed expression by the following stages. He would start with a conceptualization for a subject and paint it in one session, perhaps in three or four hours. Then he would create a whole series of paintings for the subject, trying to

get closer and closer to his vision, until he was satisfied.

In the same way, by continually revising, refining, and elaborating your mind map, you keep your thinking active and get closer and closer to the ultimate answer. Readily revise your mind map by adding new thoughts or eliminating elements that seem extraneous.

Mind mapping allows you to group and regroup concepts, encouraging comparisons. Moving and synthesizing concepts into new clusters often provokes new ideas. How would you describe the figure below?

● ● ● ●   ● ● ● ●   ● ● ● ●

They are twelve separate and unrelated dots. However, because of the way they are clustered, we perceive them as separate groups of dots. In fact, it is almost impossible to see them any other way. By organizing the dots into clusters, one gives them a new identity. This is what happens when you graphically map your thinking. When you organize your thoughts into clusters, you give them a new identity and the process of idea evolution can really begin.

In the dot illustration, you can also choose to focus on one specific dot or one group of dots or on three separate groups of dots. Similarly, when you map your subject, you can emphasize either individual thoughts, a cluster of thoughts, or the subject as a whole. Mind mapping provides an easy way to move from the general to the specific and from the specific to the general. In addition, mind mapping

- Clears your mind of mental clutter
- Focuses you on the subject
- Activates your whole brain
- Allows you to develop a detailed organization of your subject
- Demonstrates connections between isolated pieces of information
- Gives you a clear picture of both the details and the big picture
- Gives you a graphic representation of what you know about the subject, allowing you to easily identify gaps in your information
- Requires you to concentrate on your subject, which helps get information about it transferred from short-term to long-term memory

Group Mind Maps

In a group, individuals combine their energies to create a group mind map as "hard copy" for the group's brainstorming session. First, have each participant create a mind map about the subject. Having completed the individual maps, create a group map. Use wall-sized sheets of paper to record the basic structure. Cover an entire wall with paper. The drawing of the map can be done by one good mind mapper or by the whole group. Color and codes should be agreed on in advance to ensure consistency and clarity. All ideas are totally accepted and are incorporated into the map.

Variations

Once you understand the basic principles of mind mapping, try different variations until you find the method that works best for you. Following are some suggestions.

Moving mind maps. An interesting way to cluster your thoughts after mind mapping is to copy your key words from your map on index cards, group them into stacks of associated thoughts, and then tape them to a wall. This creates a moving mind map on a wall. The basic guidelines are

1. Print the key words from your mind map on index cards, one key word per card.
2. Write the central theme of the problem on a different-colored card and tape it to the wall or chalkboard.
3. Tape all the other cards to the wall or chalkboard, around the central theme card. Cluster related thoughts together. The act of transferring your thoughts onto cards makes it easier for you to group and regroup your thoughts, which facilitates comparisons. Moving your cards around into new juxtapositions often will provoke new ideas.
4. Once your cards are taped to the wall in clusters, you can test your associations, discover what's missing, and discover areas where you need more and better ideas.
5. Add cards as new thoughts and relationships occur to you.
6. If you taped the cards to a chalkboard or a large sheet of paper, you can connect related thoughts with colored arrows. On a wall, you can use stickpins and string to connect related areas.

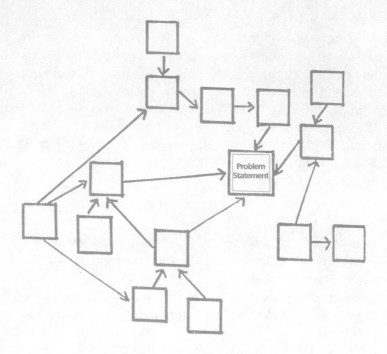

It often helps to involve yourself completely in a subject, in much the same way you might become totally absorbed in a movie or novel, before you mind map it. The Spanish artist Pablo Picasso would totally immerse himself in his subject before he painted it.

Picasso's technique

The artist, Picasso observed, paints to unload feelings, visions, and thoughts. This, he believed, was the whole secret of art. When Picasso went for a walk in the forest, he thought about nothing but the color green until he got "green indigestion." To get rid of this "full" sensation, he unloaded it into a picture. Picasso's copious work was a product of this continual refilling and emptying of his mind on canvas.

After Picasso was "filled" with his subject, he would start a work of art from some arbitrary point, proceeding in a desultory manner, and somehow end up with something novel and original. One representation of this method is found in the movie *The Mystery of Picasso*. He begins with a flower, transforms it into a fish, then into a chicken–switching back and forth from black and white to color–which he then refashions into a cat surrounded on the side by human beings. As Picasso painted, his topic changed as his thoughts changed. The true painting, he seems to indicate, can only occur after a process uncovers what is there.

To try Picasso's technique, collect as much material as you can about your problem in an easily readable form–for example, summaries of related articles and books, the experiences of others, ideas that people have given you, and competitors' actions. Read through all the material as rapidly as you can in one sitting until you are "filled" with your subject. Then, like Picasso did with his art, start from some arbitrary theme and mind map it, letting the thoughts flow while you are in this "activated" state. Refashion your map as your thoughts and topics change, just as Picasso transformed objects and switched back and forth between topics as he painted.

Finally, ask yourself what your mind map means. What have you uncovered that you didn't know was there? Do you notice any patterns? If so, what do they suggest? What solutions pop into your head? If you allow all the information to evolve naturally, new ideas will develop.

Thought cards. Pure thinking is generative and can be characterized by rapid bursts of ideas embedded in the sustained thought of the thinker. Picasso's technique activates generative thinking with mind maps. Another way to activate a rapid flow of ideas is to use index cards.

First, collect and read material as described in "Picasso's technique." After you have read through all the material as rapidly as you can and "filled" yourself, write your thoughts on index cards as quickly as you can. Write one thought per card, using key words or phrases. Write anything that comes to mind as quickly as you can. Keep writing until your thoughts stop. Then, arrange the cards in stacks of associated thoughts. Go through them again and add new cards as new thoughts occur to you.

Write the subject or problem on a card and tape it to the wall or chalkboard. Tape all the other cards to the wall around the subject cards. Cluster related thoughts together. Once your cards are taped to the wall, look for associations, connections, gaps, and areas where you need more information. Keep grouping and regrouping your cards into new juxtapositions until you get the inspiration you need.

Picasso's technique begins by filling yourself with information from a variety of sources about the subject and then mind mapping associations. Eventually, thoughts are clustered and organized into common components or themes. The themes evolve from the map. An alternative is to first determine your subject's basic themes or components and then map each separate theme.

Theme Mapping

When Charles Darwin first set out to solve the problem of evolution, he simply was not ready for natural selection. He initially organized his thinking around eight significant themes of the problem. Over time, he rejected some of his themes–the idea of direct adaptation, for instance. Other ideas were emphasized, like the idea of continuity, or were confirmed for the first time–like the idea that change is continuous. Some were recognized, such as the frequency of variation. These themes brought about shifts in his thinking. He played the critic, surveying his own positions; the inventor, devising new solutions and ideas; and the learner, accumulating new facts not prominent before.

The original method of mind mapping is simply to map lots of thoughts and then weed out the ones that are nonsensical or unrealistic by revising the map several times. The major themes and ideas evolve over time in mind mapping. In theme mapping, the goal is to map more realistic and theme-related thoughts and ideas from the outset by establishing a structure of connected themes in advance. Here are the guidelines:

1. *Subject.* Print or draw your subject or problem in the center of a large sheet of paper.

2. *Themes.* List the significant themes, components, or dimensions of your subject. The optimal number of themes for a manageable map is between six and eight. If you have more than eight, make additional maps. Ask questions: What are my specific objectives? What are the constants in my problem? If my subject were a book, what would the chapter headings be? What are the dimensions of my problem? For example, suppose you wanted to improve brainstorming. If brainstorming were a book, what would the chapter headings be?

3. *Branches.* Print the significant themes around the subject and connect them to the subject with straight lines. For example, if your subject is "Improving Brainstorming Sessions," your themes might be "People," "Environment," "Resources," "Facilitator," and "Rules." In the example to follow, the themes are connected to the subject as branches.

4. *Mind map.* Now extend your thinking by mind mapping (see mind-map guidelines) each theme as a separate branch. Free associate and make associations. For example, the theme "Rules" leads to the key thoughts of "Defer judgment," "Quantity," "Quota," "Freewheel," "Hitchhiking on other ideas," "Combine ideas," and so on.

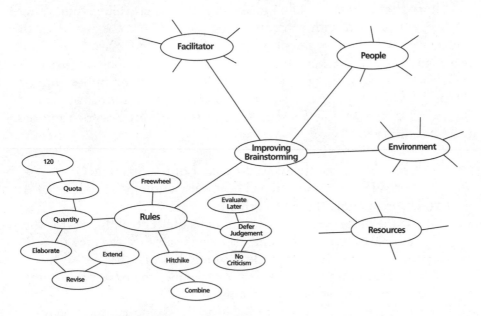

   The idea is to extend each theme as far as you can. When you've finished mapping each separate theme, look for links and connections between the separate themes. Explore each theme for possible new interpretations and ideas.

   The strategy of organizing creative thinking around core themes is a favorite of many creative thinkers, including the major poet T. S. Eliot. His poem *The Waste Land* is arguably the most famous and influential poem of this century. Eliot started with the central theme of "the decline of self and civilization" and branched out on an amazing number of subthemes. Each of the lines, and certainly each of the stanzas, is pregnant with meaning and could itself launch a separate poem on a separate topic. This strategy not only conveyed to the reader a universe of poetry but provided several different universes, each with an enormous number of entry points for the audience.

Lotus Blossom

Eliot's strategy was to start with a theme, subdivide it into sub-themes, and then to make variations on each of the subthemes. Yasuo Matsumura of Clover Management Research in Chiba City, Japan, developed Lotus Blossom, a creative-thinking technique that diagrammatically mimics T. S. Eliot's strategy. You start with a central theme and expand into subthemes and ideas until you've created several different subthemes, each with separate entry points. In Lotus Blossom, the petals around the core of the blossom are figuratively "peeled back" one at a time, revealing a key component or subtheme. This approach is pursued in ever-widening circles until the problem or opportunity is comprehensively explored. The cluster of themes and subthemes that are developed in one way or another provide several different possibilities. The guidelines are

1. Write the central theme in the center of the diagram.
2. Write ideas or applications in the surrounding circles labeled *A* to *H* surrounding the central theme.
3. Use the ideas written in the circles as the central themes for the surrounding lotus blossom petals or boxes. Thus, the idea or application you wrote in circle A would become the central theme for the lower-middle box A. It now becomes the basis for generating eight new ideas or applications.
4. Continue the process until the lotus blossom diagram is completed.

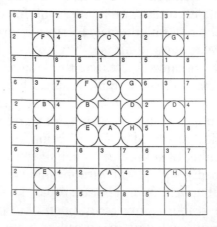

Suppose, for example, you want to create more value for your organization by increasing productivity or decreasing costs. You would

write "Add Value" in the center box. Next, write the eight most significant areas in your organization where you can increase productivity or
decrease costs in the circles labeled *A* to *H* that surround your central
box. Also write the same significant areas in the circles with the corre-
sponding letters spread around the diagram.

    Each area now represents a main theme that ties together the sur-
rounding boxes. For instance, in the sample diagram, the word "technology" in the circle labeled *A* serves as the theme for the lower-middle
group of boxes.

    For each theme, try to think of eight ways to add value. Think of
eight ideas or ways you can use technology to increase productivity or
reduce expenses, eight ideas or ways to make personnel more productive
or ways to decrease expenses, eight ideas or ways to create more value
for your delivery methods, and so on. If you complete the entire diagram, you'll have sixty-four new ideas or ways to increase productivity
or decrease expenses.

6	3	7	6	3	7	6	3	7
2	F Suppliers	4	2	C Travel Expenses	4	2	G Partner ships	4
5	1	8	5	1	8	5	1	8
6	3	7	F Suppliers	C Travel Expenses	G Partner ships	6	3	7
2	B Evaluation	4	B Evaluation	Add Value	D Delivery Methods	2	D Delivery Methods	4
5	1	8	E Facilities	A Technology	H Personnel	5	1	8
6	3	7	6	3	7	6	3	7
2	E Facilities	4	2	A Technology	4	2	H Personnel	4
5	1	8	5	1	8	5	1	8

In Lotus Blossom, ideas evolve into other ideas and applications. Because the components of the technique are dynamic, the ideas seem to flow outward with a momentum all their own.

Another dynamic thinking strategy is systemic thinking. Reality is made up of curves, but we're biased to see a straight-line, cause-effect view of the world. Geniuses tend to operate more in terms of "loops of interaction" or "mutual interaction" than linear or mechanical cause and effect. This thinking strategy typically allows them to track whole systems of interacting elements.

Freud, for instance, viewed mental processes as "merely isolated acts and parts of the whole psychic entity" and claimed that the "meaning" of a symptom could only be found in its relation to the larger system. Einstein rejected the mechanical statistical approaches to physics because he thought they ignored the deeper dynamics of the system and focused too much on the results and not enough on the processes. Freud and Einstein both believed that unless you looked at the whole system and all of its components you may miss the key relationships and how they interact.

System Mapping

Consider nature's creations. Nature doesn't just make leaves; it makes branches and trees and roots to go with them. It makes whole systems of interacting elements. Similarly, Edison didn't just invent an electric lightbulb–other people had invented electrified lamps. He invented a whole practical system for electric lighting, including dynamos, conduits, and a means for dividing up current that could illuminate a large number of bulbs.

A strategy to think systematically is system mapping. System mapping will shift us from focusing on the parts to seeing the whole, and from reacting to static "snapshots" of the problem to creating new possible futures by seeing new relationships and connections between the different components.

When you have a good sense, a good map, of how all the different components interact, you'll begin to see the deeper dynamics of the problem and will begin to look at it in a different way. Following are guidelines on how to make a system map:

1. Write a single word or short phrase that identifies your subject. Place it in the middle of the page and circle it. Your subject can be

anything: declining sales, training and development, marketing, future markets, corporate reorganization, and so on.

Example: An insurance agency that customizes and brokers insurance packages between insurance providers and corporations is interested in looking for ways to improve business possibilities. Their subject is "Improving Business."

2. Identify major components. These are the major areas of the domain that need to be considered. There are usually three to six major areas (for example, company, competition, environment, customer) that need to be considered. According to Buckminster Fuller, three elements are the minimum number of elements necessary to have a structure or pattern. Even when the number of variables is small, if the elements all mutually influence and relate to one another, quite sophisticated interactions can be stimulated. Freud's ability to handle a great deal of complexity with his simple model of the ego, id, and superego; Walt Disney's ability to play the role of the Dreamer, Realist, and Critic when creating ideas; and Einstein's famous $E=MC^2$ exemplify dynamic models based on three interrelated elements.

Draw your major components as outlying circles and link them back to the central subject.

Example: The major components for the insurance agency are "Our Company," "Insurance Providers," the "Corporate Customer," and the "Environment."

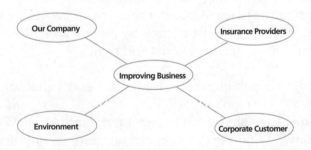

3. Identify the influences on each component. Every influence, whether positive or negative, is both cause and effect. Nothing is ever influenced in just one direction. Geniuses focus more on "relationships" between objects than on the objects themselves. In his theory of gravitational attraction, Isaac Newton pointed out

there is not one operation by which the sun attracts Jupiter and another by which Jupiter attracts the sun, but one operation by which the sun and Jupiter endeavor to approach each other.

The idea is to identify and link as many influences as possible to each component.

Some examples of common influencers are

A. Things that influence a company: product design, suppliers, workforce, management, materials, methods, machinery, financial performance, distribution channels, marketing, sales personnel

B. Things that influence a customer: competition, economy, needs, goals

C. Things that influence the environment: economy, technology, demographics

D. In our example, the influencers of our insurance company are technologies, cost-cutting procedures, competition, management, operations, and services.

The key to seeing reality is seeing circles of influence rather than straight lines. By linking influences to the major components, we break out of the reactive mindset that comes inevitably from linear thinking. Every circle tells a story. By mapping the flow of influence, you can see major patterns and trends.

4. Identify and link important factors for each influence. This step prompts a questioning process that often reveals trends and new developments. What has an impact on the influence? What's happening now? What are the recent trends and developments? What are the recent changes that are affecting the influence? List as many as possible and link to each influence.

Example: In our example, the important factors for the influence "Technologies" on the "Customers" component are "Fax," "Networks," "Database," "Internet," "Teleconference," and "EDI."

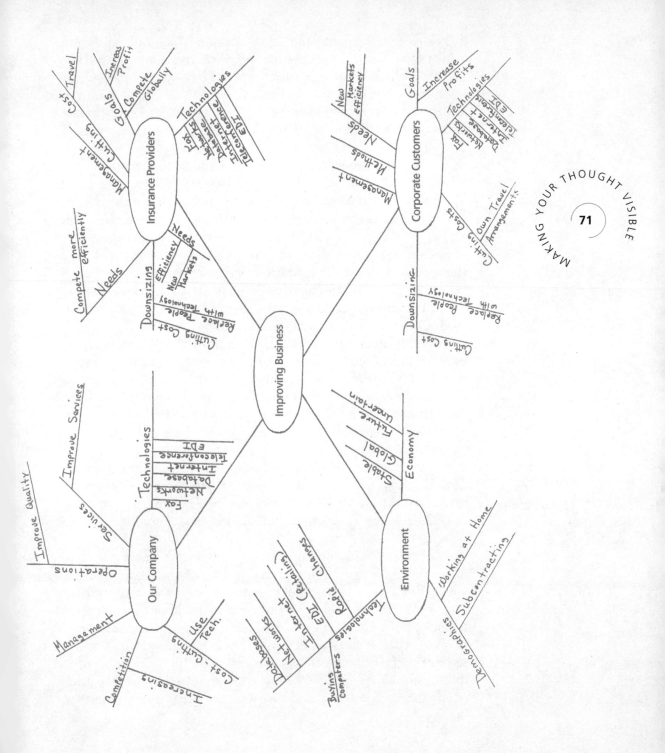

5. Prioritize influences and factors. Decide which influences and which factors or changes are having the biggest impact on the mess, or which influences are capable of having the biggest influence. Use color pens to color code the influences: Red–major; Green–moderate, Yellow–none. In our example the major influences are "Downsizing," "Cost-Cutting," and "Technologies."

6. Analyze the major impact items. Are the factors positive or negative? Why did the changes happen? Do they reflect a trend or a short-term event? What are all the possible causes of the change? Color code each item as to its impact. In our example, the agency realizes that the advances in technology will give the insurance providers and corporations the means to eliminate the middleman, the agency. Soon, the corporations will use their own computer power to scan a comprehensive database and select and customize an optimal insurance package for themselves, in the process cutting out the insurance agency.

If the insurance agency had used traditional brainstorming, listing linear cause-effect chains, they may not have seen the interrelationships between technology and cost-cutting that dominate their domain. Imagine the difficulties using everyday English to describe the domain's components, the influences upon the components, the major factors upon the influences, and the interrelationships between them.

However, when the agency maps and explores the relationship of technology and cost-cutting on them, the customer insurance providers, the corporate customer, and the environment, the chances are very good that it will identify it as a major challenge.

7. Brainstorm. Select an impact item factor and generate as many ideas, possibilities, or solutions as possible. In our example, the agency realizes that the changes in technology and corporate interest in cost-cutting is a long-term trend that will not be influenced by any changes in their services. They decide to brainstorm for ways to redefine their services to include fast, customized solutions to clients' emerging business problems, new kinds of value-added information, new specialized niche services, and ways to significantly improve personalized customer service in everything they do.

System mapping helps us to restructure the problem. In other words, one may suddenly look at a problem in a different way and be able to see it in terms of a different question. In our example, the insurance agency started out looking for ways to improve their existing services and ended up redefining their business.

System mapping has several benefits:

• The map tells a story. The main skill is to see the "story" that the map tells: how the components of the subject interrelate, how patterns of change are emerging, and how those patterns might be influenced. Einstein did no experiments, gathered no new information, and invented nothing new before he created the theory of relativity. What Einstein did was to tell a "new" story about how space, time, and energy interrelated and how those concepts influence and are influenced.

• The map helps us to see and keep "the big picture." The great sculptor Auguste Rodin saw the task of genius as keeping his "global idea." Rodin said it was necessary for him to maintain energetically his global idea so as to remain unceasingly close to it and closely connect with it the smallest details of his thought.

• The map helps us to see the relationships and connections between major factors, rather than linear cause-effect chains. Mozart's musical genius didn't come simply from his ability to recognize and play specific notes and manipulate qualities of sound such as tempo, volume, and tone. His gift involved perceiving and representing deep patterns, relationships, and universals through sound.

• The map helps us to identify processes of change rather than a series of unrelated static snapshots. Leonardo da Vinci's genius was the ability to see the "processes of the results" rather than the "results of the process."

• The system map allows us to see the details. For Freud, it was the details that seem contrary to the context or typical cultural assumptions that so often became key elements in his creative thinking. The strength of Freud's strategy, and of his genius, was to be able to find what was significant in the clusters of details that most people overlooked. Freud believed that the ideal reasoner would, when once shown a single fact in all its bearings, deduce from it not only all the events which led up to it, but also all the results which would follow from it. For example, Freud's study of Leonardo da Vinci's memory is an expression of the belief that a part of any system is in some way an expression of the whole.

Imagine yourself in a large auditorium. Above, you see many lights. Each bulb is separate from the others, and you may think of them, regarded that way, as so many separate entities. But now consider further. Each of these separate lightbulbs is a vehicle of light, and the light is not many but one. The light, which is one, appears through many different bulbs.

Similarly, when you look at a subject, you may think of its components as separate from each other and think of them as separate entities. System mapping gives you a way to visibly see how the components interact with each other to make the subject what it is. The subject, which is one, appears through different components, influences, and factors.

Diagramming Extreme Conditions

System mapping consists of two processing stages: a generative phase, in which the subject is mapped, followed by an exploratory phase, in which the map is explored for possible interpretations and ideas. Once the dynamics of a subject are represented, insight is gained and ideas begin to flow. Another way to visually represent the dynamics of your subject or situation is to diagram its extreme conditions.

Leonardo da Vinci observed that to really understand a subject, you should examine it under extreme conditions. He would first identify the significant factors of his subject, either through observation or imagination, and then explore the interaction of these factors under various conditions–especially extreme ones. For example, to understand human anatomy, da Vinci investigated a variety of questions: When a person puts on weight, what organs put on weight first? When the body is starved, what is the last organ to shrink? When you push your subject to its extremes, you'll quickly see its essential parts, crucial relationships, and driving principles.

Force Field Analysis

Force field analysis is a powerful technique that was developed by Kurt Lewin, a social psychologist, to visually identify how positive and negative forces dynamically influence subjects or situations by pushing them to one extreme or the other. We tend to see subjects as static and fixed. Yet the world is in a constant state of flux and subjects and relationships are dynamic and fluid. Positive and negative forces are constantly pushing and pulling a subject to one extreme or the other. Force field analysis is a way to explore the forces in order to devise a practical means of getting at them. This technique can help you

- Better define what your challenge is
- Make a careful assessment of all relevant factors
- Identify strengths you can maximize
- Identify weaknesses you can minimize
- Add more strengths

To make a force field diagram:

1. Write the challenge you are trying to solve.

2. Determine the extremes. On the left side of the sheet, describe the worst-case scenario. On the same line, at the right, describe the best-case scenario.

3. In the center, list all the significant factors or conditions of the subject or situation. It is helpful to list as many significant factors as you can when constructing the diagram.

4. As you list the conditions, you will find some of the forces pushing you to the best case while other forces are pulling you toward catastrophe. Draw a line that reflects whether you are being pushed or pulled by that factor and place an X where you feel you are at present.

5. Finally, examine all the Xs and place an X on the general continuum that extends from the "Best-Case Scenario" to the "Worst-Case Scenario." This gives you a snapshot of where you are at this time.

In the example below, the situation being analyzed is creative thinking. An individual is interested in becoming more of a creative thinker and decides to analyze her creativity. She describes her best case scenario as "Becoming Leonardo da Vinci," and her worst case is "Becoming a Dunce." In the middle, she listed her significant factors for creative thinking.

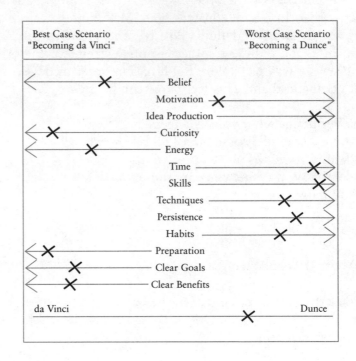

Some of the factors are being "pulled" toward the best case, and some are pushed toward the worst case. There are three options for moving the X toward the best-case scenario:

1. Minimize or eliminate your negatives.
2. Maximize your positives.
3. Add more positive forces.

In the example, one could choose to develop ways to minimize the negatives by working on them. For example, she might increase her idea production by giving herself a daily idea quota, allocate one hour each day for creative thinking, read books on creative thinking to learn the techniques, start practicing creative-thinking habits, such as learning how to take risks, or become more persistent by refusing to give up on an idea until she makes it work.

Or, she could choose to further strengthen some of the positive forces by putting still more energy into her creative-thinking efforts, improving her preparation by learning as much as she can about her subject, and asking her supervisor to make creative thinking one of her measurable goals in her job performance. She could also create new positive forces to further outweigh the negative forces; for instance, she might work on her drawing skills so she could represent her subjects visually as well as verbally and add that force to her analysis.

The particular value of the analysis grows out of the way the factors are diagrammed and assessed. In our example, the X on the "da Vinci" to "Dunce" general continuum is drifting toward the "Dunce." The factors that relate to specific thinking skills, idea production, and techniques are moving toward the worst-case scenario. Eventually the dynamic nature of the component factors makes it clear that one must create active ideas and actions to reverse the forces and move the factors toward the best-case scenario. For example, to dramatically improve her creative thinking (move the X toward the best-case scenario), our subject could enroll in a creative-thinking class at a local college, attend open-enrollment seminars on creativity, and ask her supervisor to bring in a creativity expert to conduct on-site workshops for her and other employees.

When Mozart composed, he started with the large structure of his musical composition–its shape and basic dynamics. Once having fixed the significant details of the overall structure, Mozart would go back and adjust and refine the details toward a "best-case scenario" for his musical composition. Sometimes this activity would inspire him to add a new musical dimension to the piece, which he would excitedly move to integrate into the whole composition. This is something like the way factors are worked on in force field analysis.

Let's consider the probability of getting a major sale. The first thing we do is construct a force field analysis with the best-case scenario of closing the sale and the worst-case scenario of losing the sale. Then the factors are listed and diagrammed as follows.

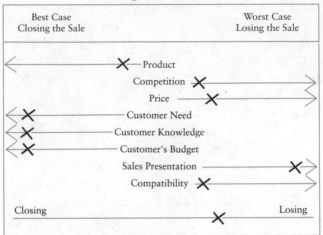

Getting a Major Sale

In this situation, we have the superior product; however, our price is higher; our competition is perceived by the customer to be superior; we gave a poor sales presentation; and there is a sense that the customer does not like the salesperson. We have a good chance of losing the sale unless we take specific actions.

To improve our chances, we might

• Offer packaged financing to offset the price differential

• Bring in support personnel (product managers, engineers, etc.) to offset the poor sales presentation and the perceived dislike of the salesperson

• Emphasize our customer service to offset the perception of a superior competitor

• Bring in testimonials from satisfied customers

A force field analysis of the sales situation allows us to realistically assess our probability of getting the sale and gives us the chance to create alternative ideas to move the forces in a positive direction. Just as Mozart would be inspired to integrate a new musical dimension into his composition as a result of his refinements, our analysis inspires us to integrate packaged financing, support personnel, and customer service (new dimensions) into the sales situation.

Visual Brainstorming

Creative geniuses use a great diversity of graphic means in shaping and communicating their thoughts. Some use diagrams or maps. Others build three-dimensional, physical models. For example, Francis Crick and James Watson built and experimented with single- and double-chained three-dimensional models that led to the discovery that the DNA molecule is in the shape of a "double helix," winning them the Nobel Prize in 1962. And still others, like Martha Graham, use simple, fragmentary schematic drawings and sketches.

Martha Graham, a creative genius in modern dance, defied the conventions of traditional ballet and created her own dance vocabulary with simple drawings and sketches. Her notebooks are full of drawings and sketches of her ideas and thoughts, which enabled her to conceptualize them without using words. Virtually each new dance proved more daring than its predecessors.

Composer John Corigliano, whose much-lauded works include *The Ghosts of Versailles*, prepares for a big commission in a similar way. In the building of a piece of music, at first, he creates no music or words at all. Instead, he sketches his ideas and thoughts and sometimes just draws abstract shapes.

In the illustration below, I've visually arranged the letter *T*, the number eight, and the letter *P* into a visual synthesis. Most people easily interpret this as a mallet striking balls through a hoop in a game of croquet. The dynamics of the drawing immediately suggest a particular interpretation.

If I had asked you to synthesize the *T*, eight, and *P* into a game of croquet, you would have found it difficult, if not impossible, to do so without drawing or sketching various possibilities. In fact, if you read a detailed description of how you can combine a *T*, eight, and *P* to represent

a game of croquet, you would still find it impossible to understand without visualizing and drawing it.

We know more than we can tell in words. For example, we know our best friend's face and can recognize it among a million faces, yet we usually cannot tell how we recognize a face. So much of our knowledge simply cannot be put into words. In fact, experiments have demonstrated that when people were asked to describe their best friend's face in writing before identifying it, the written description significantly interfered with the ability to recognize it. In this instance, a written description constrains the ability to recognize the face. However, if asked to draw or sketch that best friend's face, people were able to conceptualize what he or she looks like and, thus, find it more quickly.

Visual brainstorming is an attempt to use drawings and sketches to conceptualize and capture ideas. The basic idea is to draw a sketch of how the problem might be solved. The sketches may be abstract, symbolic, or realistic. Draw the solution to your problem. Then review and revise it by modifying it or by making a new sketch or drawing. Keep modifying or making new sketches as long as you can. Finally, construct a final solution from one of the sketches or from parts of different sketches.

Groups

Participants are allowed five minutes to draw sketches of a problem solution. The sketches may be abstract, symbolic, or realistic. No talking is permitted. After five minutes, the participants pass their sketches to the person on their right. They review the sketch they receive, add features, modify the drawing, or make a new sketch on the same page. They then pass this drawing to the person on their right. This process of modifying and passing the modified sketches continues for about thirty minutes. Finally, the participants collect and examine all the drawings and select a final solution or construct a final solution from parts of different sketches.

PART II
THINKING WHAT NO ONE ELSE IS THINKING

Creative genius operates similarly to Darwin's theory of biological evolution. According to Darwin, nature creates many possibilities through blind "trial and error" and then lets the process of natural selection decide which species survive. In nature, 95 percent of new species fail and die within a short period of time. Genius is analogous to biological evolution in that it requires the unpredictable generation of a large quantity of alternatives and conjectures. From this quantity of alternatives and conjectures, the genius retains the best ideas for further development and communication. The first strategy, "Thinking Fluently," in Part II presents how geniuses produce prodigious quantities of ideas.

An important aspect of this theory is that, as in evolution, you need some means of producing variation in your ideas, and for this variation to be truly effective, it must be "blind." To count as "blind," the variations are shaped by chance or unrelated factors. In nature, a gene pool totally lacking in variation would be unable to adapt to changing circumstances, with consequences that would be fatal to the species' survival. In time, the genetically encoded wisdom would convert to foolishness. A comparable process operates within us. Every individual has the ability to create ideas based on his or her existing patterns of thinking, on the way he or she was taught to think. But without any provision for variations, ideas eventually stagnate and lose their adaptive advantages. As I said before, if you always think the way you've always thought, you'll always get what you've always got. The same old, same old ideas.

Speak the following words aloud: joke, joke, joke. Now, what is the white of an egg called? Your brain organizes incoming information according to your existing patterns of thinking, selecting a thinking pattern to process the information. If you said "yolk," you were fooled by the pattern created by the repetition of the word "joke." The answer is "albumen," which is the white part of the egg.

Our minds build up patterns that enable us to simplify and cope with a complex world, based on our experiences in life, education, and work that have been successful in the past. We look at 6 X 6 and 36 appears automatically, without conscious thought. We examine a new product for our company and know it is a good design at an appropriate price. We look at a business plan and know that the financial projections are not good. We do these things routinely, because of our thinking patterns, based on our past experiences. In addition, these thinking patterns help us perform repetitive tasks precisely, such as driving an automobile or making a sales presentation. But this same patterning makes it hard for us to come up with new ideas and creative solutions to problems, especially when confronted with unusual data.

Creativity implies a deviance from past experiences and procedures. For example, cut a cake into eight slices using no more than three cuts. Most people have trouble coming up with one solution because of their past experiences cutting cakes. To solve this, you need to change the way you think about cakes, a piece of cake and how to cut a cake. One solution is to cut the cake in half and stack the one half on top of the other. Cut this piece in half, stack the pieces on top of one another and cut them. Or cut the cake into quarters and then slice the cake horizontally through the quarters. Or cut the cake as illustrated below.

When you break out of your established patterns and ignore the conventional wisdom, you'll discover that there are many solutions.

In nature, a genetic mutation is a variation that is created by a random or chance event that ignores the conventional wisdom contained in parental chromosomes. Nature then lets the process of natural selection decide which variations survive and thrive. An analogous process operates within geniuses. Creative geniuses produce a rich variety of original ideas and solutions because they ignore conventional ways of thinking and look for different ways to think about problems. They deliberately change the way they think by provoking different thinking patterns that incorporate chance and unrelated factors into their thinking. These different thinking patterns enable them to look at the same information as everyone else and see something different.

The strategies in Part II enabled creative geniuses to produce a rich variety of original ideas and creative solutions to problems by provoking different thinking patterns. They include several strategies:

- Combining things in novel ways in "Making Novel Combinations"
- Using random stimuli in "Connecting the Unconnected"
- Thinking in opposites in "Looking at the Other Side"
- Thinking metaphorically and analogically in "Looking in Other Worlds"
- Actively seeking the accidental discovery in "Finding What You're Not Looking For"

The strategies do not reproduce the creative experience; they only suggest it. To illustrate, let us say that you accept my notion that the best way to see my neighborhood is to stand on the roof of my house. This does not reproduce the experience; it is a suggestion. To realize the experience, you cannot will yourself to fly up to the roof. You need a specific tool, such as a ladder, that allows you to get on the roof and look around. In the same way, when you accept my notion that geniuses get ideas by combining things in novel ways, you cannot will yourself to suddenly start thinking this way. You need specific techniques to show you how to do it. This is why each strategy contains specific techniques and practical tools with precise instructions on how to implement the strategy to get the ideas you need in your business and personal life.

These strategies liberate your creativity by breaking up your conventional thinking patterns and stimulating new thinking patterns by juxtaposing unlikely information. Illustration A shows a conventional thinking pattern, which shows thought moving linearly from a problem to a solution. This is how we've been taught to think. When confronted with a problem, we analytically select the most promising approach based on past experiences in life, education, and work, exclude all other approaches, and work within a clearly defined direction toward a conventional solution.

Illustration A

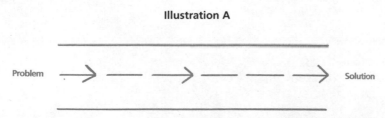

Problem → → → Solution

Illustration B shows how a genius will break up this conventional thinking pattern by introducing random stimuli. This action provokes new thinking patterns that lead to the formation of new ideas and concepts that you cannot get using the conventional way of thinking.

Illustration B

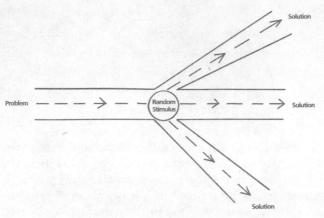

This part concludes with a final strategy, "Awakening the Collaborative Spirit," which presents conditions for open and honest collaborative thinking in group brainstorming sessions.

STRATEGY THREE: THINKING FLUENTLY

A distinguishing characteristic of genius is immense productivity. All geniuses produce. Bach wrote a cantata every week, even when he was sick or exhausted. Mozart produced more than six hundred pieces of music. Einstein is best known for his paper on relativity, but he published 248 other papers. Darwin is known for his theory of evolution, but he wrote 119 other publications in his lifetime. Freud published 330 papers and Maslow 165. Rembrandt produced around 650 paintings and 2,000 drawings and Picasso executed more than 20,000 works. Shakespeare wrote 154 sonnets. Some were masterpieces, while others were no better than his contemporaries could have written, and some were simply bad. In fact, more bad poems were composed by the major poets than the minor poets. They composed more bad poems than minor poets simply because they produced more poetry.

The common misconception that phenomenal creative geniuses contribute only a few selective masterworks is plain wrong. Thomas Edison may be best known for his incandescent lightbulb and phonograph, but he held 1,093 patents, still the record. Edison looked at creativity as simply good, honest hard work. "Genius," he once said, "is 1 percent inspiration and 99 percent perspiration." It took him nine thousand experiments to perfect the lightbulb and fifty thousand to invent the storage-cell battery. Once, when an assistant asked why he continued to persist trying to discover a long-lasting filament for the lightbulb after thousands of failures, Edison explained he didn't understand the question. In his mind, he hadn't failed once. Instead, he discovered thousands of things that didn't work.

True-North Thinking

Geniuses produce because they think fluently. Fluency of thought means generating quantities of ideas. To think fluently, it's necessary to organize your thinking around a set number of principles, which I call "True-North Thinking." True North is a standard against which all courses are measured. A run-of-the-mill compass points to magnetic north, which shifts over time. Only a gyrocompass points to "true north," an unyielding spot that won't lead ships astray. Only if you organize your thinking around a set of True-North thinking principles when you brainstorm for ideas will true idea production follow. These principles are timeless, timely, solid.

The True-North principles for creative thinking are

- Defer judgment while generating ideas.
- Generate as many ideas as possible.
- Record ideas as they occur.
- Elaborate or improve upon the ideas.

Defer Judgment

When looking for ideas, either alone or with a group, it is essential not to judge, evaluate, or criticize ideas as they are generated. Nothing kills creativity more quickly or more absolutely than critical, judgmental thinking.

This is difficult for us to do. We have been educated and conditioned to be critical, judgmental creatures, and we judge new thoughts and ideas instinctively and immediately. Only humans can try to come up with new ideas while simultaneously coming up with all the reasons why the ideas won't work. It's like driving a car with your foot on the gas and your foot on the brake at the same time. Consequently, whenever we brainstorm for ideas, we spend most of our time imagining all the reasons why an idea can't work or can't be done, instead of generating as many ideas as we can. Judging, it seems, is safer than attempting to generate something new, and people often concentrate on judging ideas, to the exclusion of generating them. Difficulties arise when people judge ideas too early and reject them before all their implications are considered.

Below is a diagram of a person evaluating ideas as they are offered. The person thinks of idea A and rejects it as unsound. Then the person thinks of ideas B and C and rejects both out of hand. Eventually, the person moves toward idea D, which is a safe, conservative idea that compares favorably with the person's past experiences and carries no risk. Once an idea is judged, creative thought crystallizes and stops. Few new ideas are generated, and eventually, thoughts are channeled to weak, safe, conservative ideas.

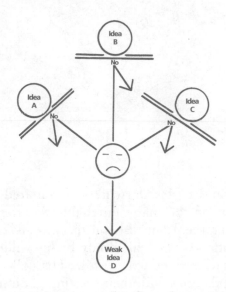

The next diagram represents the thought process of a person who does not evaluate ideas as they are offered. Here, the person is able to think fluidly and freely, freewheel, hitchhike, piggyback, and combine ideas to create even more ideas, until the breakthrough "eureka" idea is achieved. Nonjudgmental thinking is dynamic and fluid. Ideas bounce off each other to trigger additional ideas and combinations of ideas, multiplying the possibilities.

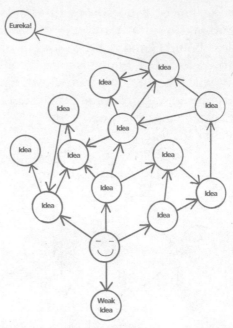

Francis Darwin, Charles Darwin's son, admired his father's ability to reserve judgment on the many untenable theories that occurred to him, not condemning them out of hand the way his colleagues did. His richness of imagination was equaled only by his willingness to consider what others did not consider worthwhile. His colleagues would compare new ideas and theories with their existing patterns of experience. If the ideas didn't fit, they would reject them out of hand. Conversely, Darwin would consider all ideas and theories to see where they led. His colleagues' thought was static. Darwin's was dynamic and fluid. This willingness to consider what others called "fool's experiments" led to his theory of evolution.

Possibility thinking

The secret to deferring judgment while generating a lot of ideas is to separate your thinking into two stages: possibility thinking and practicality thinking. Possibility thinking is the raw generation of ideas, without judgment or evaluation of any kind. You turn off your internal critic. Your internal critic is that part of your mind that is constantly telling you why something can't work or can't be done. The strategy is to generate as many ideas, both obvious and novel, as possible, without criticism of any kind.

After you've created the maximum number of ideas possible, you change your strategy to practicality thinking, the evaluation and judgment of ideas, to find the ideas that have the most value to you. Edison once declared that he constructed three thousand different theories in connection with electric lighting, each one of them reasonable, before he decided on the one theory that was the most practical and profitable. His first goal was to construct as many possibilities as he could, and then he turned to the business of evaluation to find the one that was the most practical and profitable. Possibility thinking and practicality thinking are two separate mental operations, without a compromise, in-between position.

Quantity

Edison's New Jersey laboratory contains a staggering display of hundreds of phonograph horns of every shape, size, and material. Some were round, square, angular, thin, short, squat while others are curved and as long as six feet. This collection of rejected ideas is a visual testament to Edison's thinking strategy—in essence, to explore every conceivable possibility. For every brilliant idea Edison had, he had many duds, like the horse-drawn contraption that would collect snow and ice in the winter and compress it into blocks that families could use in the summer as a refrigerant.

Quantity breeds quality

Imagine a pearl diver on an island in the South Seas. He pushes his canoe off from shore, paddles out into the lagoon, dives deep into the water, picks an oyster off the bottom, surfaces, climbs into his boat, paddles to shore, and opens the shell. Finding nothing inside but an oyster, he pushes his canoe off again and begins paddling into the lagoon.

What an incredible waste of time. The reasonable thing to do is not to paddle back to shore with one oyster, but to dive again and again, to fill up the canoe with oysters and then return to shore. Pearls are rare—a diver must open many oysters before finding one. Only a foolish person would waste time and energy making a separate trip for each oyster. It's the same with producing ideas. Many times we'll produce one or two ideas and proceed as if they are the answers. But creative ideas, like pearls, occur infrequently. So the sensible thing to do is to produce many ideas before we evaluate. Just as a good idea may stop you from going on to discover a great one, a great idea may stop you from discovering the right one.

Increasing your idea production requires conscious effort. Suppose I asked you to spend three minutes thinking of alternative uses for the common brick. No doubt, you would come up with some cases, but my hunch is not very many. The average adult comes up with three to six ideas. However, if I asked you to list forty uses for the brick as fast as you can, you would have quite a few in a short period of time.

Quota

A quota and time limit focused your energy in a way that guaranteed profluency of thought. The quota is not only more effective at focusing your energy, but also a more productive method of generating alternatives. To meet the quota, you find yourself listing all the usual uses for a brick (build a wall, fireplace, outdoor barbecue, and so on) as well as listing everything that comes to mind (anchor, projectiles in riots, ballast, device to hold down newspaper, a tool for leveling dirt, material for sculptures, doorstop, and so on) as you stretch your imagination to meet the quota. By causing us to exert effort, a quota allows us to generate more imaginative alternatives than we otherwise would.

Thomas Edison guaranteed productivity by giving himself and his assistants idea quotas. His own personal quota was one minor invention every ten days and a major invention every six months. A way to guarantee productivity of your creative thought is to give yourself an idea quota, for example, an idea quota of 40 ideas if you're looking for ideas alone or a quota of 120 ideas if a group is brainstorming for ideas. By forcing yourself to come up with forty ideas, you put your internal critic on hold and write everything down, including the obvious and weak. The first third will be the same old, same old ideas. The second third will be more interesting and the last third will show more insight, curiosity, and complexity.

Initial ideas are usually poorer in quality than later ideas. Just as water must run from a faucet for a while to be crystal clear, cool, and free of particles, so thought must flow before it becomes creative. Early ideas are usually not true ideas. Exactly why this is so is not known, but one hypothesis is that familiar and safe responses lie closest to the surface of our consciousness, and therefore, are naturally thought of first. Creative thinking depends on continuing the flow of ideas long enough to purge the common, habitual ones and produce the unusual and imaginative.

Following is a list of five words. Write the first association that occurs to you for each word. Now do this five more times and for each time write an association that is different from the association you gave the same word on the previous occasions.

	1	2	3	4	5	6

Fish

Military

Government

Ocean

Automobile

You will note that the latter associations are much more original and unique than the earlier ones. The first responses are the common dominant associations you have for that word. By arranging to give responses that are not common or dominant, you experience an increase in originality and imaginativeness of the responses.

Researchers have discovered an interesting correlation between the birth order of human beings and revolutionary creativity, as well. Firstborn children tend to become conservatives, and "laterborns," like Darwin, are more likely to become free thinkers. Firstborns tend to identify more with established tradition than their siblings do. They try to dominate their siblings. Laterborns are more open to experience, because this openness aids them, as latecomers to the family, in finding an unoccupied niche. Their openness tends to make them more imaginative and creative. From their ranks have come the bold explorers and revolutionary creators. Darwin, Marx, Jefferson, Joan of Arc, Rousseau, Lenin, Virginia Woolf, and Bill Gates typify the behavior of laterborns.

When you wish to create something new or to come up with a creative solution to a problem, it is often necessary to distance yourself from your firstborn ideas as well. If I want to surprise my wife on Valentine's Day, I know that I must disregard the first idea that comes to mind for what to do. I probably will have to disregard the second, third, and fourth as well. In order to come up with something creative, we must get beyond our habitual response to intentionally create something new.

List your ideas.

When you give yourself a quota, you force yourself to list your ideas. Leonardo da Vinci had a mania for listing and cataloging his thoughts in little notebooks that he carried everywhere. The thousands of pages of lists that he made constitute the raw material for a huge encyclopedia on creativity. A habit to consciously cultivate is to always write or list your ideas when brainstorming. List making will help you permanently capture your thoughts and ideas, speed up your thinking, keep you focused, and will force you to dwell upon alternatives.

Listing ideas also helps you remember them. We have all had the experience of looking up a phone number, then being distracted before dialing and forgetting the number in a matter of seconds. What is happening is that new information is bumping out older information before your mind can ready older information for long-term storage in your memory.

Read the first series of numbers, cover the numbers, and recall them. Chances are you remembered them correctly. Now, read the second series, cover them, and see how many you can recall. Chances are you had difficulty recalling this series.

7 9 1 4 0

2 6 5 8 9 3 1 4 7 0 5 3 9

Psychologists have demonstrated that the human brain is only able to retain about five to nine chunks of information at a time. After about twelve seconds, however, recall is poor, and after twenty seconds the information will disappear entirely, unless you keep repeating it to yourself or write it down. (In fact, by the time you finish reading this chapter, you will have forgotten the first series of numbers as well.) Writing signals your brain that this piece of information is more crucial than others and should be stored in long-term memory. If you don't list your ideas, you'll spend all your mental energy trying to resurrect old thoughts instead of generating new ones.

Without looking at your watch, draw a picture of it as accurately as you can. Now compare your drawing with your watch. If you're like most of us, your drawing is not an accurate representation. You probably discovered many missing details. Even though this is an instrument we look at several times a day, our mental image of it is weak.

Writing or listing your ideas as they occur also speeds up your thinking and focuses your attention on your subject.

• **Speed**. Writing ideas speeds up thought. Many of us harbor the illusion that we are fast thinkers. Visualize the alphabet in capital letters. How many letters have curved lines? Observe how your brain thinks. First, you see the *A*, then *B*, and so forth and so on. It's like watching a slide show. First, one, then the next, one after the other, one at a time until you're finished scanning the entire alphabet. This is as fast as your brain thinks. You think no faster than the speed of life. Visualize a tennis match. Now, speed it up 100 times. Difficult, isn't it? We think sequentially, not simultaneously. Incidentally, there are eleven letters with curved lines in the alphabet.

• **Focus**. Writing ideas focuses your attention. Another common illusion is the belief that we can perform multiple tasks at the same time. For example, I can write a work report, listen to a football game, and pay attention to my child at the same time. If you believe that, try counting by sevens while at the same time counting backwards by three. You'll find that you can only do this by alternating. Your thinking is occupied by one topic until it switches to another. Try thinking of what you did yesterday and what you will do tomorrow. Notice how you do this sequentially, not simultaneously.

Listing ideas is one of the simplest methods of increasing your conceptual ability, because it does not require a change in behavior. It's also surprisingly powerful, because it utilizes the compulsive side of most of us in a way that makes us into more fluent and flexible thinkers.

Elaborate on Your Ideas

Contrary to popular belief, Thomas Edison did not invent the lightbulb; his genius, rather, was to perfect the lightbulb as a consumer item. He took an idea and elaborated on it. Not satisfied with just the lightbulb, he invented a whole practical system for electric lighting, including dynamos, conduits, and a means for dividing up current that could illuminate large numbers of bulbs. Later, when Alexander Graham Bell announced his work on the telephone in 1876, Edison immediately went to work on ways to elaborate on Bell's work. Out of this work, the phonograph, the device that made Edison a celebrity, emerged one year later.

Pyotr Tchaikovsky, the brilliant Russian composer, set down his ideas in moments of intense ardor and then spent many days improving, extending, or condensing his ideas. Paul Valery, the French poet, asserted that stubborn elaboration was an important component of creativity and took great exception to the suggestion that poets receive the best part of their work from muses. He called that a concept of savages. His own labor was stubborn, we know–Valery made 250 typed drafts of his masterpiece, "La Jeune Parque."

In 1845 Edgar Allan Poe published "The Raven." One year later, Poe published the critical essay "The Philosophy of Composition," which recounted the process by which this poem emerged. We might have expected Poe, as a poet in the romantic age, to describe the flash of divine inspiration by which the entire poem appeared at once–in an ecstatic frenzy. Yet Poe wrote that no one point in its composition is referable to divine guidance. Instead, the work proceeded methodically, step by step, to its completion, as he made constant modifications about every choice, from the poem's length and themes down to single words.

Even small changes are significant. You meet a friend you haven't seen in a while. The friend looks different. You say, "What happened to you? Did you lose weight?" But you're wrong. You learn to your embarrassment that it's because he has grown a mustache or she has a new hair color. Of course. How could you have missed it?

You missed it because you view your friend as a whole, so that every part of your visual image inextricably affected every other part. Change one part and the whole seemed changed. It's the same with ideas and concepts. We view an idea as a whole, "a gestalt," so that any change, no matter how minor, affects the whole and the way we see it. Consider how Manco changed the whole gestalt of their duct tape by simply changing its name to Duck™ tape, or how the Japanese engineer Yuma Shiraishi developed a whole new entertainment concept–the home VCR–by simply suggesting that videotapes needed to be long enough for a feature-length movie. This simple modification changed the whole gestalt of video machines and lead to the VCR revolution.

Constantly improve your ideas and the ideas of others by elaborating on them, adding detail, depth, and dimensions. Physicist Ed Witten has been called the most brilliant physicist of his generation. He is the master of string theory, a field as arcane as it is fundamental: It promises to explain what matter is. Never satisfied, he wakes up each morning with the intention of improving his ideas. After you've emptied your "box" and generated as many ideas as you can, extend your ideas by elaborating on them by combining or modifying them in some fashion.

SCAMPER

Elaborate on your ideas by applying a checklist of nine creative-thinking principles that were first formally suggested by Alex Osborn and later arranged by Bob Eberle into the following mnemonic.

S = Substitute?
C = Combine?
A = Adapt?
M = Magnify? Modify?
P = Put to other uses?
E = Eliminate?
R = Rearrange? Reverse?

SCAMPER is based on the notion that everything new is some addition or modification of something that already exists. You take a subject and change it into something else. (For example, drilled petroleum becomes chemical feedstock becomes synthetic rubber becomes automobile tires. Natural gas becomes polyethylene becomes milk jugs. Mined ore becomes metal becomes wire becomes parts of a motor.)

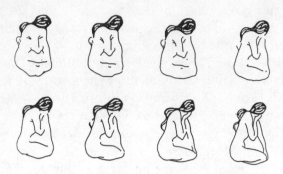

Isolate the subject you want to think about and ask a checklist of questions to see what new ideas and thoughts emerge. Think about any subject, from improving the ordinary paper clip to reorganizing your corporation, and apply the SCAMPER checklist of questions. You'll find that ideas start popping up almost involuntarily, when you ask the right questions:

Can I substitute something?
Can I combine it with something else?
Can I adapt something to your subject?
Can I magnify or add to it?
Can I modify or change it in some fashion?
Can I put it to some other use?
Can I eliminate something from it?
Can I rearrange it?
What happens when I reverse it?

Substitute something? Substitution is a sound way to develop alternative ideas to anything that exists. Think up ways of changing *this* for *that* and *that* for *this*. The scientist Paul Ehrlich kept substituting one color for another–well over five hundred colors–until he found the right dye to color the veins of laboratory mice. You can substitute things, places, procedures, people, ideas, and even emotions. Ask,

Can I substitute something? Who else? What else?
Can the rules be changed?
Other ingredient? Other material? Other power? Other place?

Other approach?

What else instead? What other part instead of this?

Combine it with something else? Much of creative thinking involves combining previously unrelated ideas or subjects to make something new. This process is called synthesis and is regarded by many experts as the essence of creativity. Gregor Mendel created a whole new scientific discipline, genetics, by combining mathematics with biology.

What can be combined?

Can we combine purposes?

How about an assortment? A blend? An alloy? An ensemble?

Combine units? Combine materials? What other article could be merged with this?

How could we package a combination?

What can be combined to multiply possible uses?

Combine appeals?

Adapt something to it? One of the paradoxes of creativity is that, in order to think originally, we must first familiarize ourselves with the ideas of others. Thomas Edison put it this way: "Make it a habit to keep on the lookout for novel and interesting ideas that others have used successfully. Your idea needs to be original only in its adaptation to the problem you are working on." Ask,

What else is like this? What other ideas does it suggest?

Does the past offer a parallel?

What could I copy? Whom could I emulate?

What idea could I incorporate?

What other process could be adapted? What else could be adapted?

What different contexts can I put my concept in?

What ideas outside my field can I incorporate?

Magnify it? An easy way to create a new idea is to take a subject and add something to it. Japanese engineer Yuma Shiraishi made the home VCR possible by figuring out how to lengthen videotapes so they would be long enough for feature-length movies. Ask,

What can be magnified, made larger, or extended?

What can be exaggerated? Overstated?

What can be added? More time? Stronger? Higher? Longer?

How about greater frequency? Extra features? What can be duplicated?

What can add extra value?

How can I carry it to a dramatic extreme?

Modify it? What can be modified? Just about any aspect of anything. The hub-and-spoke transportation system that makes Federal Express work was a feature of at least three air freight services as early as 1930. What Fred Smith did was to modify the dimensions, process, and purposes of the system and turn an old idea into an elegant concept. Ask,

How can this be altered for the better? What can be modified?

Is there a new twist?

Change meaning, color, motion, sound, odor, form, shape? Change name?

What changes can be made in the plans? In the process? In marketing? Other changes?

What other form could this take? What other package? Can the package be combined with the form?

Put it to some other use? A subject takes its meaning from its context. Change the context, and you change the meaning. George Washington Carver, botanist and chemist, discovered over three hundred different uses for the lowly peanut. Ask,

What else can this be used for?

Are there new ways to use this as is?

Other uses if modified?

What else can be made from this?

Other extension? Other markets?

Eliminate? Sometimes subtracting something from your subject yields new ideas. Trimming down ideas, objects, and processes may gradually narrow the subject down to its truly necessary part or function—or spotlight a part that's appropriate for some other use. Ask,

What if this were smaller? Understate?

What should I omit? Delete? Subtract? What's not necessary?

Should I divide it? Split it up? Separate it into different parts?

Streamline? Make miniature? Condense? Compact?

Can the rules be eliminated?

Rearrange it into something else? Creativity, it could be said, consists largely of rearranging what we know in order to find out what we do not know. Rearrangement usually offers countless alternatives for ideas, goods, and services. A baseball manager, for example, can shuffle the lineup 362,880 times. Ask,

What other arrangement might be better?

Interchange components?

Other pattern? Other layout? Other sequence? Change the order?

Transpose cause and effect?

Change pace? Change schedule?

Reverse it to see what happens? Reversing your perspective opens your thinking. Look at opposites, and you'll see things you normally miss. Ask, "What is the opposite of this?" to find a new way of looking at things. The historical breakthroughs of Columbus and Copernicus were the polar opposites of the current beliefs of their day. Ask,

What are the opposites?

What are the negatives?

Can I transpose positive and negative?

Should I turn it around? Up instead of down? Down instead of up?

Consider it backwards?

Reverse roles?

Do the unexpected?

To a genius, all ideas are in a state of constant flux. There can be no such thing as an ultimate idea, just as there cannot be the ultimate poem that would make all further poems unnecessary or the ultimate symphony that would render all further musical composition redundant and unnecessary.

All ideas can be improved by elaborating upon them. Most people feel that there must be inadequacy or fault before we look for ways to improve things. Geniuses, on the other hand, don't need inadequacy as justification for improving something. They look for ways to elaborate or improve ideas any time they want to. For example, a physicist learned of the invention of the electron microscope. It was touted as the perfect microscope. He immediately worked out three different ways by which it could be built. Later he checked the patent and found one of his methods was superior and made the original patent obsolete overnight.

Take it apart

An easy way to elaborate on your ideas is to take them apart and improve or change one part at a time. Imagine renovating a house with many rooms. Each of the rooms is part of the function of the house, and we tend to think of one "house" instead of a building composed of many rooms. To change the nature of the house, you do not blow it up and build a different one. It is much more productive to shift your focus from the one "house" to the many separate "rooms" and improve one room at a time. By converting a few rooms, you can convert a large house made up of many rooms into a mansion. Every idea is a house of many rooms. To elaborate on your idea, take the problem and improve one part at a time.

In the illustration, a target is split into two halves which creates the illusion of a white square in the middle. Separating the target into two parts created something new.

In a similar way, dividing a subject into its separate parts is a good way to change your fixation on a subject and see its components in a new way. Leonardo da Vinci felt it was essential to learn how to separate the parts from the whole. For example, seeing is one of the most rapid operations possible: It embraces an infinity of forms, yet it fixes on but one object at a time. To read a text, one has to consider the words one by one, then the sentences the words make up, not the total number of letters written on the page. Leonardo believed that, to understand things, you begin with the detail and move from one detail to another.

Moving from one detail to another leads to original or novel ideas through the assembling of all the possibilities. Try listing the attributes (attributes are characteristics, parts, or dimensions) of your subject and then focusing your attention on each attribute in turn. Think of ways to change or improve each attribute by asking yourself the SCAMPER questions. For example, if you wanted to develop a new office procedure or work flow, you could first identify and list all the steps taken. Then go through the checklist of questions to trigger ideas on how to improve or change each step.

Suppose you wanted to improve the common toaster. You would do the following:

1. List the attributes on a sheet of paper. Some of the attributes of a toaster are
   - Made of metal or plastic
   - Uses outside power source
   - Operated by pushing a lever down
   - Toast "pops" up when done
   - Heated coils
   - Toast bread vertically

2. For each attribute, ask, "How else can this be accomplished? and "Why does this have to be this way?" Come up with as many alternatives as you can for each attribute.

3. See if you can change or improve each attribute by asking the SCAMPER questions. You might end up with something like a see-through toaster with heat-resistant glass sides that let the user see the bread as it toasts. The sides can be removed for easy cleaning. In addition, the toaster pivots to allow for both vertical and horizontal open-face toasting.

Listing attributes helps you think beyond your stereotypical notions of things. We usually describe an object by its function, a description that grows out of our experience and observation. But the function of an object is not inherent in the object itself. Instead, it comes from our association with it. In one experiment, a group of subjects were first taught how to use tools in their conventional ways–for example, pliers to grip and unfasten wires or a paper clip to hold papers together. Then they were presented with problems that could only be solved through using the tools in unconventional ways. They solved 11 percent of the problems. Another group was given the same tools without instruction and presented the same problems. They scored 97 percent successes.

Because the one group was fixated on the ordinary, conventional uses of tools, they were unable to use the tools in unconventional and novel ways to solve the problems. Focusing on attributes helps clear away this fixation on stereotypic functions. Often, if you consider the attributes of subjects, you'll come up with different conclusions than if you operate with your stereotypes.

By examining "steel shank" as a separate attribute, we can move away from our stereotypic label of a screwdriver and come up with new applications. Possible other uses include probe, pointer, plug, shoe horn, paint-can opener, weapon, measuring rod, tool to remove paper jams from copiers, prying device, minidowel, telephone dialer, and so on.

Just the act of listing attributes focuses your thinking and helps overcome deeply entrenched patterns of thought. Suppose you were given a candle, a corkboard, and a box of tacks. Can you fasten the candle in such a way that it does not drip on the floor?

Typically, when given a candle, a corkboard, and a box of tacks and asked to fasten the candle on the wall so that it does not drip on the floor, most people have great difficulty coming up with a solution. However, when people are given a candle, corkboard, and the thumbtacks and the box separately, most solve the problem quickly. In the first case, the box containing the tacks is subject to a particular association. Participants see it only as a container for tacks, not as a possible wall fixture for the candle. When it is separated out, participants quickly are able to see how they could use it to solve the problem by tacking the box to the wall as a platform and placing the candle on top. (The function of any object is not inherent in the object itself but develops from our observation and association with it.)

Count the *F*s in the following sentence:

FINISHED FILES ARE THE RE-SULT OF YEARS OF SCIENTIF-IC STUDY COMBINED WITH THE EXPERIENCE OF YEARS.

If you found less than six, you probably ignored the *F*s in the word "of." If so, you are probably thinking, "Of course, it was right before my eyes the whole time." Ordinarily we do not make the fullest use of our ability to see. We look at a subject and do not see the details. And the details sometimes contain the germ of an idea that will lead to a creative breakthrough. George Westinghouse took the workings of a simple well in his backyard apart and examined the separate parts. He then modified some of the parts and reassembled them into an efficient way to transmit clean natural gas to homes and industry, creating the natural-gas industry. In music, the Russian composer Igor Stravinsky, took specific details from folk music and reassembled the details into different patterns and invented a new artistic style that began with his pathbreaking work *Petrushka*.

In the figure below, we see the dot to which the arrow is pointing as part of the diagonal line, even though it is actually closer to the vertical line. We tend to ignore the relationship with the vertical line and see the dot only as a continuation of the diagonal one. This illustrates the principle of common fate: Events that seem to be continuous are likely to be seen as a single entity rather than as discrete events.

The genius of French artists Georges Seurat and Paul Cézanne was in their realization that even color itself was not continuous. This was contrary to the prevailing technique of shading from one patch to another through intermediate tones as if nature was one continuous whole. Seurat and Cézanne believed that color transitions do not exist in nature, because each little patch of color is an independent experience that had to be independently painted. They broke down the discrete experiences of nature as tiny independent "dots" and then grouped them in various ways to act on each other and create stunning new artistic experiences that revolutionized the way artists perceived the world.

Breaking nature down into independent particles and then focusing on one particle at a time helped Seurat and Cézanne break their stereotypical notions and discover new relationships and experiences. In the same way, listing the attributes of a subject and then focusing on one attribute at a time helps us to break our stereotypical notion of a subject as a continuous whole and to discover relationships that we would otherwise miss. For example, suppose we want to improve the revolving door of the kind used in office buildings and department stores. We could list the attributes of a revolving door and then focus on each attribute one at a time. The following attributes might be listed:

- Has individual compartments
- Pushing it manually creates the energy to move it
- Made of glass to see through
- One or more people pushing it around at a time

The attribute "pushing it manually creates the energy" inspires one to think of ways to harness all that energy that is being voluntarily created by thousands of people pushing through the door each day. This triggers the idea of modifying the revolving door to make electricity from the force of people pushing it around. Separating the revolving door into attributes broke our stereotypical notion of a revolving door and inspired us to think of energy and of a creative way to use the door to harness that energy.

Written Records

Another habit to cultivate is keeping a written record of your creative attempts in a notebook, on file cards, or in your computer. A record not only guarantees that the thoughts and ideas will last, since they are committed to paper or computer files, but will goad you into other thoughts and ideas. The simple act of recording his ideas enabled Leonardo da Vinci to dwell on his ideas and improve them over time by elaborating on them. Thus, Leonardo was able to take simple concepts and work them into incredible complex inventions that were years ahead of their time, such as the helicopter, the bicycle, and the diving suit.

Edison's Notebooks

Leonardo da Vinci was Thomas Edison's spiritual mentor, and Edison's notebooks illustrate the strength of their spiritual kinship. Following da Vinci's example, Edison relentlessly recorded and illustrated every step of his voyage to discovery in his 3,500 notebooks that were discovered after his death in 1931. Keeping a written record of his work was a significant key to his genius. His notebooks got him into the following habits:

• They enabled him to cross-fertilize ideas, techniques, and conceptual models by transferring them from one problem to the next. For example, when it became clear in 1900 that an iron-ore mining venture in which Edison was financially committed was failing and on the brink of bankruptcy, he spent a weekend poring over his notebooks and came up with a detailed plan to redirect the company's efforts toward the manufacture of Portland cement, which could capitalize on the same model as the iron-ore company.

• Whenever he succeeded with a new idea, Edison would review his notebooks to rethink ideas and inventions he'd abandoned in the past in the light of what he'd recently learned. If he was mentally blocked working on a new idea, he would review his notebooks to see if there was some thought or insight that could trigger a new approach. For example, Edison took his unsuccessful work to develop an undersea telegraph cable—variable resistance and incorporated it into the design of a telephone transmitter that adapted to the changing sound waves of the caller's voice. This technique instantly became the industry standard.

• Edison would often jot down his observations of the natural world, failed patents and research papers written by other inventors, and ideas others had come up with in other fields. He would also routinely comb a wide variety of diverse publications for novel ideas that sparked his interest and record them in his notebooks. He made it a habit to look out for novel and interesting ideas that others had used successfully on other problems in other fields. To Edison, an idea needed to be original only in its adaptation to the problem he was working on.

• Edison also studied his notebooks of past inventions and ideas to use as springboards for other inventions and ideas in their own right. To Edison, his diagrams and notes on the telephone (sounds transmitted) suggested the phonograph (sounds recorded), which, in turn, suggested motion pictures (images recorded). Simple in retrospect, isn't it? Genius usually is.

Walt Whitman was another genius who collected ideas to stimulate his creative potential. His journals describe an ingenious technique he developed for recording ideas. Any time an idea would strike his imagination, he would write it down on a small slip of paper. He placed these slips into various envelopes that he titled according to the subject area each envelope contained. In order to have a place for each new idea he encountered, Whitman kept ideas in many different envelopes.

Whitman, whenever he felt a need to spawn new thoughts or perspectives, would select the various envelopes pertaining to his current subject or interests. He retrieved ideas from the envelopes, randomly at times, or on other occasions, only those ideas relevant to his subject; then he would "weave" these ideas together as if he were creating an idea tapestry. These idea tapestries often became the foundation for a new poem or essay.

Following are guidelines for keeping a written record:

1. Collect all interesting ideas that you encounter from brainstorming sessions, ideas you read about, or ideas you create.

2. Record them thematically in a notebook, in your computer, or on note cards, and file them by subject (organizational improvement, sales presentations, new markets, new product ideas, etc.) in a file box. In the event you need further information about an

idea, indicate the source where you found the idea. Cross-reference any ideas that may fit into several different categories.

3. Once you have developed a fairly extensive idea base, use it to glean insight when you have a problem.

Whenever you experience a problem, retrieve ideas from your file that you feel may apply to your need. Spread the ideas out before you and review them. Use the following suggestions to select the ideas most suited to your needs:

1. Select ideas containing attributes closely related to your subject's attributes.

2. Once you have selected several ideas from the larger group, prepare to apply the ideas to your current needs. You may realize that the entire idea applies or only one procedure or portion of the idea applies. Likewise, ideas may have to be modified in order to apply them to the situation.

3. Combine and apply appropriate attributes or procedures from two or more ideas.

Geniuses recognize the essential merits and attributes of a good idea and can adapt these elements to their subjects, thereby "creating" a new idea. Many original ideas are secondhand, consciously or unconsciously drawn from a million outside sources and used by the garnerer with pride and satisfaction. Henry Ford, founder of the Ford Motor Company, once said that his simple genius was the ability to create something new from the ideas and inventions of others.

Mind Popping

When you keep a historical record of your ideas and problems, you initiate a phenomenon that George Mandler, a leading researcher in the problems of consciousness, calls "mind popping." Mind popping is when a solution or idea seems to appear, after a period of incubation, out of nowhere.

Very possibly, the act of recording your thoughts and ideas about a particular problem plants the information into your long-term memory and into your unconscious. While consciousness plays the important role in our daily lives of restricting the boundaries of our actions, in the unconscious we can activate complexes of information without boundary. Information held in long-term memory can be processed in parallel in the unconscious and find its way into conscious thought. An innovative idea emerges not in any real-time sequence but in a "mind-popping" explosion of thought.

Suppose your notebook contains

• Information about the problem you are working on
• Information about other ideas, concepts, and problems you are currently working on

By periodically reviewing your notebook, you activate all the recorded information in your conscious and subconscious mind. You've now set up a mental system of network thinking where ideas, images, and concepts from completely unrelated problems combine to catalyze the nascent moment of creativity. This necessarily nonlinear thought process can occur unconsciously–and not necessarily in real time.

Concepts combine like light rays focusing at a point and pop into your consciousness. In the illustration below, *A* represents the brain cell connections of an average brain working on a problem, while *B* represents the brain cell connections of a brain that is constantly stimulated by recording and reviewing of information.

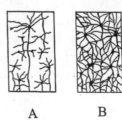

A   B

Recording your work plants the information in your subconscious mind and somehow activates relevant patterns so it can be processed into a mind-popping solution, even after a long delay during which the problem is abandoned. In the 1970s, Frank Wilczek of the Institute for Advanced Study, in Princeton, New Jersey, deduced how the nuclei of atoms stay together, one of those rare "knowing the mind of God" discoveries. His breakthrough occurred when he was reviewing a totally different problem–in fact, a completely different force of nature. He suddenly experienced a "mind pop" and realized that a failed approach in one area would be successful in another.

Archimedes got his sudden insight about the principle of displacement while daydreaming in his bath. According to legend, he was so excited by his discovery that he rushed naked through the streets, shouting, "Eureka!" (I've found it.) Henri Poincaré, a French genius, spoke of incredible ideas and insights that came to him with suddenness and immediate certainty out of the blue. So dramatic are the ideas that arrive that the precise moment in which the idea arrived can be remembered in unusual detail. Darwin could point to the exact spot on a road where he arrived at the solution for the origin of species while riding in his carriage and thinking of some other subject. Other geniuses offer similar experiences. Like a sudden flash of lightning, ideas and solutions seemingly appear out of nowhere.

That this is a commonplace phenomenon was shown in a survey of distinguished scientists conducted over a half-century ago. A majority of the scientists reported that they got their best ideas and insights when not thinking about the problem. Ideas came while walking, recreating, or working on some other unrelated problem. This suggests how the creative act came to be associated with "divine inspiration," for the illumination appears to be involuntary.

The more problems, ideas, and thoughts that you record and review from time to time, the more complex becomes the network of information in your mind. Think of thoughts as atoms hanging by hooks on the sides of your mind. When you think about a subject, some of these thoughts are released and put into motion in your subconscious mind. The more work you put into thinking about a problem, the more information you put into your long-term memory by systematically recording it, the more thoughts are put into random motion. Your subconscious mind never rests. When you quit thinking about the subject and decide to forget it, your subconscious mind doesn't quit working. The thoughts keep flashing freely in every direction through your subconscious. They are colliding, combining, and recombining millions of times. Typically, many combinations are of little or no value, but occasionally, a combination is made that is appreciated by your subconscious as a good combination and delivered up to the conscious mind as a "mind-popping" idea.

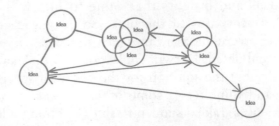

Our conscious minds are sometimes blocked from creating new ideas because we are too fixated. When we discontinue work on the problem for a period of time, our fixation fades, allowing our subconscious minds to freely create new possibilities. This is what happened to Nobel laureate Melvin Calvin. While idly sitting in his car waiting for his wife to complete an errand, he found the answer to a puzzling inconsistency in his research on photosynthesis. It occurred quite suddenly and suddenly also, in a matter of seconds, the path of carbon became apparent to him.

To experience "mind popping," try the following experiment. Write a letter to your unconscious about a problem you have been working on. Make the letter as detailed as possible. Describe the problem, what steps you have taken, the gaps, what is needed, what the obstacles are, the ideal solution, and so on. Instruct your subconscious to find the solution. Write "Your mission is to find the solution to the problem. I would like the solution in two days." Seal the letter and put it away. Forget it. Open the letter in two days. If the problem still has not been solved, write on the bottom of the letter, "Let me know the minute you solve this." Sooner or later, when you are most relaxed and removed, ideas and solutions will pop up from your subconscious.

Your mind also works when you are sleeping. The reason most creative people give for their morning work schedule was expressed by Balzac, the great French novelist, who said he wanted to take advantage of the fact that his brain works while he sleeps. Once asked where he found his melodies, Johann Sebastian Bach, one of the giants of musical history, said that the problem is not finding them, it's getting up in the morning and not stepping on them. Thomas Edison sometimes slept on a table in his laboratory so that he could start work as soon as he woke up and not forget anything.

Try this exercise before you go to sleep. Take a few minutes and review a problem that you are stuck on. Write down the key words on a sheet of paper and put the paper on your bed stand. Forget the problem and go to sleep. When you wake up, look at the paper. You will probably think of new insights, will see the problem more clearly, and may get a "mind popping" idea.

Summary

We think of a creative genius as a mysterious person who spontaneously creates ideas out of the blue. This is not so. This is not how a creative genius gets ideas. He or she get ideas by working hard and incorporating deliberate thinking practices.

Creative geniuses think fluently and flexibly. Fluent thinking means to generate quantities of ideas and flexible thinking means to think beyond the ordinary and conventional nature of things. Geniuses are fluent thinkers because of the following practices. They

- Defer judgment when looking for ideas
- Generate as many ideas as possible
- List their ideas as they occur and keep a written record
- Constantly elaborate or improve their ideas
- Allow their subconscious to generate ideas by incubating their subject

Geniuses are flexible thinkers because they extend their thinking by incorporating random, chance, and unrelated factors into their thinking processes. The next strategies in Part II show how geniuses produce original ideas and creative solutions to problems using random, chance, and unrelated factors.

STRATEGY FOUR: MAKING NOVEL COMBINATIONS

In his book *Scientific Genius*, psychologist Dean Keith Simonton of the University of California at Davis suggests that geniuses are geniuses because they form more novel combinations than the merely talented. He suggests that, in a loose sense, genius and chance are synonymous. His theory has etymology behind it: *cogito*–"I think"–originally connoted "shake together"; *intelligo,* the root of *intelligence,* means to "select among." This is a clear, early intuition about the utility of permitting ideas and thoughts to randomly combine with each other and the utility of selecting from the many the few to retain.

In the illustration, the square seems to be deformed (the sides seem to be bent). It is not. The sides of the square are perfectly straight. Place a straight edge along the sides of the square to determine this for yourself. Combining a perfect square with a circular background changes our perception of the figure.

Creativity takes place in the perceptual phase of thinking. This is where our perceptions and concepts are formed, and this is where they have to be changed. Combining a square with a circular background changed our perception of the square. In the same way, combining information in novel ways increases your perceptual possibilities to create something original.

Consider Einstein's equation, $E=mc^2$. Einstein did not invent the concepts of energy, mass, or the speed of light. Rather, he combined these concepts in a novel and useful way. By combining the concepts in a different way, he was able to look at the same information as everyone else and see something different. Einstein vaguely referred to the way he thought as "combinatory play" in response to a survey that was conducted by the brilliant French mathematician Jacques Hadamard in 1945. To Einstein, this combinatory play seemed to be the essential feature in his creative thought.

Like the highly intelligent child with pailfuls of Legos building blocks, a genius is constantly combining and recombining ideas, images, and other various thoughts. Think for a moment about hydrogen and oxygen. Put them together in the right combination and you have something different from either of the gases alone. You could not have predicted that ice would float, a hot shower would feel so relaxing, or a cool drink would be so refreshing. Simple concepts are like these simple gases. Alone, they have known and obvious properties. Put them together, and seemingly magical transformations can occur. But it is not magic; it is simply a creative aspect of ordinary cognition.

Because geniuses are willing to entertain novel combinations, they are able to discard accepted ideas of what is possible and imagine what is actually possible. In 1448 Johannes Gutenberg combined the mechanisms for pressing wine and punching coins to produce movable type, which made printing practical. His method of producing movable type endured almost unchanged for five centuries. The laws of heredity on which the modern science of genetics is based are the result of the work of Gregor Mendel, who combined mathematics and biology to create this new science. Thomas Edison's invention of a practical system of lighting involved combining wiring in parallel circuits with high-resistance filaments in his bulbs, two things that were not considered possible.

Think of your mind as a bowl of ice cream with a flat surface. Imagine pouring hot water from a spoon on the ice cream and then gently tipping it so that it runs off. After many repetitions of this process, the surface of the ice cream would be full of ruts. When information enters the mind, it flows, like water, into the preformed ruts. After a while, it takes only a small amount of information to activate an entire rut. This is the pattern-recognition and pattern-completion process of the brain. Even if much of the information is out of the rut, the mind will automatically correct and complete the information to select and activate a pattern.

When we sit down and try to will new ideas or solutions, we tend to keep coming up with the same old ideas. Information is activating the same old ruts making the same old connections, producing the same old ideas over and over again. Or to put it another way, if you always think what you've always thought, you'll always get what you've always got.

Creativity occurs when we tilt the bowl of ice cream and force the water (information) out of the ruts and get it flowing in a new direction. You tilt the bowl of ice cream by combining information in different ways. These new combinations give you different ways to focus your attention and different ways to interpret whatever you are focusing on. It is these different ways of focusing your attention and different ways of interpreting what you are focusing on that lead to new insights, original ideas, and creative solutions.

A number of techniques follow that are designed to help you get original and novel ideas through the chance combination of dissimilar subjects, ideas, concepts, and thoughts. The first technique is modeled after one of Leonardo da Vinci's favorite thinking strategies. He believed that once you listed a set of distinctions, you could generate new possibilities by combining them in various ways, or fill in holes and missing links by anticipating features that have not yet been encountered. Combining key elements for the purpose of constructing something new was a cornerstone of his genius.

Da Vinci's Technique

Leonardo's grotesque heads and famous caricatures are examples of the random variations of the human face made of different combinations of a set number of features. He would first list facial characteristics (heads, eyes, noses, etc.) and then, beneath each, list variations. Next he would mix and match the different variations to create original and grotesque caricatures. Below is a hypothetical example of a box similar to one that da Vinci might have constructed:

Heads	Eyes	Noses	Mouths	Chins
bullet	goggle-eyed	parrot-beak	pinched	double chin
skeletal	sunken	hooked	harelipped	slack-jaw
dome-like	bulging	thick-snub	wafer-thin	latern-jaw
beetle-brow	squinty	beak-like	drooping	sagging
bell-shaped	beady	cigar-shape	blubber-lipped	angular
egg-shaped	slanty	lumpy	bow-like	chunky
furrowed	swollen	broad	beefy	projecting
forehead	red eyes	fibrous	twisted	receding

While the number of items in each category is relatively small, there are thousands of possible combinations of the listed features. The circled features indicate only one out of thousands of different groupings of features that could be used for an original grotesque head.

From his notebooks, it is clear that da Vinci used this strategy in his production of art and invention. He advised to be on the watch to take the best parts of many beautiful faces, rather than create what you consider to be a beautiful face. It is intriguing to speculate that the *Mona Lisa*, probably the most admired portrait in the world, is a result of da Vinci combining the best parts of the most beautiful faces that he observed and systemized. Perhaps this is why admirers find so many different expressions in the mix of features on the face of the woman in the painting. It is especially interesting to consider this possibility in the light of the fact that there is so little agreement about the actual identity of the subject.

One can almost see Leonardo composing a matrix of elements (apostles, types of reactions, conditions, facial expressions, types of situations) and experimenting with their variations and combinations until he found the right configuration to create that once-in-a-lifetime masterpiece–*The Last Supper*. Many other artists before him had made their own versions of Jesus Christ having his last meal with the twelve apostles. When Leonardo painted the picture, however, the scene came alive with new meaning that no one else was able to give nor has been able to give since.

Leonardo da Vinci would analyze the structure of a subject and then separate the major parameters ("parameter" means a characteristic, factor, variable, or aspect). He would then list variations for each parameter and combine them. By coming up with different combinations of the variations of the parameters, he created new ideas.

Think of the parameters as card suits (hearts, spades, clubs, and diamonds) and the variations as the different cards within each suit. By experimenting with different combinations of the variations, you create new ideas.

To use da Vinci's technique, follow these procedures:

1. Specify the challenge.

2. Separate the parameters of the challenge. The parameters are the fundamental framework of the challenge. You choose the nature and the number of parameters that you wish to use in your box. A good question to ask yourself when selecting parameters is "Would the challenge still exist without the parameter I'm considering adding to the box?"

3. Below each parameter, list as many variations for the parameters as you wish. The complexity of the box is determined by the number of parameters and the number of variations used. The more variations and the more variety to the variations of each parameter, the more likely the box will contain a viable idea. For instance, a box with ten parameters, each of which has ten variations, produces ten billion combinations of the parameters and the variations.

4. When you are finished listing variations, make random runs through the parameters and the variations for the parameters,

selecting one or more from each column, and assemble the combinations into entirely new forms. During this step, all of the combinations can be examined with respect to the challenge to be solved. If you are working with ten or more parameters, you may find it helpful to randomly examine the entire group, and then gradually restrict yourself to portions that appear to be particularly fruitful.

Let's look at an example. A car-wash owner wanted to find an idea for a new market or new market extension. He analyzed the activity of "product washing" and decided to work with four parameters: "method of washing," "products washed," "equipment used," and "other products sold."

He listed the parameters and listed five variations for each parameter. He listed four parameters on top. Under each parameter he listed five variations for each parameter. He randomly chose one or more items from each parameter and connected them to form a new business.

		New Business Extension for Car Washes		
	Method	Products Washed	Equipment	Products Sold
1	Full	Cars	Sprays	Related Products
2	Self	Trucks	Conveyors	Novelties
3	Hand	Houses	Stalls	Discount Books
4	Mobile	Clothes	Dryers	Edible Goods
5	Combination	Dogs	Brushes	Cigarettes

New Business: The random combination of parameters ("self," "dogs," "brushes," "stalls," "sprayers," "dryers," "related products") inspired an idea for a new business. The new business he created was a self-service dog wash. The self-service dog wash has ramps leading to waist-high tubs where owners spray the dogs, scrub them with brushes provided by the wash, shampoo them, and blow-dry them. In addition to the wash, he also sells his own line of dog products, such as shampoos and conditioners. Pet owners now wash their dogs, while their cars are being washed in the full-service car wash.

Five alternatives for each parameter generates 3,125 possible different combinations. If only 10 percent prove useful, that would yield 312 new ideas. In theory, if you list the appropriate parameters and variations, you should have all of the possible combinations for a specified challenge. In practice, your parameters may be incomplete or a critical variation for a parameter may not have been described. When you feel this may be the case, you should reconsider the parameters you specified and adjust the parameters or the variations accordingly.

We tend to see the elements of our subject as one continuous "whole" and do not see many of the relationships between the elements, even the obvious ones. They become almost invisible because of the way we perceive things. Yet these relationships are often the links to new ideas. When you break down a subject into different parts and combine the parts in various ways, you restructure your perception of the subject. This perceptual restructuring leads to new insights, ideas, and new lines of speculation.

Gestalt psychologist Wolfgang Köhler demonstrated perceptual restructuring with animals. He would present an ape with a problem in which bananas were displayed out of reach and could only be obtained by using techniques new in the ape's experience. For example, Köhler would give an ape boxes to play with for a few days. Then he would hang bananas from the ceiling out of the ape's reach. When he placed the boxes behind the ape, it would try all the familiar ways of reaching the fruit and fail. When he placed the boxes in front of the ape so that they were visible, the ape would sit and think and suddenly have an insight and use the boxes to stand on to reach the bananas. What happened was that the visibility of the information restructured the ape's perception. It suddenly saw the boxes not as playthings but as supports to build a structure. It saw the relationship between the boxes and bananas.

In the same way, when you combine and recombine information in different ways, you perceptually restructure the way you see the information. In addition, the greater the number of combinations you are able to generate, the more likely it is that some combination will serve as an associative link to ideas you could not come up with using your usual way of thinking (A, B, and D may become associated because each in some way is associated with C). For example, the three words "surprise," "line," and "birthday" in combination serve as an associative link to the word "party." That is, "surprise party," "party line," and "birthday party." In the car wash example, an associative link was made from the information that was listed to the idea of a bird wash. The bird wash is a miniature clamp device that holds the bird securely in an upright stance so it can be gently washed and hosed (much like a car wash). It's designed to help workers cleanse birds who are damaged from oil spills at sea. It's expected to save thousands of birds that now expire from the rough handling during cleanup operations.

A food company wanted new ideas for products and markets for tuna. Following are the parameters they used and their variations. They used the parameters "uses for tuna fish," "kinds of containers," "products used with tuna fish," and "how tuna is seasoned."

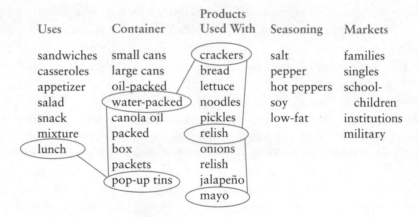

Uses	Container	Products Used With	Seasoning	Markets
sandwiches	small cans	crackers	salt	families
casseroles	large cans	bread	pepper	singles
appetizer	oil-packed	lettuce	hot peppers	school-
salad	water-packed	noodles	soy	children
snack	canola oil	pickles	low-fat	institutions
mixture	packed	relish		military
lunch	box	onions		
	packets	relish		
	pop-up tins	jalapeño		
		mayo		

These variables triggered many new ideas. One idea that was marketed was portable, single-serve, pull-top cans of water-packed tuna with packets of mayo and pickle relish, whole wheat crackers, and a mixing spoon. Other ideas included canola-oil tuna for variety and tuna mix-ins, which are low-fat seasoning packets that require no mayo.

The food company also saw an associative link between mayo and tuna that inspired them to work on developing a synthetic mayo that can be premixed and canned with the tuna, instead of being packaged separately. The food company broke apart their challenge into discrete parts, which opened the way for them to see the parts from all sides at once and to recombine those parts in new ways.

In the world of art, Pablo Picasso's *Les Demoiselles d'Avignon* represents cubism as the final breaking of the painting and the world into discrete parts, which also opened the way for Picasso to recombine the parts in new and startling ways. The figures in the painting were perceived to be the first figures in Western art to have been painted from all sides at once. As cubism conquered the exhibition halls, Picasso also showed how to combine the parts of a painting with the parts of the world into a new art form, which he called a collage.

Inventive Problem Solving

The mathematician Henri Poincaré believed that invention in problem solving consisted of constructing a large number of various combinations of possibilities and the essential ability to select those that are most likely to be useful.

A useful technique for escaping from the fixed parts of a problem is to break the parts down into still smaller parts and then recombine these smaller units to form larger novel units. It is usually much easier to put together subparts in different formations than to divide the situation into novel parts from the first.

The number of different ways in which something can be looked at is limited not only by the rigidity of the available units of description but also by the number of available relationships. The larger the repertoire of relationships that can be handled with confidence, the more original can be the lines of division, the ways of looking at a situation.

1. First, select the parameters or dimensions. You can select as many as you want. It's suggested that you select at least four.

2. List as many variations as you can for each parameter.
(See the example below.)

3. Make random runs linking one or more variations in each column with one or more in other columns.

4. Force each random combination of variations into new ideas.

5. Keep trying different combinations.

For example, a Midwestern town wanted a more reliable way to warn people about approaching dangers, such as floods, tornadoes, earthquakes, and so on. The parameters they selected were

- How to locate people
- How to get their attention
- How to deliver the desired message
- How to get the desired reaction from the citizens

They then randomly linked the variations to trigger ideas. One of the combinations ("Bells," "Telephone," "Find protection," "Information") with "all the ways to locate people" triggered the idea to make an arrangement with the telephone company to cause all the telephones throughout the city (including cell phones and public phones) to ring. When answered, the phones relay a prerecorded message informing people about the particular emergency and instructing people what to do. Additionally, they employed a mass-media advertising campaign that told of the danger alert system and how it works.

Locate People	Getting Attention	Deliver Message	Desired Reaction
Homes	Bells	Telephone	Find protection
Schools	Messengers	Advertise	Seek help
Hospitals	Firehouse Sirens	In person	Evacuate
Nursing homes	P.A. System	Penny Savers	Help others
Places of business	Mass media	Newspapers	Information
Public transit	Traffic lights	Pagers	Inform others
Private transit	E-mail	E-mail	Do nothing
Public parks	Electric lights	Radio-TV	
		Web site	

Suppose you want to create a new product promotion. The parameters for a new marketing campaign might be

- Ways to get attention
- Ways to get people to act
- Themes
- Markets
- Ways to surprise people

Under each parameter list as many variations as you can. Then make random runs linking one or more variations in each column with one or more in other columns. Keep trying different combinations until you get the ideas you want.

When you look into a kaleidoscope, you see a pattern. If you then add a new piece of crystal and manipulate the drum, you have a multitude of new patterns. When you make random combinations linking varia-tions together, it's like adding crystals to a kaleidoscope. You create a multitude of new possibilities.

Key-Word Combinations

Creative thinking is often a matter of forming new associations, new syntheses, or new combinations of elements of existing knowledge, rather than producing something that is new in every respect. Take the following elements: speedy messenger service, discounted jets for sale, and empty skies at night. Fred Smith combined these elements and created Federal Express.

Look for new ideas in your business by analyzing the variables of your business, listing components, and making random combinations:

1. First, ask, "What is our business?" and "What should our business be?" These questions will help focus your attention. For example, the business of a publisher is not producing books, it's information and entertainment, and the business of a telephone company is not providing telephones, it's service.

2. Next, define the variables of your business. For instance, some variables for a typical business are products, services, markets, functions, technologies, pricing, distribution, management, and so on. Select four or five that you believe to be the most significant.

3. Under each variable, list the attributes or components. Create a key-word index. Use key words to describe the components or attributes of each variable.

Following is a key-word index for a business book publisher.

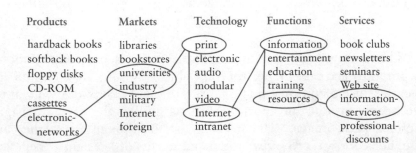

Products	Markets	Technology	Functions	Services
hardback books	libraries	print	information	book clubs
softback books	bookstores	electronic	entertainment	newsletters
floppy disks	universities	audio	education	seminars
CD-ROM	industry	modular	training	Web site
cassettes	military	video	resources	information-services
electronic-networks	Internet	Internet		professional-discounts
	foreign	intranet		

4. Mix and match your products, functions, markets, technologies, and services in various ways to explore new ideas, for instance, connecting electronic networks, information, resources, Internet, print, and information services to trigger the idea of an electronic data bank. The bank would contain all the information from the publisher's backlist of business books. The information would be sold as a business resource by way of a computer network for businesses and over the Internet.

In key-word combinations, we predetermine the variables by defining our business, extend our thinking by using key words, and then make random combinations. Another interesting exercise is to write all possible characteristics, components, or dimensions for your business as key words on cards or slips of paper, one per card. Come up with as many as you can and then randomly draw them from a fishbowl, a box, or a similar container. The following are some common examples.

Communication	Character	Strength
People	Color	Quality
Cohesion	Shape	Characteristics
Design	Package	Dimensions
Movement	Size	Patterns
Position	Parts	Purpose
Materials	Image	Opportunities
Functions	Trends	Options
Obstacles	Research	Competition
Information	Environment	Value
Functions	Products	Partnership
Expense	Benefits	Success
Technology	Markets	Service
Prices	Management	Distribution
Staff	Space	Process

Whenever you are thinking about a business problem, randomly draw three to six cards from the box. List any and all thoughts that each card triggers and then combine the thoughts. Suppose we want to create a new product promotion, and we pulled the cards "design," "benefits," and "image." Under each, list the thoughts that the cards inspire. Look for ways to satisfy the requirements of "design," "benefits," and "image" in a new product promotion. Extend your thinking by listing as many thoughts as you can.

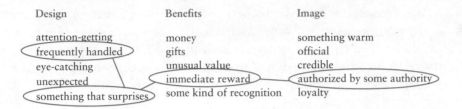

Design	Benefits	Image
attention-getting	money	something warm
frequently handled	gifts	official
eye-catching	unusual value	credible
unexpected	immediate reward	authorized by some authority
something that surprises	some kind of recognition	loyalty

Read through the thoughts and let your imagination begin to form ideas. Then make random combinations from the separate thoughts and force the combinations into new ideas. Continue making random combinations until you have the ideas you want. The key thoughts "frequently handled," "something that surprises," "immediate reward," and "authorized by some authority" combined into a new idea for the company running a grand lottery that benefits the Alzheimer's Foundation. The promotion for the lottery, the tickets, the winner's celebration would all be tied in to the product promotion.

Jacques Hadamard, the brilliant French mathematician who proved the prime number theorem, argued that invention, including mathematical invention, requires the discovery of unusual but fruitful combinations of ideas. To find such novelties, it is necessary to construct numerous random combinations. It is the random combinations of variables that allow new and exciting ideas to form and emerge.

A physicist I know makes systematic use of the idea that new associations may be formed by accidental combination. He will cut up indexes of physics textbooks and then throw the fragments into a fishbowl. Lastly, he will draw out several at a time to see whether any new useful combinations emerge. This simple technique has produced insights and ideas that he could not generate using his usual way of thinking. Cut up an index of a book in your field, for example, a marketing book if you are in marketing, and try the same technique.

Combining Existing Information

The notion that geniuses combine items of existing knowledge because they become aware of some similarity or overlap between them has been favored for some time. William James was very decisive on this point. He explained that was why Newton noticed the law of squares and Darwin noticed the survival of the fittest in nature. Their discoveries required a remarkable eye for resemblances between items of existing information and the ability to combine them in a novel way.

We possess an abundance of thoughts about most of our problems. By organizing our thoughts efficiently, we can systematically create combinations that will generate multiple solutions to problems. The following is a technique designed to help you recognize items of existing knowledge about a subject and how to combine different items:

1. Collect all available material relating to the problem.

2. Think of every factor related to the problem, regardless of its importance, and write each factor on a small card.

3. Look for connections between the cards. Group them into general categories.

4. Keep integrating and grouping them until they are reduced to four to six main groups. Place a new card on top of each group that describes the general category (the title card). These final groups are the fundamental dimensions, or parameters, of the problem.

5. On a blank sheet of paper, write the parameters across the top. Below each parameter, list its components from the cards.

6. Cut the sheet into vertical strips. Each strip will contain one parameter and its components.

7. Lay the strips side by side. If you move each strip up and down, you'll notice new relationships between the components, which in turn may trigger new ideas or creative solutions.

An optional way to display the information is to tape the title cards to a wall. Below each parameter, tape the appropriate cards. Make random runs through the parameters and their components, selecting one or more components from each column and assemble into new combinations.

Combining the Unrelated

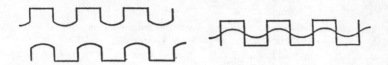

When the lines at the left are combined to form the figure on the right, we see the original two patterns only with great effort. Instead, we see a continuous wavy line running through a series of bars. Combining the lines creates a new pattern with new properties. The illustration verifies the seemingly obvious point that from a combination can emerge new properties that were not evident in either of the original lines.

It is the same with concepts and ideas. Gregory Murphy of the University of Illinois had people rate how true certain properties were of individual concepts and their combinations. One set of concepts consisted of the individual words "empty" and "store" and their combination "empty store." Consider the property "losing money." Like subjects in Murphy's study, you probably recognize that losing money is typical of "empty stores," but not of "stores" in general or of things that are "empty." Meaning changes when we combine concepts, and the more novel the combination, the more novel the new meaning. This is why genius is often marked by an interest in combining previously unrelated ideas, goods, and services, making novel combinations more likely. There are many different ways to create novel combinations:

Random Objects

Select twenty objects at random. You can select any objects, objects at home, objects at work, or objects you might find walking down the street. Or you can imagine you are in a technologically oriented science museum, walking through the Smithsonian Institute, or browsing in an electronic store and make a list of twenty objects that you would likely see. Make two lists of ten objects each on the left and right sides of the paper (see example that follows). Pick one from the left and combine it with one on the right. When you find a promising new combination, refine and elaborate it into a new invention.

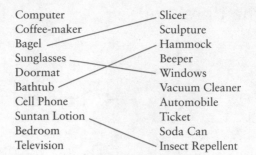

Computer
Coffee-maker
Bagel
Sunglasses
Doormat
Bathtub
Cell Phone
Suntan Lotion
Bedroom
Television

Slicer
Sculpture
Hammock
Beeper
Windows
Vacuum Cleaner
Automobile
Ticket
Soda Can
Insect Repellent

In the example, the illustrated combinations yielded the following ideas:

• Combining a bagel with slicer yields a bagel slicer with plastic sides designed to hold the bagel and prevent rotation when slicing.
• Bathtub and hammock combines into a baby tub with a simple hammock in the tub with a headrest to hold the baby's head securely, leaving the parent's hands free to do the washing.
• Sunglasses and windows combine to form the idea of tinted house windows, like tinted sunglasses, designed to change colors with ultraviolet light to help keep the house cool.
• Suntan lotion and insect repellent combines to form a new product—one lotion that protects against both the sun and insects.

You can also try the inverse heuristic to generate ideas, which states that if an object performs one function, a new artifact might be realized by combining it with an object that performs the opposite function. The claw hammer is a good example. So is a pencil with an eraser. Can you create new objects from the list of random objects by combining the object with something that performs the opposite function. How about a small cap for tightly sealing a soda can that could be attached to the lever of the pop-top device?

What is the figure in the following illustration?

It can be seen as either a duck or a rabbit. If you focus on the left you see a duck, and if you focus on the right, you see a rabbit, as the duck's beak becomes the rabbit's ears. A novel image is created by integrating two different images into one. In the same way, when we randomly combined dissimilar objects, we easily created many novel products.

Albert Rothenberg, in his book *The Emerging Goddess*, defines this as "homospatial thinking." He presents an ample number of examples drawn from the visual arts. Leonardo da Vinci, Paul Klee, Oskar Kokoschka, Henry Moore, Claes Oldenberg, and others all provide illustrations. For instance, in Klee's 1927 masterpiece painting, *Physiognomic Lightning*, the chief features of a man's face are delineated by a bolt of lightning: an integrated image ensues from two heterogeneous elements.

Rothenberg demonstrated that integrated images can stimulate superior creative ideas. Newton, according to his own story, conceived the concept of universal gravitation when he observed an apple falling and at the same time noticed the Moon in the sky. These simultaneous images inspired him to speculate if the same laws governed the falling apple and the Moon orbiting the Earth. This in turn led him to develop the laws of mechanics and establish mathematical analysis and modeling as the principal foundations of science and engineering.

Combining two dissimilar subjects creates a cognitive fusion that sometimes leads to a novel insight or idea. We combined random objects to create new products, the artists in Rothenberg's studies combined images to create stunning masterpieces; and Newton combined subjects (the apple and the Moon) from unrelated fields to create new science.

Combining Subjects from Unrelated Fields

Sigmund Freud's interest in fields that were unrelated to psychology was a key to his uncommon insights. For example, in his psychiatric practice, he used not only knowledge about the data of a person's life history and psychical mechanisms, but also knowledge about cultural patterns, literary works, and world history to make inferences and draw conclusions. His ability to synthesize elements of information from different fields contributed to his ability to see things differently from his contemporaries.

When looking for original ideas, try combining subjects from unrelated fields. Among combinations, the most fertile will often be those formed of elements drawn from domains that are far apart. For example, one entrepreneur created two lists of objects: One list contained household objects, and the other list contained objects from the world of sports. The combination of "laundry hamper" with "basketball" inspired him to create a new laundry hamper fashioned into a basketball net, approximately forty inches long, attached to a cylindrical hoop and hung on a backboard that is attached to a door. This allows kids to play basketball with dirty laundry as they "stuff" the basket. When it is full, a tug on a drawstring releases the clothes.

Another way to make random combinations with subjects from unrelated fields is to select two unrelated subjects, break each subject down by listing its attributes, and then randomly combine the attributes. Suppose, for example, you want to invent a new product. You would first select two objects that interest you. Make two lists of the objects' attributes or characteristics and randomly combine them to trigger ideas. For example, we select "bedroom" and "automobile." Some of their attributes are as follows:

Bedroom	Automobile
bed	carries passengers
place to sleep	moves
window shades	heater
located near bathroom	comes in different colors
one feels a sense of security	automatic door locks

Combining "sense of security" and "automatic door locks" inspires the idea of a master lock near the bed, which locks and unlocks all windows, doors, computer systems, and everything else in the house with one key. Combining "window shades" and "moves" triggers the idea of incorporating light sensors into window shades that automatically raise or lower the shades according to the intensity of the outside light.

Combining attributes of different subjects is a quick way to generate ingenious ideas. Suppose you wanted a new advertising campaign. Select two advertising campaigns from different fields that you liked (for example, an advertising program for a political campaign and an advertising program for a sports team). List the attributes of each program in two columns and then make random connections until you create ideas for a new campaign. Or suppose you wanted to improve office morale. Then you would identify two offices from different fields (a dentist's office and your spouse's office) that had terrific morale, list the attributes of each, and then make random connections to come up with new and different ideas to improve morale in your office.

Combining Problems

Thomas Edison's lab was a big barn with worktables throughout the room holding separate projects in progress. He would work on one project and then another. His workshop was designed to allow one project to affect a neighboring one, so that moves made here may also be tried there. This method of working allowed him to consistently rethink the way he saw his projects.

Use a notebook to do in time what Edison's workshop did in space. Work on two or more unrelated problems in parallel. One problem might be about finding the capital and resources for a new project. Another problem might be about improving the employee evaluation system, and still another might be a new advertising campaign. When you're stonewalled on one problem, move to the next. When you come up with ideas or moves that work for one problem, try the ideas or related ideas with the other as well.

Combining Words

The French poet Paul Valery believed that it takes two different thinking strategies to invent something new in writing a poem. With one strategy, you make up combinations, and with the other you choose what is important. Following are some techniques that take words and combine them in different ways.

Identify the main verb and noun in the problem you are trying to solve. Generate words similar in meaning to the main verb and noun and list them in two separate columns. Use a thesaurus. Select a word from the first list, combine it with a word from the second list, and use this combination to generate ideas. Try different combinations. For example, suppose you wanted to reduce conflict between two opposing departments. Your lists might look like this:

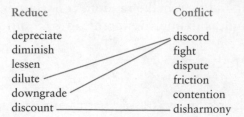

Reduce   Conflict

depreciate   discord
diminish   fight
lessen   dispute
dilute   friction
downgrade   contention
discount   disharmony

Consider the following combinations: "dilute-discord" triggers the idea to reduce the number of interactions between the departments; "downgrade-discord" triggers the thought to downgrade departmental performance ratings until the conflict diminishes, and "discount-disharmony" encourages one to ignore the conflict and hope it resolves itself.

Another way to generate ideas is to take a problem apart and randomly combine the words in different ways. Suppose you want to encourage employees to daily clean up their work areas at the office. Write the words or major phrases on slips of paper or index cards—one thought per card. For example, in our problem our words would be "encourage," "employees," "work areas," "work," "clean up," "office," and "daily." Shuffle the cards and place them face down. Randomly select two, combine the words, and try to force an idea. Keep shuffling and combining until you get the ideas you want. "Encourage-work areas" leads one to think of making the environment more pleasant by increasing the accessibility of trash receptacles. "Employees-encourage" inspires the formation of quality circle discussion groups. "Daily-office" motivates the idea of setting aside a certain time period at the end of the day for each employee to clean his or her work space.

A third technique using words is to first generate a list of nouns (five to ten or so) and another list of adjectives and verbs that pertain to your subject. Each noun should represent some aspect of or the essence of your subject. Use a thesaurus if you wish. The list of adjectives and verbs should be freely associated (write whatever adjectives and verbs come to mind). Next randomly choose a noun from the first list and combine it with an adjective or verb from the second list and use this combination to generate ideas. Try different combinations. This is the technique that I used to create the title for my book *Thinkertoys: A Handbook of Business Creativity for the 90s*. I randomly combined "toys" and "think." Then, I reversed it to "think toys." Next, I elaborated on the words to "Thinking Toys" and combined the two again into "Thinkertoys."

Here is an example of how to use this technique to discover new product or service ideas for commercial airlines. List A contains nouns that capture some aspect or essence of airliners and List B contains adjectives and verbs.

Nouns	Adjectives and Verbs
glasses for drinks	jump
first class	novel
baggage	eat
ticket	board
meal tray	connecting
overhead compartments	talking

Combining "meal tray" with "eat" prompted the idea of organic, edible meal trays. The edible trays made out of soybean starches and proteins would not be meant for human consumption, but rather to be collected and distributed for cattle and other livestock as part of the national recycling effort. You could possibly get soybean farmers to finance the research and development.

Combine Ideas

J. Bronowski, the author of the book *The Ascent of Man*, claimed that "a genius is a person who has two great ideas." The work of genius arises from the person's ability to get them to fit together. In 1979, physicist Alan Guth was puzzling over magnetic monopoles–hypothetical chunks of magnetic north poles divorced from any south. He was also playing around with a totally different idea, the odd notion of "false vacuums" freezing and unifying the forces of nature. Combining these two unlikely subjects, he hit upon no less than a new theory of genesis. His "inflation theory" posits that the universe began in a hyper-explosion that makes the big bang look like a whimper. It answers mysteries of cosmology on which earlier theories had been mute.

The mathematician Gregory Chaitin once proved that no program can generate a number more complex than itself, any more than a one-hundred-pound woman can give birth to a two-hundred-pound child. An idea grows by annexing its neighbor. Perhaps the two ideas catalyze each other like two chemicals that both need to be present in order for a new concept, product, or idea to form. Combining ideas into still more and better ideas will help your mind work to the peak of its creative efficiency.

Try this strategy to combine ideas. Collect all your ideas and put them into two columns, column A and column B. Either list them on paper or write them on cards, and put them into two piles or tape them onto the wall in two columns. Randomly connect one idea from column A and one idea from column B. Try to combine the two into one idea. See how many viable combinations you can make.

In a group brainstorming session, ask each participant to silently write or print five or six ideas on index cards. Then have each participant prioritize their ideas and select one. The facilitator collects and places the leftover cards face up on a table. Next, ask the participants to come to the table, review the leftover ideas, select one and then return to their seat. This is also done silently and should take about five to ten minutes. Finally, ask each participant to combine their idea with the one they selected from the leftover pile to create a new idea.

Combine elements of extreme ideas

Leonardo da Vinci believed that to really know how things work, you should examine them under critical conditions. He believed in pushing concepts to the extreme in his imagination. Create two opposite extreme ideas. For instance, what idea would you create if you had all the resources (people, money, time, etc.) in the world? Then, ask what idea would you create if you had no resources? And then try to combine the two into something practical. Think of the elements and attributes of each extreme and then make random connections between the two lists of extremes.

Suppose you want to reward employees for ideas that increase productivity. One extreme would be to award each employee one million dollars for each idea. The other extreme would be to award each employee a penny. The combination of the two extremes inspires a "Penny for Your Ideas" campaign. Buy a gum-ball machine and place it in your office filled with colored gum balls. For every idea (or every five or ten ideas) award the contributor a penny for use in the machine. Award a cash prize according to the color of the gumball that comes out ($2 for green, $5 for yellow, $100 for red, etc.)

Combine Multiple Perspectives

Genius comes from a passionate commitment to the integration of multiple perspectives. When one excels in several different areas and then is able to synthesize them, one begins to approach genius. Through the integration of multiple perspectives, the deeper structures of ideas become revealed to us. The discovery of the deep structure beneath the many and varied surface structures is the core criterion of genius.

SIL

SIL is a German acronym which means "successive integration of problem elements." SIL is another of the many brainwriting techniques that were developed at the Batelle Institute in Frankfurt, Germany. It first involves silent individual generation of ideas about a previously stated problem. It differs from most other methods in that ideas are generated by progressively integrating previous ideas. The guidelines are:

1. Each individual in the group silently writes ideas.
2. Two of the group members read one of their ideas out loud.
3. The remaining group members try to integrate the two ideas into one idea.
4. A third member reads an idea and the group attempts to integrate it with the one formed in step three.
5. This process of reading and integrating ideas continues until all the ideas have been read and integrated into one final solution. While it may not be possible to integrate all ideas, at least it ensures that all ideas get a fair hearing.

The Exquisite Corpse

This is a technique used by surrealist artists to create conceptual combinations in art. Artists in a group would take turns, each contributing any word that occurred to them in a "sentence," without seeing what the others had written. The resulting sentence would eventually become a combination of concepts that they would study and interpret, hoping to get a novel insight or a glimpse of some deeper meaning. It was thought that the juxtaposed words of individuals would approach the freedom of thought consciousness constrains. The technique is named "The Exquisite Corpse" after a sentence that happened to contain those words.

Following is a group game based on this technique; it is designed to procure and combine unrelated concepts. The group discusses a problem or subject for five to ten minutes. Then, each participant silently writes one word on a card. The group then tries to combine the cards into a sentence (words can be added by the group to help the sentence make sense). Lastly, the group is invited to study the final sentence and build an idea or ideas from it.

Combine Talent

Look for ways to combine talent. Howard Gardner hypothesized in his book *Creating Minds* that, without the stimulation and critique offered by close friends, Einstein might not have completed his innovative work. He appreciated the opportunity to try out his ideas on others such as his wife Mileva and Michaelangelo Besso, an engineer he befriended at the patent office. Einstein thanked Besso explicitly for a conversation that led to the special theory of relativity, and scholars have speculated that Mileva may have aided in the development of his most original ideas. In his passionate letters to her, Einstein spoke of "our theory." Einstein's friends and wife helped stimulate his thinking by offering diverse viewpoints and critiques.

In the world of art, Pablo Picasso and Georges Braque, by combining their talents, invented cubism. Perhaps either one of them, working alone, might have invented it. But without question, the particular form cubism took and its speed in transforming the artistic world resulted from this combination of talent of two artists, still not thirty years of age. As a more proficient depicter of the natural and the human worlds, Picasso may have been responsible for the stronger representational aspects, the focus on objects with their idiosyncratic peculiarities, whereas Braque pushed more toward abstraction. Their combination of contrasting talents inspired cubism's paradoxical properties.

Look for ways to maximize the many different and diverse talents in group brainstorming sessions. You could divide the group into smaller groups by gender, work experience, departments, geographical regions, education, and so on. Have each group brainstorm for ideas and then combine the groups to share ideas and to look for ways to combine them. For example, you might divide a large group into three groups: very experienced, moderately experienced, and little or no experience. Or divide a group by position, for example, salespeople, customer service representatives, and service personnel. Have each group separately generate ideas and then combine the groups to successively integrate the ideas using the SIL guidelines on page 135.

Left-Brainers and Right-Brainers

An interesting way to combine talent is to divide the group into left-brain (rational) thinkers and right-brain (intuitive) thinkers. Ask the left-brainers to come up with practical, conventional, and logical ideas; ask the right-brainers to come up with far-out, unconventional, and illogical ideas. Using the SIL guidelines, have the group successively integrate the logical ideas with the unconventional.

Combining Domains

Many breakthroughs are based on combining information from different domains that are usually not thought of as related. Integration, synthesis both across and within domains, is the norm rather than the exception. Ravi Shankar found ways to integrate and harmonize the music of India and Europe; Paul Klee combined the influences of cubism, children's drawings, and primitive art to fashion his own unique artistic style; Salvador Dali integrated Einstein's theory of relativity into his masterpiece *Nature Morte Vivante*, which artistically depicts several different objects simultaneously in motion and rest. And almost all scientists cross and recross the boundaries of physics, chemistry, and biology in the work that turns out to be their most creative.

Another way to combine talent is to elicit advice and information about your subject from people who work in different domains. Interestingly, Leonardo da Vinci met and worked with Niccolò Machiavelli, the Italian political theorist, in Florence in 1503. The two men worked on several projects together, including a novel weapon of war: the diversion of a river. Professor Roger Masters of Dartmouth College speculates that Leonardo introduced Machiavelli to the concept of applied science. Years later, Machiavelli combined what he learned from Leonardo with his own insights about politics into a new political and social order that some believe–this author included–ultimately sparked the development of modern industrial society.

Jonas Salk, developer of the vaccine that eradicated polio, made it a standard practice to interact with men and women from very different domains. He felt this practice helped to bring out ideas that could not arise in his own mind or in the minds of people in his own restricted domain. Look for ways to elicit ideas from people in other fields. Ask three to five people who work in other departments or professions for their ideas about your problem. Ask your dentist, your accountant, your mechanic, etc. Describe the problem and ask how they would solve it. Listen intently and write down the ideas before you forget them. Then, at a later time, try integrating all or parts of their ideas into your idea.

This is what Robert Bunsen, the chemist who invented the familiar Bunsen burner, did with his problem. He used the color of a chemical sample in a gas flame for a rough determination of the elements it contained. He was puzzled by the many shortcomings of the technique that he and his colleagues were unable to overcome, despite their vast knowledge of chemistry. Finally, he casually described the problem to a friend, Kirchhoff, a physicist, who immediately suggested using a prism to display the entire spectrum and thus get detailed information. This suggestion was the breakthrough that led to the science of spectrography and later to the modern science of cosmology.

If you're brainstorming a business problem in a group, try asking another department to join yours. For example, if you are in advertising and want to create a new product advertising campaign, ask people from manufacturing to join your session. Separate the advertising and manufacturing people into two groups. Each group brainstorms for ideas separately. Then combine the groups and integrate the ideas.

Physicists in a university assembled a huge magnet for a research project. The magnet was highly polished because of the required accuracy of the experiment. Accidentally, the magnet attracted some iron powder that the physicists were unable to remove without damaging the magnet in some way. They asked other teachers in an interdepartmental meeting for their ideas and suggestions. An art instructor came up with the solution immediately, which was to use modeling clay to remove the powder.

STRATEGY FIVE: CONNECTING THE UNCONNECTED

If one particular thinking strategy stands out for creative geniuses, it is the ability to make juxtapositions that elude most people. Call it a facility to connect the unconnected that enables them to see relationships to which others are blind. They set their imaginations in motion by using unrelated stimuli and forcing connections with their subject.

In the illustration, figure B appears larger than figure A. It is not. They are both the same size. If you cut out figure A, you will find that it fits exactly over figure B.

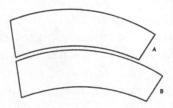

Juxtaposing the smaller arc of *A* to the larger arc of *B* makes the upper figure seem smaller. The juxtaposition of the arcs creates a connection between the arcs that changes our perception of their size. We do not see the arcs (equal in size) as they are, but as we *think* they are (unequal).

In a similar way, you can change your thinking patterns by connecting your subject with something that is not related. These different patterns catch your brain's processing by surprise and will change your perception of your subject. Suppose you want a new way to display expiration dates on packages of perishable food and you randomly pair this with autumn. Leaves change color in the autumn. Forcing a connection between "changing colors" with expiration dates triggers the idea of "smart labels" that change color when the food is exposed to unrefrigerated temperatures for too long. The label would signal the consumer—even though a calendar expiration date might be months away. Our notion of "expiration" dates was changed by making a connection with something that was unrelated (autumn), which triggered a new thought pattern and a new idea.

Leonardo da Vinci wrote how he "connected the unconnected" to get his creative inspiration in his notebooks. He wrote about this strategy in a mirror-image reversed script "secret" handwriting that he taught himself. To read his handwriting, you have to use a mirror. It was his way of protecting his thinking strategy from prying eyes. He suggested that you will find inspiration for marvelous ideas if you look into the stains of walls, ashes of a fire, the shape of clouds, patterns in mud, or in similar places. He would imagine seeing trees, battles, landscapes, figures with lively movements, etc., and then excite his mind by forcing connections between the subjects and events he imagined and his subject. According to his notebooks, da Vinci would even sometimes throw a paint-filled sponge against the wall and contemplate the stains.

The metaphors that Leonardo formed by forcing connections between two totally unrelated subjects were extremely creative and imaginative. Once he was standing by a well and noticed a stone that hit the water at the same moment that a bell went off in a nearby church tower. He noticed the stone caused circles that spread until they disappeared. By simultaneously concentrating on the circles in the water and the sound of the bell, he made the connection that led to his discovery that sound travels in "waves." This kind of tremendous insight could only happen through a connection between sight and sound made by the imagination.

Leonardo's knack for making remote connections was certainly at the basis of his genius for forming analogies between totally different systems. He associated the movement of water with the movement of human hair, thus becoming the first person to illustrate in extraordinary detail the many invisible subtleties of water in motion. His observations led to the discovery of a fact of nature that came to be called the law of continuity.

Leonardo da Vinci discovered that the human brain cannot deliberately concentrate on two separate objects or ideas, no matter how dissimilar, without eventually forming a connection between them. No two inputs can remain separate in your mind, no matter how remote they are from each other. In tetherball, a ball is fastened to a slender cord suspended from the top of a pole. Players bat the ball around the pole, attempting to wind its cord around the pole above a certain point. Obviously, a tethered ball on a long string is able to move in many different directions, but it cannot get away from the pole. If you whack at it long enough, eventually you will wind the cord around the pole. This is a closed system. Like the tetherball, if you focus on two subjects for a period of time, you will see relationships and connections that will trigger new ideas and thoughts that you cannot get using your usual way of thinking.

Samuel Morse, for example, became stumped trying to figure out how to produce a signal strong enough to be received over great distances. Larger generators were not sufficient. One day he saw tired horses being exchanged at a relay station. He made the connection between relay stations for horses and strong signals and solved the problem. The solution was to give the traveling signal periodic boosts of power. This made the coast-to-coast telegraph possible. Nikola Tesla made a connection between the setting sun and a motor. His insight was to have the motor's magnetic field rotate inside the motor just as the sun (from our perspective) rotates. He created the AC motor, with electrical current that reverses direction many times per second.

In more recent times, a materials scientist laboring to improve steel made the connection between the abalone, a sea creature, and steel. He became intrigued with the iridescent yet tough shell of an abalone. He discovered it was made of simple calcium carbonate, the stuff of chalk, and that the same material may make superhard ceramics possible. It's expected that the superhard ceramics will be used for lining the pistons in cars and in producing steels that "heal" themselves when cracked.

Thinking Unpredictably

In the following illustration, two figures (A) are given to someone with the instructions to arrange them into a recognizable shape that can be described to someone who cannot see the shapes. The figures are usually arranged into a rectangle (B). Then another figure (C) is added and the task is to arrange all three figures into a recognizable shape. The result is almost always another rectangle (D).

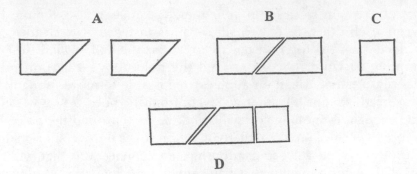

The first pattern makes the second rectangle almost inevitable. We've activated the rectangle pattern, which dominates our thinking and produces another predictable rectangle when given a new piece of information. A square pattern (see A below) is just as good an arrangement, yet few people see it until it's pointed out. This example illustrates how our conventional thinking patterns dominate our thinking and block out new ideas and creativity.

You can change your patterns by changing your focus and thinking about something that is not related. For example, two additional figures (C) are added. Taking (B) apart and integrating the figures in (C) gives us the arrangement in (D). The addition of something (C) that was not related to the original problem activated different thinking patterns and inspired us to think of squares (D). We can now go back and arrange the original figures (B) into a square (A). It is the same with creative thinking. To get original ideas, you need to look at your subject in an unpredictable way.

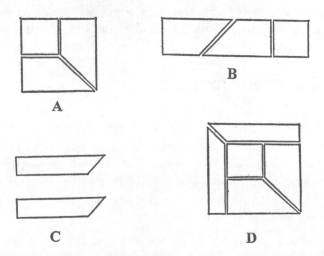

It is impossible to think unpredictably by looking harder and longer in the same direction. When your attention is focused on a subject, a few patterns are highly activated in your brain and dominate your thinking. These patterns produce only predictable ideas, no matter how hard you try. In fact, the harder you try, the stronger the same patterns become. If, however, you change your focus and think about something that is not related, different, unusual patterns are activated. If one of these newer patterns relates to one of the first patterns, a connection will be made. This connection will lead to the discovery of an original idea or thought, what some people call "divine" inspiration.

Focus on your subject in a different way by forcing relationships with something that is not related. DuPont developed and manufactured Nomex, a fire-resistant fiber. Its tight structure made it impervious to dye. Potential customers (it could be used in the interior of airplanes) would not buy the material unless DuPont could manufacture a colored version. A DuPont chemist compared Nomex to a "mine shaft" in a gold mine–a subject that had nothing to do with Nomex. What is the connection between a "tight structure" and a "mine shaft"? To excavate minerals, miners dig a hole into the earth and use props to keep the hole from collapsing. Expanding on this thought, the chemist figured out a way to chemically "prop" open holes in Nomex as it is being manufactured so they could later be filled with dyes.

In nature, a gene pool that is totally lacking in variation would be totally unable to adapt to changing circumstances. In time, the genetically encoded wisdom would convert to foolishness, with consequences that would be fatal to the species' survival. A comparable process operates within us as individuals. We all have a rich repertoire of ideas and concepts that enable us to survive and prosper. But without any provision for the variation of ideas, our usual ideas become stagnate and lose their advantages. For this variation to be truly effective, it must be "blind."

Einstein learned how to stimulate "blind variation" in his creative ideas by allowing his imagination to play freely and generate new connections and combinations of associations. His genius was the ability to voluntarily reproduce images and elements of thought at will and to explore relevant connections between those images and elements of thought and his subject. Einstein's genius had more to do with how he processed information than with the amount of knowledge that he had.

A major characteristic of creative genius is the ability to generate a host of associations and connections between dissimilar subjects. This is difficult for most of us to do voluntarily because we have not been taught to process information in creative ways. When we use our imaginations to develop new ideas, those ideas are heavily structured in predictable ways by the properties of existing categories and concepts. We have not been taught how to process information by connecting remotely associated subjects through trial and error. This is true for inventors, artists, writers, scientists, designers, businesspeople, or everyday people fantasizing about a better life.

Techniques

Following are a series of techniques that incorporate the thinking strategy of "connecting the unconnected" to generate novel and unpredictable ideas. The techniques provide a means of producing blind variation of ideas through the use of unrelated stimuli, such as random words, random objects, pictures, magazines and newspapers, colors, wishes, and fantasies.

Random Words

This technique provides a means of producing blind variation of ideas through the use of random words to produce a rich variety of unpredictable ideas. Imagine dropping a stone in a pond. You see a wave emanate outward in a plane. The stone jostles the water molecules, which, in turn, jostle neighboring water molecules. Thus, waves of relayed jostling molecules are propagated by the action of the stone. Yet the waves are essences of neither the stone nor the water. Each wave is distinct and measurable and has its own integrity as it visibly grows and travels outward. The consequence is a new pattern of events that has a life of its own, independent of the stone that initiated the action. By dropping a stone into the pond, you created something that did not exist before: a wave.

In the same way, in order to get original ideas, you need a way to create new sets of patterns in your mind. You need one pattern reacting with another set of patterns to create a new pattern. The "random word" technique generates an almost infinite source of new patterns to react with the patterns in your mind. Random words provide rich sources of connection-making material. They are like pebbles being dropped in a pond. They stimulate waves of associations and connections, some of which may help you to a breakthrough idea. There are several ways to select a random word:

Random Words List (on page 148). You can close your eyes and randomly put your finger on one of the groups of words (each group contains five words) titled "Random Words" that follow this section. The words in "Random Words" are connection-rich. Each word will trigger other words and images that are linked to the "special" word. What you should not do is read the list and select the most likely one for your purposes.

Random Draw. Cut up the "Random Words" list into fragments and throw them into a fishbowl or box. Add your own words to the collection. Draw out random words whenever you use this technique.

Dictionary. You can retrieve random words from a dictionary by opening it, by chance, at any page, closing your eyes, and randomly putting your finger on a word. Another way is to think of a page number (page 22) and then think of a position of the word on that page (say the tenth word down). Open the dictionary to page 22 and proceed to the tenth word down. If the word is not a noun, continue down the list until you reach the first noun.

Other resources. You can use any other resource (magazine, newspapers, books, telephone yellow pages, etc.). Close your eyes and stab your finger at a page. Take the noun closest to your finger.

Now, how would we use random words to generate ideas? Suppose our challenge is to improve the automobile. The group of random words we blindly drew from the "Random Words" list are

nose
Apollo 13
soap
dice
electrical outlet

1. List characteristics. Work with one word at a time. Draw a picture of the word to involve the right hemisphere of your brain and then list the characteristics of the words. Think of a variety of things that are associated with your word and list them.

For example, a nose has some of the following characteristics:
- Different shapes and sizes
- Sometimes decorated with pins and jewels
- Has two nostrils
- Can be repaired easily if broken
- Hair inside
- Decays with death

2. **Force connections.** Make a forced connection between each characteristic and the challenge you are working on. In forcing connections between remote subjects, metaphorical-analogical thinking opens up new pathways of creative thinking. Ask questions such as

- How is this like my problem?
- What if my problem were a . . . ?
- What are the similarities?
- . . . is like the solution to my problem because . . . ?
- How is . . . like an idea that might solve my problem?

Example: Connecting "A nose has two nostrils" with "improving the car" triggers the idea of building a car with two separate power sources: a car with battery or electric power for city driving and liquid fuel for long distances.

3. **What is its essence?** What is the principle or essence of your random word? Can you build an idea around it? For example, the essence of a nose might be "smell." Forcing a connection between "smell" and "improving the automobile" inspires the idea of incorporating a cartridge in the auto during manufacturing that warns the driver of malfunctions with various odors. If you smell orange blossoms, for example, it's time to have your brakes checked, or if you smell cinnamon, you might have a gasoline leak, and so on.

   For each random word, list the principle or essence, characteristics, features, and aspects, and force connections with the challenge. Another example is derived from the random words "*Apollo 13*." Astronauts used the LEM as an emergency alternative power source in *Apollo 13* in order to return to earth. Connecting this thought with the automobile led to the redesign of the automobile engine so that it can be used as an emergency power generator for the house during power failures. You could plug the house into the car.

4. **Create many connections.** When using the "Random Words" list, use all five words in the group and force as many connections as possible. Allow yourself five minutes for each word when you try it. Five minutes should be ample time to stimulate ideas. You should find that long after the fixed time period of five minutes, further connections and ideas are still occurring.

One of the hallmarks of geniuses is that they consciously form many connections and associations between dissimilar subjects. Chance discoveries favor the open, active mind that is consciously searching for connections. James Watt was not the first person to notice steam escaping from a teapot, but he was the first to make a connection between steam and transportation, and he invented the high-pressure steam engine. George de Mestral was not the first to notice how cockleburs stick to clothes, but he was the one who made the connection between cockleburs and fasteners and invented Velcro. Arthur Frye at 3M made the connection between a bookmark and a temporary glue that was originally invented for bulletin boards and created the Post-it note. An IBM engineer, while watching his daughter playing with building blocks, made a connection between play blocks and computer keyboards and created a collapsible keyboard for laptops.

The emergence of new ideas through "random" or chance connections may be illustrated by an analogy with paper clips. Imagine you have a pile of paper clips. You open out the clips a little and put them together in a box. If you toss them long enough and vigorously enough, you create a chain. A chain has been formed by the chance interaction and intertwining of the clips. The pattern of the chain is always unexpected and usually original. The more clips you toss, the more likely the pattern will be novel and original. Once the pattern has been formed, you can modify or elaborate on it as well, by trimming or adding more clips.

The more connections you make, the more likely the chance of an original idea. Consider someone who can attend to two subjects—*A* and *B*—at the same time. That person has a chance of thinking of a creative connection *AB*. A person who attends to three subjects—*A*, *B* and *C*—has three potential connections: *AB, AC,* and *BC.* Someone who attends to four subjects has six possible creative connections. Such a person should be six times more likely to think of a creative idea than the person who attends to two and so on.

Random Words

bench	shaft	football	knot	hook
envelope	prison	bridge	seed	magnet
broom	bag	rope	weed	spaghetti
radio	chain	pulley	bruise	disco
landlord	torpedo	toe	toilet	thumbtack
cashier	ladle	woman	closet	tie
toast	insect	plow	shirt	sink
soup	rose	mattress	pocket	bifocals
hair dye	fly	sunset	pipe	television
beer	fossil	gate	rubber	Jell-O
shoe	butter	clock	cancer	eye
egg	nut	rash	plane	pot
meat	twig	car	pill	wedding ring
cup	bird	road	ticket	wine
umbrella	sword	zoo	tool	taxes
hook	motor	museum	hammer	pig
door	monster	painting	circle	hoe
window	dog	sand	needle	mouse
roof	field	menu	rag	wok
lake	gun	index	smoke	gondola
violin	acid	book	referee	coconut
candy	stamp	ashtray	sky	telephone
gutter	beetle	lighter	ocean	sleet
computer	sun	hip	pepper	toll
paint	summer	mouse	valve	notebook
man	ice	poster	triangle	dictionary
glue	dust	aisle	thermostat	file
water	bible	milk	tube	lobby
bottle	drum	horse	octopus	clouds
neon light	fog	tide	smoke	volcano

suitcase	money	lunch meat	clay	dinner
fish	magazine	liquor	gourmet	label
lamp	screwdriver	pilot	roast	laboratory
library	VCR	lipstick	heat	sandpaper
university	stereo	caviar	limo	wedge
fulcrum	ink	perfume	campfire	sundial
outdoor grill	ditches	gum	fireworks	squirrel
canister	razor	cheese	tomato	mustache
chimney	tea	flame	tongue	organ
rotating spit	eyedropper	fruit	fracture	molar
toxic waste	actor	ham	watermelon	ghetto
coffee	homeless	highway	Christmas	bag lady
ashes	person	lingerie	politician	ghost
groundhog	queen	jelly bean	quail	athlete
rib cage	artist	bubble	handball	herd
	storm			
parking lot		choirboy	AK-47	flute
lungs	Indian	pet	donut	rod
speech	snake	hair dye	mama	constitution
math	fox	eraser	peanut	handkerchief
war	lobster	bikini	dance	key
	Satan			
brunch		canyon	song	trophy
ailing boats	balloon	cards	congress	zodiac
mirrors	sauce	button	arrow	turkey
burdock	acne	riot jacket	honey	surf
sludge	crystal	film	bath	refrigerator
	shrimp			
wastebasket		runway	igloo	dragon
watch	army	flamingo	tub	turtle
flag	beet	police	ruler	seaweed
helmet	brick	white house	nomad	goulash
cactus	prostitute	lava	subway	mud
	catsup			
cowboy		rainforest	Mass	worm
tavern	explosives	island	missing link	planet
butterfly	diamond	sunrise	vein	opera
cube	camel	plastic	truck	chameleon
X ray	leaf	Hindu	monk	wart
	train			

olive	doorbell	griddle	soap	wagon
map	marble	candle	dice	magnifying
coupon	knot	banjo	electrical	glass
foam	pump	anteater	outlet	wire
nosebleed	umpire	tent	nose	dock
			Apollo 13	rock
mushroom	shark	funeral		top
gasoline	onion	gear	bookmark	cursor
music	garage	carpet	torch	tire
recess	rum	Windsurfer™	tomb	drawer
rain	attic	champagne	can	sock
			gold	
hockey	fireplace	salmon		taxi
eel	deli	underwear	ear	zebra
rocket	knapsack	diaper	beans	elevator
barge	circus	lug	spark plug	stairs
trash	ant	microphone	bat	branch
			lawn mower	
pyramid	clamp	paperweight		ladder
dome	wrench	griddle	pothole	bus
chapel	bum	rifle	bookends	toy
thunder	software	paper clip	fly	hair
caterpillars	star	EKG	cufflinks	rubber band
			belt	
jaguar	crown	copier		pond
firefly	curb	desk	tile	dream
wasp	fingerprint	vibrator	piano	pencil
moon	guerrilla	earrings	skyline	steak
moss	iodine	shower	creek	template
			snow	
panda	jam	podium		compass
stomach	silver	scotch	biology	tattoo
brush	microscope	hat	cow	insulation
gland	nail	jet	bandage	legs
intestine	piston	soda	calendar	wheat
			calculator	
roach	priest	stoplight		bread
exhibition	doctor	confession	cake	paper
holocaust	salt	roulette	fence	soda
tax	mouth	spaceship	toothbrush	insurance
lamb	horizon	judge	rainbow	pennant
			apartment	

chess
stew
waiter
goose
sandwich

buffalo
kite
hoop
archer
hunter

laundry
toolbox
chopsticks
bathrobe
conscience

child
eagle
costume
heaven
brain

parachute
pudding
parsley
ape
sidewalk

sneakers
chair
gutters
zipper
want ads

ballet
shotgun
dirt
cream
skin

chalk
pool table
jar
bracelet
satellite

minnow
society
examination
Genesis
skin

vodka
suicide
maid
comb
picture

vest
crab
lottery
rake
soldier

spoon
swing
skates
curtain
wax

boot
helicopter
fishing pole
rice
puddle

sin
shadow
cells
hand
sex

frame
Jeep
Rolex
mailbox
shampoo

disk
necklace
flashlight
monument
dam

hose
golf
fortune
  cookie
change
atlas

wind
comic
roller
mat
Volkswagen

fire
poem
blood
castle
psychology

pendant
rail
megaphone
skyscraper
skyline

teacher
bank
China
fan
steering
  wheel

phone book
cuffs
vacuum
courthouse
chips

safari
lightning
sculpture
board
keyboard

Holy Grail
symbol
globe
mow
cross

hubcap
carton
sugar
match
deadbolt

fig
pole
oceanfront
townhouse
angel

intersection
parent
blueprint
forest
wigwam

steam
saucer
Broadway
remote
  controller

silk
earthquake
supermarket
leash
teabag

blindfold
teeth
flowers
whale
chocolate

noodles
theater
mast
cabin
bone

mantle
ball bearings
lock
terrorist
dishwasher

drill
orange
tobacco
myth
journey

iceberg
snail
jungle
log cabin
syrup

boxing glove
noose
jeans
aerial
crayons

pipe cleaner	medal	bleach	easel	celebrity
ribbon	fountain	cord	flood	leather
pencil	fingernail	pliers	cockroach	snowflake
sharpener	beard	magician	frying pan	salad
battery	student	faucet	crewcut	senator
wheel	thumb	mason	hell	bomb
baton	basket	jewels	miracle	airport
orchestra	purse	lap	palm tree	cornmeal
suspenders	arch	sweater	choir	cornstalks
brassiere	cloak	band	frankfurter	manure
tractor	block	frost	trivia	trumpet
candlestick	screen	girdle	crust	cone
newspaper	vase	stove	oasis	temperature
secretary	basement	hotel	stream	howitzer
salesman	logo	nipple	hostage	rally
wallpaper	torso	RV	dandruff	merchant
tower	pickle	grandfather	rib	box
kitchen	pigeon	clock	popovers	willow
magnifier	whip	cruise liner	dope	stick
garden	lint	stage	frog	canteen
		binoculars		
general	meatball		pilot	gourd
eyebrow	tape	audience	milkshake	polyester
chapter	coffin	fur	wheelbarrow	Stetson
catalog	meadow	juice	level	minute
bonnet	cyclone	buffet	aunt	IRA
		husband		
butcher	lips		pimple	office
dinette	watermelon	bacteria	pizzeria	wand
bed	knee	spirit	balcony	graph
locker	swamp	sauna	communist	amplifier
professor	furnace	monopoly	hedge	line
		mold		
cereal	bingo		thesaurus	bagel
cotton	weeds	teenager	workshop	beef
brochure	paper	handcuffs	cheesecake	floor
mime	studio	Tinkertoys	gang	barn
elbow	patch	chess	shelf	dolphin
		scaffold		

aircraft carrier
submarine
reef
casino
revolution

bow
kneecap
borscht
raincoat
dawn

steam engine
cliff
seam
tumor
zone

office
psychology
Easter
scar
dancer

hero
fear
hamburger
welfare
Vaseline

media
laughter
principal
script
contract

forecast
grid
herring
warrior
occult

putter
bush
tugboat
bonds
glove

wig
deodorizer
news
display
Internet

leopard
team
staple
hearing aid
expressway

breeze
postcard
beets
photograph
scalp

cremation
network
scripture
anchor
cauliflower

packrat
cult
dime
robotics
engineer

tar
maple
classroom
pope
statistician

bomber
textbook
border
sagebrush
aluminum

shutter
safety pin
cargo
lemon
garter

mustard seed
symbol
logo
United
   Nations
grammar

fertilizer
feast
cigar
ornament
disease

poppy
horseradish
group
strip
spinach

dividend
hospital
tank
sonar
sardine

binding
scab
detective
England
dumpling

prune
poker
gravy
mulch
poetry

nude
trial
traveler
fraction
sausage

headhunter
matchsticks
fat
rabbit
duck

words
cartridge
dwarf
shuttle
DC-10

bulletin
plum
check
checkers
FAA

wildfires
bluebells
vinyl
brakes
cavity

pornography
landfill
wages
vacation
dial

CIA
mosquito
cherry
rattlesnake
saxophone

auditorium
timer
dill
cork
condom

microwave
rhinoceros
marshmallow
scarecrow
beam

scallop
pumpkin
plumber
lounge lizard
official

eggshell
Peace Corps
fugitive
gully
Hawaii

lantern
sulfur
alligator
cobra
cattails

giraffe
ranch
vampire
emerald
confederacy

cradle	Olympics	liver	parakeet	ostrich
alphabet	trout	shield	pig hock	tent
lettuce	scissors	fuel	excrement	gold
reindeer	sand dune	Japan	vines	jazz
paintbrush	forehead	lacrosse	telescope	DNA

dynamite	Jerusalem
beam	muffler
supertanker	resume
astrodome	chuckhole
cheetah	jellyfish

Random Objects

Just as water flows down slopes, settles in hollows, and is confined to riverbeds, so information flows down your usual thinking channels, and by its very flow, increases the probability of triggering the same old ideas. If you deliberately dam up the old channels, you force the information to seek out and take to new and better patterns of flow. Another way to dam up the old channels and cut new ones in your mind is to make connections between your subject and random objects.

This is what happened to NASA engineer James Crocker when the Hubble telescope failed and embarrassed NASA. In the shower of a German hotel room, James Crocker was contemplating the Hubble disaster while showering and looking at the showerhead, which could be extended to adjust to the user's height. He made the connection between the showerhead and the Hubble problem and invented the idea of placing corrective mirrors on automated arms that could reach inside the telescope and adjust to the correct position. His idea turned the Hubble from a disaster into a NASA triumph.

Following are guidelines for making connections with random objects:

1. Generate a list of five objects that are unrelated to the problem. Imagine you are in the Smithsonian Institute, a science museum, a natural history museum, the White House, France, an airplane, or some other interesting location. List objects or things that interest you.

2. Select the first object and describe what comes to mind. Write just a word or phrase. Draw a picture to get your right brain involved.

3. Study it and list all of its descriptive characteristics (specific parts, relationships, what it does, its essence, etc.).

4. Examine each characteristic and use it as a stimulus for suggesting ideas by forcing connections between the characteristics and your challenge.

5. Continue this process with all the characteristics for the object.

6. Test different ways to connect characteristics and your problem.

7. Select another object and repeat the process.

8. Examine all the ideas and select the most promising.

Thought Walk

Jean-Jacques Rousseau, the famous French philosopher, did his best thinking on trips he made alone and on foot. Similarly, Johann Wolfgang von Goethe took a walk whenever he wanted to think and come up with new ideas. During his long hikes in the mountains of Berchtesgaden, Sigmund Freud worked out his imposing structure of the unconscious, preconscious, and conscious that has bound the twentieth-century psyche ever since. In fact, he told his good friend Wilhelm Fliess, a Berlin doctor, that his book *The Interpretation of Dreams* was designed to have the effect of one of his hikes through a concealed pass in a dark forest that opens out on a view of the plain. Taking a walk stimulated and refreshed these men in their thinking.

Instead of imagining objects, take a walk around your home or workplace and the surrounding grounds. Come back with four or five things or objects (or a list of objects) that interested you during your walk. (For example, children skipping rope, a pebble, a bag of jelly beans, a drinking fountain, and so on.) Study the objects and list their characteristics. Then brainstorm for ideas using the procedures outlined previously in "Random Objects."

If you are brainstorming in a group, ask each person to take a "thought walk" and come back with four or five things or objects (or a list). Ask each participant to silently list the characteristics and to build ideas around the characteristics. The group shares ideas and then elaborates on them into still more ideas.

A few months back, a group of engineers were looking for ways to safely and efficiently remove ice from power lines during ice storms, but they were stonewalled. They decided to take a "thought walk" around the hotel. One of the engineers came back with a jar of honey he purchased in the gift shop. He suggested putting honey pots on top of each power pole. He said this would attract bears. The bears would climb the poles to get the honey, and their climbing would cause the poles to sway and the ice to vibrate off the wires. Working with the principle of vibration, they got the idea of bringing in helicopters to hover over the lines. Their hovering vibrated the ice off the power lines.

Idea Bank

Max Planck, the creator of quantum physics, said new ideas are not generated by deduction, but by a creative imagination that enables one to make unusual associations. Make it a practice to collect and store interesting items like a packrat and use the items to stimulate your imagination. Keep a container (coffee can, shoe box, desk drawer, file folder, etc.) of interesting advertisements, quotes, articles, designs, ideas, questions, cartoons, pictures, doodles, poems, interesting words, and other intriguing items that might trigger additional ideas by association.

When you are working on a challenge, shake up the container and pull an item, at random, to see what connections, links, and intriguing associations you can discover between the item and your subject. Suppose you wanted to improve your business organization and you drew a picture about DNA. What is the connection between DNA, a nucleic acid that carries genetic information in the cell, and a business organization? One might, for example, write out the values and goals of the business as a DNA organizational code that is so tightly compressed that it acts like a mathematical formula. It will lock in the organization to prescribed values and rules of action. Employees will know what the code is and what the rules are.

The great American author, F. Scott Fitzgerald, once remarked that he achieved his ideas and insights by holding two dissimilar subjects or ideas in his head at the same time. The contradiction caused by the dissimilarities created a tension within him. This tension inspired him to overcome the contradiction with a creative idea or insight. This is the principle behind the "Idea Bank." When you draw two dissimilar subjects (random stimuli) from the bank, you will experience an almost instinctive desire to overcome the contradictions by making connections between the two. These connections trigger new ideas. Other sources of random stimuli are newspapers and magazines.

Newspapers and Magazines

Newspapers and magazines are excellent sources for random stimuli that can be used to initiate new ideas. Pick up your favorite newspaper or magazine and open to one of the following sections:

- Classifieds
- Front page
- Editorials
- Sports
- Comics
- Business
- Arts
- Fashion

Put the problem aside and forget the problem while you browse through the newspaper or magazine. List phrases, pictures, or other things that catch your eye but have nothing to do with the problem. Select another section. Keep browsing and listing until you have a list of five to ten interesting items. Connect your problem with something from your list to get new ideas.

Randomly pick up a magazine and select and read one article, no matter how remote the article is from your challenge. Then force connections and links between the subject matter in the article and your challenge by thinking metaphorically. Ask yourself, "What are the similarities between this article and my problem? What connections can I make? What new questions does it inspire? What in this article is like a solution to my problem?"

An engineer needed to place a large generator into an excavated area. The usual way to do this was with a heavy crane, which costs $5,000 to lease. He brainstormed for alternative ways to move the generator in the hope of saving the money. Leafing through a travel magazine, he read about Eskimos and the construction of igloos. He connected the article to his problem and came up with an ingenious solution. He trucked in blocks of ice and placed the ice in the excavated area. Next, he pushed the generator onto the ice and placed the generator over the location for it. When the ice melted, the generator settled perfectly into the location. The chances of picking up the magazine and leafing to the Eskimo article is a little like playing roulette, the ultimate game of chance.

Imagine that you are invited to play roulette with someone else's money. You can keep your winnings but your losses are paid for you. It's a game of chance you cannot lose. You can never be sure of winning on any particular bet, but you know that if you played long enough you would win, sooner or later. Chances are, you would play as often as possible despite the unpredictability of the game. You would play as often as you could, in order to increase your chance of winning.

Using this model, it is possible to see what can be done about randomly connecting unrelated subjects in thinking. The first step is to be aware that there is the possibility of this thinking strategy. The second step is to learn how to do it. The third step is to use this strategy as often as you can and to get rid of any inhibitions that interfere with your using it. The more times you use it and the more different ways you use it, the more you increase your chances of coming up with original ideas and creative solutions to problems.

You Can Connect Anything

Psychologists have found that if you put people in a room with a contraption of lightbulbs wired to blink on and off at random, they will quickly discern what they believe are patterns, theories for predicting which bulb will be next to blink. We invent elaborate architectures in our minds to invent patterns to make connections.

Try an experiment. Pick eight random words and give the list to someone or to a small group (for example: "flowerpot," "baby," "glass," "grasshopper," "coffeepot," "box," "toast," and "garage"). Ask them to divide the words into two groups without giving them any rationale for the division. You'll discover that people will come up with some very creative classifications. They'll group them according to "words with the letter o," "things that touch water," "objects made in factories," and so on. No one ever says there is no connection. They invent one. Our minds are incredible connection-making and connection-recognizing machines.

Max Ernst, the surrealist artist, became fascinated with the random patterns he saw in wooden floors. He developed a technique where he would place paper on the wood and rub it with graphite to make a tracing that he would sometimes embellish with painting. His technique of turning random patterns of wood into art inspired other surrealist painters to work with other natural patterns and transform them into meaningful pieces of art.

When you make a connection between two unrelated subjects, your imagination will leap to fill the gaps in order to make sense of it. Suppose you are watching a mime impersonating a man taking his dog out for a walk. The mime's arm is outstretched as though holding the dog's leash. As the mime's arm is jerked back and forth, you "see" the dog straining at the leash to sniff this or that. The dog and the leash become the most real parts of the scene, even though there is no dog or leash. In the same way, when you make connections between your subject and something that is totally unrelated, your imagination fills in the gaps to create new ideas. This willingness to use your imagination to fill in the gaps produces the unpredictable idea. This is why Einstein claimed that imagination is more important than knowledge and why Sigmund Freud used a healthy dose of imagination and "free creation" in his interpretive work.

When Freud's father died, Freud closed the eyes of his father's corpse, which was a Jewish son's traditional duty at the time. He thought a lot about closing his father's eyes and what it could mean. He remembered a book he had once read about the legend of King Oedipus, which was the story of a man who tore out his own eyes. He made an imaginative connection between the action of "closing eyes" and his theories of psychological repression. Within a few months, he came up with a new theory of repressed sexual fantasy, popularly known as the Oedipus complex, which posits that people repress sexual impulses toward one parent and hatred toward the other. This insight became his crowning moment in the field at that time.

Freud's act when his father died inspired a whole new line of thinking that led to one of his famous theories. His imagination allowed him to force a connection between the act of closing eyes and psychoanalytic theory. If you declare that you are going to pay attention to some random stimuli, you can force connections between anything and your subject. You could select a color, blue, for example, and then walk around and list all the blue things you see for the next few minutes (sky, wall, telephone, pen, shirt, and so on). Then list characteristics and force connections. Or you may select a shape, for example, a circle, and focus on circular things that you see. Or you could make connections between your five senses and your subject.

Five Senses

Psychologists have long sensed an association between the senses and creativity. Artists and poets, in particular, have taken the unity of senses for granted. Think of any poem, and you'll discover that the metaphoric stimulation of one sense elicits a certain response. A description of a sound, for example, might elicit a certain emotion that gives the poem meaning. After generating ideas, try using the five senses to generate new possibilities. Concentrating on our senses takes us from our main track of thinking and deposits us on side tracks. These side tracks sometimes lead to original thoughts and ideas. The guidelines for this exercise are

1. Write down the five senses: sight, smell, taste, touch, and hearing.

2. Select one of your ideas and force a connection between the idea with each of the five senses. Suppose you are trying to reduce employee turnover and one of your ideas is that employees should have more involvement with their jobs. Apply the five senses to the idea to extend your thinking. For example:

Sight. Initiate more activity. Get people meeting in small groups. Have open doors, open areas for interaction. Use brightly colored bulletin boards and other information exchange facilitators.
Hearing. Pipe in classical music. Hang a large bell outside the boss's door. Whenever something is accomplished or a company goal is reached, the boss rings the bell.
Smell. Provide snacks, such as popcorn, that have enticing odors to invite interaction in a gathering place.
Taste. Provide occasional pizza and potluck lunches where people meet and talk shop and develop relationships. Have managers make custom hot fudge sundaes every Friday for employees to celebrate the week.
Touch. Provide clean, inviting surroundings with soft, comfortable areas and sound-absorbent dividers.

Visuals

Applying your senses to your subject gets you thinking about the problem in different dimensions. Consider the sense of sight. Pictures, photographs and illustrations are excellent sources of unrelated stimuli. Years back, a designer, working to invent a new light fixture, leafed through an issue of *National Geographic* and got his inspiration for a new idea from a picture of a monkey. He imagined a monkey running around a home with a light wherever it was needed. This image led to the invention of track lighting. Use images to help with your problems:

1. Browse through newspapers and magazines. Select two or three interesting pictures at random.

2. Describe one of the pictures in detail. List descriptors. Include physical references and action-oriented statements. List everything that comes to mind (imagery, feelings, words, phrases, etc.). If you think of absurd material, list that too.

3. Force connections between each descriptor and your challenge.

4. List your ideas.

The CEO of a Japanese perfume company asked his executives for ideas that would enable the company to survive poor economic times. Disappointed with their suggestions, he gave each of them a picture of a king crab and instructed them to study it and to look for ideas from the crab they could apply to their business. Some of their connections and ideas were

"A crab can rejuvenate lost claws. We must develop back-up product lines in case our primary line falters."
"A crab can see 360 degrees. We must improve our market intelligence."
"A crab moves slowly. We cannot afford this. We must downsize so we can react more speedily to the market."

"A crab has distinct features. We need to develop a distinctive package that differentiates our perfume more clearly."

"A crab is a scavenger. We need to allocate resources to see what other uses and markets we can find for our products."

Picture Portfolios

Use picture portfolios to stimulate discussion and ideas in group brainstorming sessions. Following are guidelines:

1. Read a problem statement aloud and ask the group to verbally brainstorm solutions.

2. Give each group member a folder containing eight to ten pictures that are not related to the problem area.

3. Instruct the group members to examine each picture and silently write down any new ideas or modifications of previous ideas suggested by the pictures.

4. After a designated period, ask the group members to read their ideas aloud.

5. As each idea is read, ask the group members to discuss it and try to develop new ideas or modifications. Record all new ideas as they are suggested.

6. Collect and evaluate.

An interesting twist is to provide participants with instant-film cameras and ask them to take a stroll and photograph interesting objects and scenes. Use the photos as prompts. A group of managers from various departments met to seek better ways to mesh functions. One of their photographs showed birds looking at a pond of goldfish. To some it seemed that the birds were trying to communicate with the fish who could not hear them. As they discussed the photo, they realized they saw themselves as the unheard birds. Marketers felt that the researchers were preoccupied with scientific rather than commercial matters while the researchers felt that marketing was deaf to new technical insights. The teams of marketers and researchers now meet quarterly to learn "how to talk to each other."

Children's Drawings

The great landscape artist J. M. W. Turner used an unusual technique to stimulate his imagination. Whenever he visited friends who had young children, he would give the children watercolors and paper to make drawings. Sometimes he would suggest a general theme, and other times he would let them draw anything they wanted. The results were original and spontaneous expressions of primary consciousness. Turner would then take the drawings, observe them with an open mind, and create his own visual impressions from the children's work, in much the same way Leonardo da Vinci imagined faces and scenes among stains on the wall. Turner would use these visual impressions to inspire his imagination to create new perspectives for the familiar landscape.

If you or your friends have young children, try Turner's technique. Provide them drawing materials and ask them to make drawings. You could suggest a general theme. For example, if your problem is how to organize your company more effectively, you might suggest that they make drawings of people at work; or if you're worried about your job security, ask them to make drawings of people in danger. Or let them draw anything they want. Take the drawings and observe the images, patterns, and colors with an open mind. Then force connections between the images and your subject.

The Dreamer, the Realist, and the Critic

Imagine a creature living on another planet with a different atmosphere in a distant solar system. Take a moment and draw a picture of the creature that you imagine.

Most people draw creatures that resemble life as we understand it, even though we're free to think up anything. Namely, creatures with sense organs to see, hear, and smell, and arms and legs with bilateral symmetry. Rather than creating something that's idiosyncratic and unpredictable, most people create creatures that have a great deal in common with one another and with the properties of typical earth animals.

There is no reason why animals on other planets would have to resemble animals on earth. People drawing space creatures could have tapped into any existing knowledge base, such as rock formations, tumbleweed, or clouds, to get an idea for the general shape of their space creature, and each person could access something different and novel. But most people draw animals that have similar properties to animals on earth.

What we're exhibiting is a phenomenon called structured imagination. Structured imagination refers to the fact that even when we use our imagination to develop new ideas, those ideas are heavily structured in highly predictable ways according to existing concepts, categories, and stereotypes.

Research shows that we call up typical instances of a concept faster than less typical ones. To see this for yourself, quickly name the first five birds you can think of. Your list is likely to be populated with very typical birds, such as robins, bluejays, and sparrows, and less likely to contain unusual birds, such as pelicans, ostriches, and penguins.

Because more typical instances of a concept spring to mind first, we naturally tend to seize on them as starting points in developing new ideas. And because the most typical members of a concept are the ones that have all of its central properties, this can reduce innovation even further. For instance, robins fly, lay eggs, and build their nests in trees, but penguins do not. If you base a novel alien on the more typical robin, it will resemble a stereotyped bird more than if you base it on a penguin.

We need ways to open and expand our minds to explore the outer limits and dazzling variety of our concepts and concoct ideas that are wonderfully unusual. One approach is a creative-thinking technique used by Walt Disney that allowed his vivid imagination to explore extraordinary ideas and concepts. This approach allowed him to produce fantastical ideas, uncritically and unrestrained. Later, he would engineer these fantasies into feasible ideas and then evaluate them. He would shift his perspective three times by playing three separate and distinct roles: the dreamer, the realist, and the critic.

On the first day, he would play the dreamer and dream up fantasies and wishful visions. He would let his imagination soar, without worrying about how to implement his conceptions. His fantasy analogies permitted him to connect words, concepts, and ideas with apparently irrelevant objects and events. The result was a rich treasure of associations, an imagination avalanche with whole mountains of ideas crashing down.

The next day, he would try to engineer his fantasies back to earth by playing the realist. As a realist, he would look for ways to work his conceptions into something workable and practical.

Finally, on the last day, he would play the part of the critic and poke holes in his ideas. Is it feasible? Can you translate the idea's features into customer benefits? If so, can you make money with it?

Play the dreamer, realist, and critic using the following guidelines:

1. You are the Dreamer. Imagine you have a magic wand that will grant you any wish you desire. What wishes would you create to solve your problem? List at least three to five, especially things that normally wouldn't be possible. Try to make each wish more improbable than the last.

   Example: A community wants to raise more money by more efficient policing of parking meters. My wishes are

   • I wish we had an honor code. Everyone keeps track of their parking time and sends the money to the police department once a month.
   • I wish police officers could see cars leave parking spots so others would not be able to pirate unexpired time on the meter.
   • I wish cars "vaporized" when time expired on the meter.

2. Select one of the wishes.

   Example: I wish police officers could see cars leave parking spots so others would not be able to pirate unexpired time on the meter.

3. Realist. Play the realist by working the wish into a practical idea. What is the principal feature of the wish? What features about the wish appeal to you? Extract a principle, feature, or some aspect of the wish.

Examples of features and aspects of the wish:
- The principle is "seeing."
- Others won't be able to pirate "unexpired time."
- We will provide new jobs. We have to hire more parking officers to watch the meters.
- This system would modify behavior. Motorists would no longer spend time looking for unexpired meters.

4. Extract one principle or aspect and try to engineer it into a practical idea.

Example: "Seeing." How can you work "seeing" into an idea that will lead to the more efficient policing of parking meters?

Imagineered Idea: Manufacture a parking meter with infrared sensors and lithium-powered computer chips to "see" parking spaces. When a car leaves, the remaining time on the meter is erased.

5. You are the Critic. Play the part of the critic by poking holes in the idea.

Example: The "seeing" meter is technologically possible. The major drawback is cost, as such a meter will cost at least four times the cost of a normal meter. The cost, however, will be more than offset by the more efficient collection of revenues.

You can now go back and engineer other features of the same wish into workable ideas or go back and work with one of the other wishes. Generate as many workable ideas as you can from the wishes.

Wishes

There is a clear relationship between wishful thinking and creativity. You are more likely to have a creative idea when you are wishing than when your thinking is extremely intellectual. Wishes help us deliberately oversimplify. This tactic has a long and distinguished history in science and the arts. Scientists play fast and loose with recalcitrant details. Newtonian physics was overthrown by Einstein, but it is still a good approximation for almost all purposes. No physicist objects when

NASA uses Newtonian physics to calculate the forces at liftoff and the orbital trajectory of the space shuttle, but strictly speaking, this is a deliberate use of a false theory in order to make calculations possible. Following are guidelines for a group brainstorming session using wishes:

1. The group leader writes the topic on a card or Post-it note and posts it on the wall or chalkboard.

2. Ask participants to imagine they have a magic wand. The wand will grant them any wish they desire. What wishes do they have about the subject, especially things that would not normally be possible? Participants silently list wishes for two or three minutes.

3. Participants select one wish and write it on a card or Post-it note.

4. The wish cards are collected and posted around the topic card. The group leader organizes the cards and places related ones together.

5. Select one wish. Select the wish that's most interesting to the group.

   Example: Automobile windshields must be constantly cleared when there is any bad weather at all (rain, sleet, snow, ice, frost, dirt, etc.). Wipers and washer fluid help some, but grime rarely can be eliminated completely. A group of engineers brainstormed for ways to improve the windshield. The wish they decided to work with was, What if a windshield could clean itself?

6. The group brainstorms for ways to make the wish a reality. How can you approximate the wish by achieving something similar to the desired effect? Ask what specific features or aspects of the wish appeal to the group. Then try to figure out feasible changes or actions that embody these specific features. Ask "could we," "how about," and "what if" type questions.

   Example: One of the engineers noted that camera lenses seem to be self-cleaning. Lenses are coated with titanium dioxide. When the sun's rays hit the coating, they set off a chemical reaction that strips the lens of organic matter. The engineers decided to see if they could adopt this process to the automobile windshield.

7. List and elaborate on the ideas.

Example: The engineers discovered that titanium dioxide could not be applied directly to windshields because of sodium in the glass. They solved this by coating glass first with acid to purge the sodium and then applying the titanium dioxide. This process keeps the windshields clean of everything but large bird droppings.

8. Select another wish. Select the wish that's most unique to the group and go through the same exercise.

9. Continue working the wishes until the group has generated a sufficient number of ideas.

The more interesting and unique the wish, the greater the possibilities are for an original idea or twist. A frozen-fish processor's line of frozen fish tasted bland and boring. He tried everything, including keeping the fish alive until the last moment. Food chemists told him the answer lies in keeping the fish moving. However, the fish remained inactive no matter how, or how much, the water was disturbed.

The owner waved his magic wand and wished he could "pluck" a fish out of the ocean at the last moment and process it immediately. This wish inspired him to think of the natural habitat of fish, which includes predators. This was the crucial connection—predators are the reason fish keep moving around. He thought, "Why not put predators in the holding tanks with the fish?" The fish kept moving to escape the predators and retained vitality and flavor. Of course, some fish failed to escape and were lost, but this was a small price to pay for tasty frozen fish.

Any process will do as long as it can introduce unforeseen variation for later selection and refinement.

Paper Airplanes

When you are actively engaged in solving a problem, your attention is narrowly focused and your range of awareness is likely to be relatively constricted. Only a narrow range of information is looked at and utilized at any one moment. Bringing information from outside sources may provide hints and cues that expand your focus and may provide a vital link to a new perception of the problem.

For example, in a recent workshop, participants were asked to tie together the free ends of two strings that were suspended from the ceiling. The problem was that the two strings were hung so far apart from each other that they could not be reached at the same time. The desired solution involved recognizing that a pair of pliers laying in clear view could serve not only as a tool for grasping but also as a pendulum bob. When tied to one of the strings, the pliers could be swung toward the second string, thereby permitting a subject to hold onto the second string while awaiting the arrival of the first one. Most people had not solved the problem after ten minutes.

 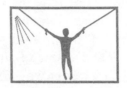

I subtly nudged one of the strings into lateral motion in front of the subjects, without saying anything. After exposure to this clue, most solved the problem within sixty seconds. What was at least as interesting, however, is that most of these subjects had no idea that the nudged-string clue had anything to do with their solving the problem.

Consciousness has a limited-capacity mode of information processing because people can be conscious of only a few things at once. So although the subjects may not have consciously noticed the lateral movement of the string, they seemed nevertheless to have been tacitly informed by it. In other words, people are able to respond productively to information that they do not consciously notice or remember. They seem to be tacitly informed by hints and cues that they may or may not remember.

An interesting way to provide cues to participants in a group is to ask each participant to silently write down three to four ideas on a sheet of paper about the subject being considered. Title the sheet "Ideas." On a separate sheet, ask participants to list their thoughts about the subject. Title the sheet "Cues." Free associate and list everything that comes to mind on the cue sheet, for example, the characteristics, components, wishes about the problem, obstacles, absurd ideas, and so on. Use a stream-of-consciousness technique and write or list everything that comes to mind.

Have everyone take the "Cues" sheet and construct a paper airplane out of it. At a given signal, everyone flies their "Cues" airplanes to another part of the room. Everyone picks up someone else's airplane.

Upon reading what's been written on the airplane, he or she takes the new "cues" and uses them to improve or elaborate on their original ideas.

Relational Words

There is an old experiment in the psychology of problem solving. Put some corn on the ground and a sheet of glass in front of the corn. Put a hungry chicken in front of the glass, so that the glass is between the chicken and the corn. The chicken will try to go straight through the glass to get to the corn. The chicken is not able to change its relationship to the corn and go around the barrier. It's wearing a relational blinder before its mind's eye and only thinks of going straight.

Humans behave this way too. There is a traffic light near my home with a left-turn lane and a straight-through lane. Every week night there is a long line of around twenty cars lined up in the left-turn lane, waiting for the light to change, and none in the straight-through lane. And, every night I drive straight through, go around the block, and wheel down the road before any of those cars get past the stoplight. Like the chicken, they, also, are wearing relational blinders and can only think of waiting in line to turn left, instead of going around the block.

The elementary statement "Take one thing in some relation to another thing" is a form of sentence used to describe the statement of a discovery, an invention, or an idea. Discovery and invention, it could be said, is nothing more than putting a couple of old things together in a new relation. Think of it as a mathematical equation with two elements of a problem on either side of a relational word. You create an elementary action statement: "Take one thing–another thing." There are sixty basic English words that can fit where the dash is and change the relationship of elements. They are the sixty words below.

about	below	near	then
above	beneath	not	though
across	beside	now	through
after	between	of	till
against	beyond	off	to
along	but	on	toward
amid	by	opposite	under
among	down	or	up
and	during	out	upon
around	except	over	when
as	for	past	where
at	from	round	while
because	if	since	with
before	in	so	within
behind	into	still	without

Blueprint

1. Break your problem apart into elements.
   Example: A team of designers wanted to improve the refrigerator. Some of the elements of the problem are "refrigerator," "door," "freezer," "electrical power source," "ice tray," "food trays," "inside light," "retaining cold air," "aesthetics," and "color."

2. Select two major problem elements.
   Example: "refrigerator," "door."

3. Select a relational word and insert it between the two problem elements. Success in problem solving comes from changing relationships between elements in a situation. Two parts of a problem concept are "forced" together with one or more relational words to produce unusual associations. The associations then are used to stimulate new ideas.
   Example: Refrigerator "without" doors.

4. Examine the combination and write down any ideas suggested.
   Example: This relationship ("without doors") inspired the invention of a refrigerator without doors. A cool-air "tornado" circulates through the interior, while vertical jets create a protective curtain,

which keeps warm air out. The refrigerator is circular in design and can be positioned anywhere, including in the center of the kitchen.

5. Repeat steps 2 and 3. Keep shuffling through different sets of relationships by changing problem elements and relational words to come up with additional ideas.

Example: In our example, the designers continued looking for additional ideas. Shuffling through a set of relationships, they settled on "refrigerator" beside "electrical power source," which inspired them to design a small battery backup power source that kicks in should there be a brief power failure.

By shuffling through a set of possible relationships and then having the wit to recognize a solution when you see one, you can successfully solve problems. For example, one of the paradoxes in business organizations is that you need to "empower" people so they can react creatively to fast-changing conditions, yet at the same time, you need to have sufficient control over the actions to achieve your organizational goals. Your problem elements might be "empowerment," "employees," "organization," "control," "goals," "react creatively," and "managing." By looking at the relationship–"Empowerment through employees"–you get the insight to invest time and energy in building trust and bonds of attachment in employees. By building commitment, trust, and bonding, the organization gains control, not by controlling employees, but by freeing them.

In tackling a problem, people commonly assume a set of boundaries to limit the solution. The boundaries of the problem are defined by assumption and then, within those boundaries, conventional thinking is used to find a solution. Very often, however, the boundaries are imaginary, and the solution may lie outside them. In 1872 Richard Dedekind was the first to reveal that mathematicians were being deceived if they thought they were working with a continuum. He demonstrated that no such thing exists for numbers. Within any numeric space, say between 1 and 5, you can increase the population all you like. To natural numbers like 2 and 3 and 4 you can add infinitely more rationals like $3/4$ or $118/119$, plus infinitely more irrationals like the square root of 2, and you'll never begin to populate the space. His work became known as the principle of discontinuity.

"Discontinuity" quickly became a key theme of modernism and a new mode of thought in the sciences, art, and invention. Physicist Ludwig Boltzmann soon demonstrated that continuity was also a statistical illusion in physics, since the behavior of atoms is unpredictable. The French painter Georges Seurat used this mode of thinking when he invented a new technique called pointillism and created the first modern painting, *Sunday Afternoon on the Island of la Grande Jatte*, out of thousands of colored dots, each no larger than an eighth of an inch. This great masterpiece contains some fifty human figures, dogs, and a monkey, all reducible to little dabs of pigment that somehow form a harmonious whole that radiates an extraordinary calm. Thomas Edison invented the movie camera, which is another triumph of discontinuity: sixteen still photos per second that the eye interprets as movement.

Reversals

Dedekind looked at the other side of continuity by reversing the way he thought about it and got the brilliant insight that led to a new mode of thinking, discovery, and art. The illustration below is made up of irregular shapes that look like puzzle pieces without meaning. However, if you focus on the background–the spaces between the shapes–the word "WEST" appears. If you have trouble seeing it, place a straightedge on the top or bottom border of the figures to make the word obvious.

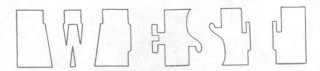

By concentrating on the background and not the shapes, you changed your perspective and saw something that you were unable to see before. This is what happens when you reverse your perspective and look at the other side of things. Suppose you are elected to host a singles elimination tennis tournament. You have 117 entrants. What is the minimum number of tennis matches that would have to be arranged for this number of entrants?

When faced with this problem most people draw diagrams showing the actual pairings in each match and the number of byes. Others try to work it out mathematically. In fact the answer is 116 matches and one can work this out at once without any complicated diagrams or math. To work it out, reverse your thinking from the winners of each match to the losers. Since there can only be one winner in a singles elimination tennis tournament, there must be 116 losers. Each loser can only lose once so there must be 116 matches.

The tendency in the tennis problem is to focus on the winners and not the losers. Reversing your thinking leads you to consider the losers instead of the winners and the problem is rapidly solved. Reversing the way you look at things encourages you to consider things that may not be considered at all. During the Middle Ages, a number of people in a French village were dying from the Black Plague. The other villagers discovered that they had buried some people who were still alive by mistake. Their problem as they framed it was how to make sure they did not bury people who were still alive. One imaginative soul solved the problem by reversing it. He proposed making sure people were dead before they were buried by putting a stake in the coffin lid above the heart. Reversing their problem reversed their viewpoint.

Reversals break your existing patterns of thought and provoke new ones. You take things as they are and then turn them around, inside out, upside down, and back to front to see what happens. In the illustration, figure A shows two lines of equal length bounded by arrow-like angles. In figure B, the arrow-like angles are reversed on one of the lines, which changes our perception and creates the illusion of the line being shorter. It's not shorter. Measure it and you will find it is still equal in length to the other lines. The lines haven't changed, your perception of them has.

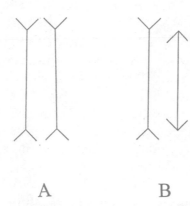

A   B

In figure A, the angles at the end of the lines seem to open up a potentially limited space. Reversing the angle seems to close off and limit the area, which changes your perception of the length of the lines.

A simple reversal of angles dramatically changes what we see in the illustration. The same perceptual changes occur when we reverse our conventional thinking patterns about problems and situations. When Henry Ford went into the automobile business, the conventional thinking was that you had to "bring people to the work." He reversed this to "bring the work to the people" and invented the assembly line. When Al Sloan became CEO of General Motors, the common assumption was that people had to pay for a car before they drove it. He reversed this to "you can drive the car before you pay for it" and he pioneered the idea of installment buying.

Years back, chemists had great difficulty putting a pleasant-tasting coating on aspirin tablets. Dipping tablets led to uneven and lumpy coats. They were stumped until they reversed their thinking. Instead of looking for ways to put something "on" the aspirin, they looked for ways to take something "off" the aspirin. This reversal led to one of the newer techniques for coating pills. The pills are immersed in a liquid and then passed onto a spinning disk. The centrifugal force on the fluid and the pills causes the two to separate, leaving a nice, even coating around the pill.

Physicist and philosopher David Bohm believed geniuses were able to think different thoughts because they could tolerate ambivalence between opposite or incompatible subjects. Thomas Edison's breakthrough invention of a practical system of lighting involved wiring his circuits in parallel and of using high-resistance filaments in his bulbs, two things that were considered impossible by conventional thinkers, in fact, were not considered at all because of an assumed incompatibility. Because Edison could tolerate the ambivalence between the two incompatible things, he could see the relationship that led to his breakthrough.

Edison always thought in terms of challenging conventional thoughts by reversing them and trying to make the reversal work. An interesting anecdote about Edison is that whenever he interviewed a job applicant, he would invite them to lunch and order the applicant a bowl of soup. If the applicant seasoned his or her soup before tasting it, he would not hire the applicant. He felt the applicant had so many built-in assumptions about everyday life that it would take too much time to train the applicant to think creatively.

In the illustration below, you can perceive four black arrowheads on a white background, or you can perceive four white arrowheads on a black background. You can choose to focus on the black or on the opposite white arrowheads. Focusing on the black arouses the notion of the white and vice versa. Similarly, any particular thought will arouse the notion of its opposite by simply adding "not" or by reversing it.

Mathematician-philosopher Bertrand Russell once astounded his colleagues by demonstrating that, in mathematical argument, every alternative leads to its opposite. You can provoke new ideas by considering the opposite of any subject or action. When bioengineers were looking for ways to improve the tomato, they identified the gene in tomatoes that ripens tomatoes. They thought that if the gene hastens ripening (black arrowhead), maybe they could use the gene to slow down the process by reversing it (white arrowhead). They copied the gene, put it in backwards, and now the gene slows down ripening, making vine-ripened tomatoes possible in winter.

Reversing Assumptions

Suppose you want to start a new restaurant and are having difficulty coming up with ideas. To initiate ideas, try the following reversals:

1. List all your assumptions about your subject.
   Example: Some common assumptions about restaurants are
   A. Restaurants have menus, either written, verbal or implied.
   B. Restaurants charge money for food.
   C. Restaurants serve food.

2. Reverse each assumption. What is its opposite?
   Example: The assumptions reversed would be
   A. Restaurants have no menus of any kind.
   B. Restaurants give food away for free.
   C. Restaurants do not serve food of any kind.

3. Ask yourself how to accomplish each reversal. How can we start a restaurant that has no menu of any kind and still have a viable business?
   Example:
   A. A restaurant with no menu. **Idea:** *The chef informs each customer what he bought that day at the meat market, vegetable market, and fish market. He asks the customers to select items that appeal and he will create a dish with those items, specifically for each customer.*
   B. A restaurant that gives away food. **Idea:** *An outdoor cafe that charges for time instead of food. Use a time stamp and charge so much for time (minutes) spent. Selected food items and beverages are free or sold at cost.*
   C. A restaurant that does not serve food. **Idea:** *Create a restaurant with a unique decor in an exotic environment and rent the location. People bring their own food and beverages (picnic baskets, etc.) and pay a service charge for the location.*

4. Select one solution and build it into a realistic idea. In our example, we decide to work with the "restaurant with no menu" reversal. We'll call the restaurant "The Creative Chef." The chef will create the dish out of the selected ingredients and name the dish after the customer. Each customer will receive a computer printout of the recipe the chef named after the customer.

Reversals destabilize your conventional thinking patterns and free information to come together in provocative new ways. For example:

• Suppose you have a glass of mint julep. Reverse this to mint julep has you. How can we accomplish this? Imagine yourself falling into a glass of mint julep. This triggers the thought of inventing a shower attachment with different scents and perfumes.
• Drivers control the parking time of their cars. Reverse this to cars control parking time. This triggers the idea of parking anywhere as long as you leave your lights on. This might be a good idea for municipalities that have problems with people who park their cars on main streets for long periods of time.
• Dentists have dental tools. Reverse this to dentists do not have dental tools. How can a dentist do dental work without tools? This provokes the idea of patients buying their own tools, which are stored by dentists in sterile compartments, to help prevent the spread of disease.
• A chair has height. Reverse this to a chair is flat. This inspires the idea of a piece of thick padding material that you could lay over something else to make it a chair–like a large rock or downed tree. In effect, you could place the pad over anything in nature to make it a chair.

Suppose two boys of different ages and skill levels are playing badminton. The older boy is much better than the younger one and wins every game. The younger boy is discouraged and refuses to play. Since this spoiled the fun for the older boy, it posed the problem of how to keep the younger boy playing. A conventional thinker would suggest offering the younger boy a handicap or exhorting him to be a good loser. A thinker who tolerates ambivalence might see that competition is the crux of the problem and would look for ideas that cooperation, the opposite of competition, would arouse. One idea is to change the game into a cooperative game, with the goal of seeing how long the two boys together could keep the bird going back and forth.

Groups

When working with a small group, ask each participant to write his or her assumptions about the subject in a numbered list. You can then

- Call out an arbitrary number, say, number three. Each person must then reverse that assumption on his or her list and figure out how to make the reversal into a viable idea.
- Ask each person to select one assumption and reverse it.
- Ask each person to reverse all their assumptions.
- Cut up the lists into slips of assumptions and put them into a paper bag. Draw one of the slips and work together as a group to reverse it into something new. Keep drawing and reversing until you get the ideas you want.

Reversals generate a lot of provocative ideas in a short period of time. In one example, a manager for a major copier company reversed her company's attitude toward the competition from noncooperation to cooperation. The conventional thinking in the copier business is not to cooperate with your competitor in any way. Consequently, her company refused to service the competitors' machines. She reversed this to a policy that publicly stated that the company would not only service the competition's machines, but would honor their service warranties as well. The policy was tremendously successful. It allowed the company to establish relationships with the competitor's customers that eventually led to new sales.

Reversals give you two different ways of looking at something. Perhaps the clearest example of the benefit to be derived from looking at things in two different ways is to be found in mathematics. Any equation is no more than the putting down of two different ways of describing something, yet the usefulness of describing a number in two ways instead of one is so great that it is one of the cornerstones of mathematics. Having the two different ways of looking at something on either side of the equals sign makes it possible to manipulate the whole thing into an answer.

Reversing Perspective

Consider the classic teaser of the mirror: Why does a mirror seem to invert left and right but not top and bottom? That is, why are the letters of a book backward when viewed in a mirror, but not upside down, and why is your left hand the double's right and your right the double's left?

When we look into a mirror, we imagine ourselves turned left to right, as if we walked around a pane of glass to look the other way. This conventional perspective is why we cannot explain what is happening with a mirror. To understand a mirror's image, you have to psychologically reverse the way you perceive your image. Imagine your nose and the back of your head reversed: If your nose points north, your double's nose points south. The problem is on the axis running through the mirror. Stand in front of the mirror with one hand pointing east and the other west. Wave the east hand. The mirror image waves its east hand. Its west hand lies to the west. Its head is up, and the feet are down. Once you look at a mirror with this perspective, you gain an understanding about the axis of the mirror.

Psychologically reversing the way we perceive our image helps us understand a mirror. In the same way, reversing your perspective about problems sometimes will lead to a different insight or a quicker, easier solution to a problem. Add up the numbers 1 to 100. The task is not difficult, but it takes time. Eventually we arrive at 5,050 as the answer. Now imagine the numbers 1 to 100 written in a row. Reverse the numbers and write them beneath the first row as follows:

1 2 3 4 5....................................95 96 97 98 99 100
100 99 98 97 96......................................6 5 4 3 2 1

Writing 1 to 100, you always increase by one. Reversing this to listing 100 to 1, you always decrease by one. Adding up each pair of numbers always gives you 101. So the total is 100 X 101 = 10,100. We've used two sets of numbers, so divide by 2 to give 5,050. Reversing the numbers allows you to visualize the rows of numbers and to understand the sequence. You can then multiply and divide in your head and arrive at the answer quickly, with little chance of error compared to the conventional method of addition.

In recent years, scientists have started looking through the other end of the telescope to find a different perspective about the origin of life. Instead of attempting to explain how the universe gave rise to life, they reversed this thinking, and now, start with life as a given and work the other way. Given that we are here, the initial conditions must have been a certain way. Reversing your problem helps you focus in a different way on the problem. If someone has been promoted ahead of you, you might define it as "This happened because the boss dislikes me." Reversed, it becomes "It happened because I dislike the boss." Does this way of looking at the problem change your perspective?

Reversals can also help you find the real causes of a problem that should be addressed. For example, suppose your sales are down and you want to increase them. Here is how to reverse the problem and identify the real causes for decreased sales:

1. **State your challenge.**
   "In what ways might I increase sales?"
2. **Reverse it.**
   "In what ways might I decrease sales?"
3. **List all the ways you can think of to make the reversal work.**
   Example: Make fewer sales calls, be rude to customers, no follow-up, poor product knowledge, provide poor service, and so on.
4. **Evaluate.** Assign a numerical rating from one to ten for everything on your list with ten being the most significant.
5. **Focus on the highest rated items.** These are the most probable causes of your problems.
   Example: "Make fewer sales calls" is the highest rated.
6. **Reverse back to get a new perspective.**
   Example: "In what ways might I increase sales by making more sales calls?"

Reversing the problem led us to the realization that the most effective way to increase our sales is to make more sales calls. Our real problem becomes to figure out how to make more sales calls.

Reverse Brainstorming

When brainstorming, a group of individuals generates as many ideas as possible without judgment or criticism of any kind. The idea is to provide an environment that encourages positive feedback. In science, "positive feedback" is not always a good thing. It will actually push systems to explode or spiral out of control. Pointing a TV camera at its own monitor gives the visual equivalent of the positive-feedback loop screech that comes from a microphone placed too near its speaker.

This is why scientists discriminate between two different types of feedback. In science "negative feedback" is the type that keeps things in check: The valve on Thomas Watt's steam engine created a negative-feedback loop because it opened when the engine was running fast in order to release steam so the machinery wouldn't explode or spiral out of control. In nature, negative feedback in evolution keeps mutation changes from spiraling out of control by wiping out many mutations to keep the design of species stable for long periods of time.

Reverse brainstorming is the critical evaluation or judgment of ideas, encouraging negative feedback. It's a particularly useful technique when a group is interested in overcoming all possible weaknesses of a particular idea. The goal is to identify weaknesses by setting up teams to oppose the plan, and then to brainstorm possible solutions. Suppose, for example, your company has developed a new five-year marketing plan for their cordless telephone. To begin the process of reverse brainstorming

1. Organize the group into teams. Each team is charged with acting as a particular competitor (or you ask the teams to construct a mythical supercompetitor). Tell them that your company's new marketing plan has been leaked. To respond to this new threat, they (the competitors) are instructed to come up with effective countermeasures to the plan.

2. Each group brainstorms for countermeasures to the plan.

3. Then the group is reassembled, and the competitor's countermeasures are discussed. The group is asked to respond to each countermeasure. Forcing people to reverse their thinking creates new thinking patterns that lead to ideas that would not normally be considered.

Reversal techniques create ambivalence, which is a fundamental but generally unrecognized aspect of creative thought. Geniuses tolerate ambivalence: for instance, the polarity in Einstein's thinking. One moment he would favor continuity and the next moment he would favor discontinuity. He could see the relationship between the two because he would tolerate the opposite. Any continuous system can be thought of as made up of a large number of discontinuous elements. Any discontinuous element is formed from a continuous background. This ability to tolerate ambivalence gives geniuses insight into nuances that are usually obscured by conventional patterns of thought.

Seeing All Sides

Dr. Albert Rothenberg, a noted researcher on the creative process, has extensively studied the use of opposites in the creative process. He identified a process he terms "Janusian thinking," a process named after Janus, a Roman god with two faces, each looking in the opposite direction. Janusian thinking is the ability to imagine two opposite or contradictory ideas, concepts, or images existing simultaneously. Imagine, if you will, your mother existing as a young baby and old woman simultaneously or your pet existing and not existing at the same time.

Rothenberg found that geniuses resorted to this mode of thinking quite often when achieving original insights. Einstein, Mozart, Edison, van Gogh, Pasteur, Joseph Conrad, and Picasso all demonstrated this ability. It was Vincent van Gogh who showed, in *Bedroom at Arles*, how one might see two different points of view at the same time. Pablo Picasso achieved his cubist perspective by mentally tearing objects apart and rearranging the elements so as to present them from a dozen points of view simultaneously. Looking back at his masterpiece, *Les Demoiselles d' Avignon*, it seems to have been the first painting in Western art to depict its subject from all sides at once. The viewer who wishes to appreciate it has to reconstruct all of the original points of view simultaneously. In other words, you have to treat the subject exactly as Picasso had treated it in order to see the beauty of the simultaneity.

In physics, Einstein was able to imagine an object in motion and at rest at the same time. To better understand the nature of this paradox, he constructed an analogy that reflected the essence of the paradox. An observer, Einstein posited, who jumps off a roof and releases any object at the same time, will discover that the object will remain, relative to the observer, in a state of rest.

Einstein realized that an observer who jumps off a roof will not, in his or her immediate vicinity, find any evidence of a gravitational field.

This apparent absence arises even though gravitation causes the observer's accelerating plunge. Einstein said this analogy was the happiest thought in his life, because it inspired the insight that led to the larger principle of general relativity. (He was looking for an analogy in nature that would allow him to bring Newton's theory of gravitation into the theory of relativity, the step making it a general theory.)

Louis Pasteur discovered the principle of immunology by discovering a paradox. Some infected chickens survived a cholera bacillus. When they and uninfected chickens were inoculated with a new virulent culture, the uninfected chickens died, but the infected chickens survived. In seeing the unexpected event of the chickens' survival as a manifestation of a principle, Pasteur needed to formulate the concept that the surviving animals were both diseased and not diseased at the same time. This prior undetected infection had therefore kept them free from disease and protected them from further infection. This paradoxical idea that disease could function to prevent disease was the original basis for the science of immunology.

Rothenberg found another illustration of Janusian thinking in Niels Bohr's thinking. Bohr believed that if you hold opposites ideas together in your mind, then you suspend your thought and your mind moves to a new level. The suspension of thought allows an intelligence beyond thought to act and create a new form. The swirling of opposites creates the conditions for a new point of view to bubble free from your mind. This ability to hold two opposites together led to Bohr's conception of the principle of complementarity, the claim that light is both a particle and a wave, which is apparently self-contradictory.

To think in terms of simultaneous opposites, convert your subject into a paradox and then find a useful analogy. Foundries clean forged metal parts by sandblasting them. The sand cleans the parts but the sand gets into the cavities and is time-consuming and expensive to clean. The paradox is that the particles must be "hard" in order to clean the parts and at the same time "not hard" in order to be removed easily. An analogue of particles which are "hard" and "not hard" is ice. One solution is to make the particles out of dry ice. The hard particles will clean the parts and later turn into gas and evaporate.

Suppose you wanted to make a lot of money. The opposite of this is that you might lack ambition. The paradox is you want to make money, but you're too lazy to do much to make it. Next, you find an analogy that contains the essence of the paradox, for example, I want light but without using electrical energy. The solution to the analogy is using natural energy from the sun. Finally, apply this principle to the problem of a lazy person making money. One solution is to go to the South Sea islands and write a travel book.

Thinking Paradoxically

Following are specific guidelines for solving problems by creating a paradox, finding an analogue, and using the unique feature of the analogue to trigger original ideas.

A CEO noted that when his high-tech company was small, people would often meet spontaneously and informally. Out of these meetings came their best ideas. With the company's rapid growth, these informal meetings (and the number of good ideas) declined. He tried the usual ways to stimulate creativity (meetings, dinners, parties, roundtables, etc.), but they did not generate novel ideas. He wanted to recreate the spontaneous creative environment.

1. **Paradox.** Convert the problem into a paradox. One of the things that distinguishes the vision of genius is its curious relationship to contraries. Niels Bohr was fascinated with the contrary dimensions of reality. Once in a heated debate over how electrons can appear in one place and then in another without any traveling in between, he declared how wonderful it was that they have met with a paradox, for now they could make intellectual progress. Ask, "What is the opposite or contradiction of the problem?" Then imagine both existing at the same time.

   Example: The paradox of the company's situation was that unless the gatherings were unorganized they wouldn't produce novel ideas.

2. **Book title.** Summarize the paradox into a book title that captures the essence and paradox of the problem. The book title should be two words, usually an adjective and a noun. Some examples of book titles are

   Sales target–*Focused Desire*
   Different level employees–*Balanced Confusion*
   Seasonal sales cycles–*Connected Pauses*
   Birth control–*Dependable Intermittence*
   Nature–*Rational Impetuousness*

Reducing the paradox into a book title makes it easier to work with and comprehend.

Example: In our example, the CEO summarized his paradox into the book title *Unorganized Gatherings*.

3. **Analogy**. Find an analogy that reflects the essence of the paradox. Think of as many analogies as you can and select the most suitable.

Example: Our CEO found a suitable analogy in nature. He thought of herring gulls, who are very unorganized scavengers but effective survivors.

4. **Unique feature**. What is the unique feature or activity of the analogue? Creative ideas often involve taking unique features from one subject and applying them to another. John Hopfield was a physicist who knew a lot about spin glass, which are magnetic substances in which the atoms have a spin and interact in either a positive or negative way with each other. Hopfield discovered that the brain is composed of neurons that are either on or off and either excite or inhibit one another. He took a set of unique features from spin glass and applied them to the brain, thereby creating his famous neural network theory.

Example: In our example, the CEO determined that the unique feature of his analogy is "scavenging." The gulls gather for an easy meal when fishers throw unwanted fish and fish parts back into the sea.

5. **Equivalent**. Use an equivalent of the "unique" feature to trigger new ideas.
Example: The equivalent of this unique feature might be to have people come together for convenient meals at attractive prices.

6. **Build into a new idea**. The company will serve inexpensive gourmet food in the company cafeteria. By subsidizing the cost of the gourmet food, the CEO encourages employees to gather there (much like the herring gulls drawn to the fishers free food) to meet informally, mingle, and exchange ideas.

W. J. J. Gordon used this strategy to develop Pringles potato chips, a matter of designing a new potato chip and package that would allow for more efficient packaging of chips without the need to fill the bag with more air than chips. The paradox was a compact chip that would not destruct. The book title that captured the essence of the paradox was *Compact Destruction*.

The analogy they worked with was bagging leaves in the fall. When you try to shove dry leaves into a plastic bag, you have a difficult time. But when the leaves are wet (unique feature), they are soft and formable. A wet leaf conforms to the shape of its neighbor with little air between them. By wetting and forming dried potato flour, the packaging problem was solved and Pringles got its start.

In another example, designers developed a flexible battery that can be folded like a sheet. They started with the paradox of a "solid battery that's elastic." Their book title was *Concrete Elasticity*. The analogue was "garbage bags," with the unique feature of "bags are blended with high-performance plastics." This analogy triggered the idea of entrapping a liquid electrolyte within an inert polymer sheet. This created an ultrathin, flexible battery that you can fold or roll up like a plastic bag. The battery will be used in camcorders, cellular phones, laptops, pagers, and games. You can even create "battery" clothing that replaces "battery packs" for powering medical devices.

Working Backward

Most of us are accustomed to converting a question (2 + 2=?) into an answer (4) according to a rigid set of rules. If you find a calculator someone has left on a desk and it says 4, you have no way of knowing how they arrived at the number. Did someone punch in 2 + 2, 3 + 1, 1 + 1 + 1 + 1, or perhaps 9 – 5, or 1,239,477 – 1,239,473? There are an infinite number of possible ways to reach 4.

Einstein is famous for visualizing his theory of relativity as a given and then working backward to what was known. Francis Crick and James Watson stunned the science community for the way they uncovered the structure DNA. While others struggled up the straight and narrow path of strict construction from the evidence (2 + 2 =), Crick and Watson made a few daring assumptions (started with 4), then worked backward, with gratifying results. In the following illustration, see if you can link up the nine dots with one straight line without lifting your writing instrument from the paper.

This problem is seemingly impossible for most people. Many of us work with the problem as given and try to solve it without success. However, if you imagine the solution and work back to the problem, you'll find that it's easily solved. Below is one imagined solution.

Now work backward to the problem and look for ways to achieve the solution. One solution is to cut the dots out, tape them in a straight line, and then link up all nine with one straight line. You might also have imagined one thick line crossing through all the dots at once. Working backward from this solution, one need only swipe through the dots with a wide paintbrush. These kinds of creative solutions probably would not have occurred to us if we worked in the conventional way with the problem.

Imagining that your problem is solved enables you to approach from the other side and work in an opposite direction. Working backward enables you to think about your problem more flexibly by changing the problem components. Following are guidelines for working backward:

1. Close your eyes, relax, and imagine the best possible solution to your problem. Feel free to fantasize any solution you can imagine.
2. Write the imagined solution on a sheet of paper. Include a brief description of how you profit from the solution, how you feel, and what you set in motion.
3. List the people, situations, or events that made the imaginary solution possible.
4. For each person, situation, or event, list specifically how each contributed to the outcome.
5. Ask yourself how these specifics were generated to solve the problem. Can you generate other alternatives?
6. List the characteristics and properties of the specifics. Do you see any deficiencies? If so, how can you overcome and improve them?
7. What are the gaps that have to be completed to realize the solution? What do you need to do to complete them? What else do you need to know?
8. Keep asking what should precede each step and continue until you work back to the problem statement.

With conventional thinking, you move forward one step at a time. Each step arises directly from the preceding step in a straight line. With thinking "backward," the steps are not sequential. You jump ahead to the conclusion and fill in the gaps afterwards. In the diagram below, conventional thinking proceeds methodically from *A* to *B* to *C* to *D* to the solution *E*. With "backward" thinking, you imagine an ideal solution, *G*, that you probably could not arrive at thinking conventionally and then work backward to *A* to figure out how to get there. When working backward from *G*, one finds a pathway from *G* to *C* to *D* to *H* to *A*. The pathway is not sequential and includes steps (*H*) that you probably would not have discovered thinking conventionally.

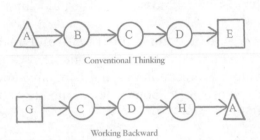

Conventional Thinking

Working Backward

Nikola Tesla, the genius who ushered in the age of electricity, would often think of something as given and work backward to the question. For example, in his work on turbines, he imagined a turbine already built and ran it "in thought" for one month. To Tesla, there was no difference whatsoever whether he "ran" something in thought or physically tested it in his shop. One month later, he disassembled the machine in his mind and noted in precise detail the wear and tear on the pieces in his imaginary machine. Later, a real turbine modeled after his imaginary one was built, run, and dissembled after one month. Remarkably, Tesla's description of where the wear and tear would occur matched the real machine in every detail.

His ability to imagine the future enabled him to create astonishing, world-transforming devices that were without theoretical precedent. Tesla's discovery of rotating magnetic fields is the basis of alternating current, which has made the widespread distribution of electric power possible. Tesla introduced us to the fundamentals of robotics and computer and missile science, and helped pave the way for such space-age technologies as satellites, microwaves, beam weapons, and nuclear power. Some experts even suggest that Ronald Reagan's Strategic

Defense Initiative was the result of secret research based on Tesla's discoveries a half century before.

By imagining a future full of glittering lights powered by electrical generators, of robots revolutionizing industry, and of global communications based on invisible waves of magnetism, Tesla was able to work backward from the future ideas "running" in his imagination to his present. This backward thinking opened up his thinking to an infinite number of different ways of making the ideas "running" in his imagination into practical realities.

Imagine working on your problem as you would in the future. Then transfer the solution back to the present and look for ways to make your idea a present-day possibility. The guidelines are

1. Select a target date in the future (2050) and imagine you are there. Write some sample future headlines that deal with governments, private lives, technology, your company, and the competition. Write a short story about a day in the life of an individual in the year 2050.

2. Generate a list of the most important things you would like to happen to your subject by the year 2050. Imagine at least five future possibilities. Ask the following:
   What is impossible now but will be possible in the year 2050 that involves my problem? What would I have that I do not have now? What information and resources would I have that I do not have now?

3. Using these possibilities, imagine the best possible solution to your problem. Write the solution in as much detail as possible. Then list the people, situations, or events that made the imaginary solution possible, and specifically, how each contributed to the outcome.

4. Ask how these specifics were generated to solve the problem. Can you generate other alternatives? List the characteristics and properties of the specifics. Transporting your subject into the future puts it into a different context and creates new relationships among the problem components. Understanding these new relationships is what is meant by insight.

5. Look for any deficiencies. If you find some, how can you overcome them? What are the gaps that have to be completed to realize the solution?

6. Keep asking what should precede each step and continue until you work back to the problem statement. By working backward from the future, we can discover what conditions would have to prevail just prior to the desired goal in order for us to achieve that goal by means of specific actions. For example, suppose we wanted to go by train from Milwaukee to Boston. The best strategy isn't necessarily to investigate train connections from Milwaukee to Chicago, from Chicago to Buffalo, from Buffalo to New York, and from New York to Boston. We can instead find out what trains come into Boston from the west during the period when we would like to arrive. We can then find out when these trains leave, say, Buffalo or New York, and in this way, plan our way back to Chicago.

Groups

A group exercise to get participants to consider desirable futures is to divide the group into teams (three or four) and have each group develop an imagined future solution. The solutions are put into separate envelopes. Each team gets an envelope with one of the future solutions in it. The team writes an immediate action that can be taken to achieve this solution and puts it into the envelope. The envelopes are passed from group to group. Each generates an action without looking at what the others have written. When all groups have addressed all the future solutions, the group leader reads the actions for achieving each solution, and the group discusses and ranks them.

The Perfect Cup of Coffee

Another way to work backward from a solution is to imagine a perfect solution, list the significant factors that would make it a possibility, and then make a graph to find out where you are at present and what you need in order to make your solution a reality. For example, suppose I wanted to brew the "perfect" cup of coffee. First I would define what I think is a "perfect cup of coffee." In this case, it's what I think the "significant" factors are for a "perfect" cup of coffee, which to me is the best tasting. In order to brew this perfect cup, I would need

- The world's best coffeemaker
- The choicest blends from the best coffee growers
- Comprehensive knowledge of how to brew coffee
- The purest spring water
- The purest sugar
- The freshest and richest cream

Next, I list the opposite for each significant factor, in order to create a continuum, and graph it as follows:

"The Perfect Cup of Coffee"		"The Worst Cup of Coffee"
Best Case		Worst Case
The World's Best Coffeemaker	✕	No Coffee Brewer or Pot
The Choicest Blends from the Best Coffee Growers	✕	Old, Stale Coffee from the Weakest Blends from the Poorest Growers
Comprehensive Knowledge on How to Brew Coffee	✕	No Information or Training on How to Brew
Purest Spring Water	✕	Ordinary Tap Water
Purest Sugar	✕	No Sugar
Freshest and Richest Cream	✕	No Cream

I place an *X* on the continuum (the vertical line represents halfway between the two extremes) to represent where I am at this point in time. For example, the *X* for a coffeemaker indicates that my coffeemaker is slightly above average, I use slightly above-average coffee blends, probably know less than the average person about brewing coffee, use average water and sugar, and milk instead of cream.

The graph illustrates what I have to do to come close to the "perfect" cup of coffee. I'll have to purchase a world-class coffeemaker, the choicest blend of coffee, the purest sugar, the freshest cream, use spring water, and research how to better brew coffee or hire a master brewer to teach me how to do it. I can choose to move all, some, or none of the Xs toward the "perfect" cup.

This inspired an entrepreneur to invent the perfect cup of coffeemaker. It makes a cup of coffee that rivals the best from any coffee house. He suggests the best beans to buy with his coffeemaker and the maker grinds the beans, meters out just the right amount of water, filters the water of impurities, and brews it at the right temperature. The appliance has such handy features as an airtight lid for the carafe, to keep out oxygen (and bitterness); a self-cleaning mechanism; and a timer.

Look at the illustration of a girl standing in the rain. Now try to imagine the girl entirely within the small circle. You will probably find that the image becomes very dense and only contains a few visible features. Now, form your image within the larger circle. Now the image becomes more clear and you can see many more details in your image of the girl in the rain.

Expanding your visual image enabled you to visualize more features. In a similar way, when you imagine a perfect or ideal solution to a problem, you dramatically expand your perception of the problem. This is because mental perception seems to share many of the same information-processing mechanisms with the human visual system. Your initial perception of a problem is narrow and small, like the image in the small circle. Expanding your perception of the problem by imagining an ideal solution enables you to visualize the features and components that are necessary to realize the perfect solution, like the image in the larger circle.

STRATEGY SEVEN: LOOKING IN OTHER WORLDS

Genius is often marked by the ability to imagine comparisons and similarities and even similar differences between parallel facts and events in different fields or "other worlds." Why is *X* like *Y*? If *X* works in a certain way, why can't *Y* work in a similar way? Alexander Graham Bell observed the similarities between the inner workings of the ear and the ability of a stout piece of membrane to move steel, and conceived the telephone. Thomas Edison invented the phonograph, in one day, after developing an analogy between a toy funnel and the motions of a paper man and sound vibrations. Moreover, the way buzzards kept their balance in flight served as an analogy for the Wright brothers when they were developing how to maneuver and stabilize an airplane.

Like a spark that jumps across a gap, an idea from one world is used to create a new idea or creative solution to a problem in another world. The idea that the solar system is continually restored came to Pierre-Simon Laplace, the brilliant French astronomer, when he considered the body's self-healing system. Many years after Laplace's insight, Bell engineers developed a technology designed to be a self-healing communication system, based on a similar analogy with a human being's circulatory system. When important telephone arteries are damaged or cut, the system will pump phone service through new channels, keeping communications alive. The self-healing network links each central office with optical fiber cable in a loop. Next, the central offices are equipped with a special switch, a special device that duplicates signals and sends them in opposite directions on the ring, ensuring that at least one arrives, even if there is a problem. If there is a problem, like the human being's circulatory system, the system is designed to go around it.

Your mind is lying in wait for some cue or suggestion that will initiate thinking about your problem in a different way. When you use analogies between your subject and a subject in another world, you produce cues and hints that will make novel combinations and connections more likely. Philo Farnsworth's interest in farming gave him the cue that led to television. One day, while sitting on a hillside in Idaho, he observed the neat rows in a nearby farm. The neat rows inspired the idea of creating a picture on a cathode-ray tube out of rows of light and dark dots. He was fourteen at the time, and the next year he presented the concept at a high-school science fair. He also demonstrated the first working model of a television set when he was twenty-one.

In the following illustration, there are two sets of parallel lines. The lines appear to have a clearly defined contour border between them. Either of the lines can be seen as covering the other. Yet, in reality, there is no border between the sets. There is nothing there. The illusion is created because our minds try to make the gaps between the lines into something meaningful.

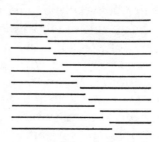

In the same way, when you imagine comparisons and similarities between dissimilar subjects and events in different worlds, your mind will struggle to look for cues and suggestions to make the comparisons meaningful. For example, suppose I want to improve the common flashlight and decide to look in another world for ideas. I look in the world of "automobiles" and choose the specific act of "replacing a flat tire." Next I draw an analogy between "improving a flashlight" and "replacing an automobile tire." What cues can we find in the world of "replacing a tire" to help us improve the flashlight?

First, describe what's involved in replacing a damaged tire. For example:

1. Read the automobile manual on how to replace the tire.
2. There is no external power source, so you have to manually crank the jack.
3. The jack is collapsible.
4. The tire tread indicates usage and damage.
5. Most tires are guaranteed for a certain number of miles.
6. The spare tire is a temporary donut tire.

The descriptions—"no external power source," "manually crank," and "collapsible"—are all cues that inspired the invention of the eternal flashlight (a flashlight that doesn't require an external power source). The light has a collapsible crank that you unfold and rotate. The cranking creates an electrical charge, which is sent to a minigenerator. Cranking the flashlight for thirty seconds will create fifteen minutes of light.

Other ideas inspired by the analogy between flashlights and replacing tires are

1. Place first-aid pamphlets in flashlights (from automobile manual).
2. Design a flashlight with a storage area for spare batteries (from spare tire).
3. Incorporate a color strip in the flashlight that changes color as the batteries discharge over time, to indicate when to replace them (from tire tread indicates usage).

You can siphon water from a bucket by sucking the water upward in a tube. This is an unconventional direction for water to travel. Once the water reaches a certain point, then the siphon forms and the water will flow naturally out of the bucket until the bucket is empty. In the same way, creating ideas for improving the flashlight by making an analogy with replacing an automobile tire is an unconventional way to think about the problem. Once your thinking reaches a certain point, then your ideas begin to flow freely like water being siphoned from a bucket.

Geniuses have a remarkable eye for resemblances and cues between two subjects in different worlds. The Harvard biologist E. O. Wilson, who shook the world with his theory that genes control culture, based his seminal theory of "sociobiology" on his observations of ant behavior in the insect world. When Gregor Mendel humbly presented the results of his experiments with plants to the Brun Society for the study of natural diseases, there was no interest at all in the matter. The genius of this simple work and the fact that the tremendously important science of genetics had been born meant nothing to the audience, who thought they were listening to yet another careful gardener with his pet gardening theories. It was many years before the report was rediscovered and given its full importance. Some of the insights into genius come, paradoxically, from studies of mentally retarded people. It seems that mentally challenged people are unable to recognize similarities and cues and make appropriate connections from one world to another.

Geniuses also demonstrate the ability to discover similar differences between subjects in different worlds. A striking example would be Helen Keller's legendary flash of insight, when she suddenly recognized the essential similarity of different experiences of water. Different kinds of relationships could be defined by considering, for example, the similarity between a young bird and a young fish, which is different from the similarity between an aging bird and an aging fish. This notion of similar differences defines a new order that cuts across various categories of experience. Newton's legendary tale about the apple and the moon was essentially a perception of the similar differences between the motion of an apple and the motion of the moon. He perceived a unity of order between two seemingly unrelated worlds–a falling apple and an orbiting moon.

Following are ways of how to look into other worlds for analogies and cues that you can use to generate original and new ideas.

Parallel Worlds

This is a structured technique that helps you imagine comparisons, similarities, and even similar differences between subjects in "other worlds." The guidelines are

1. State your challenge.
   Example: A lumberyard owner stated, "In what ways might I sell more lumber?"

2. Choose key words or a phrase in the challenge.
   Example: "Sell."

3. Choose a parallel world or distant field. The greater the distance between the parallel world and your challenge, the greater the chances of producing new thoughts and ideas. A business analogy to a business challenge is too close—analogies from television or cooking might be more likely to stimulate creative thought.
   Example: The field selected for the challenge of selling more lumber was "computers."

4. List the images and thoughts that you associate with your chosen parallel world. Then choose one or more of the particularly rich ones. Listing images will allow you to describe the analogy in as much detail as possible.
   Example: Among the images evoked by the computer field are science, multiple uses, user-friendly, hardware, software, add-ons, computer-aided design, computer schools, business uses, and recreational uses.

5. Draw analogies between the images and your subject. Look for similarities and connections. Generate as many associations as you can.
   Example: The lumberyard owner looked at a number of connections between the images and his challenge of selling more lumber, ultimately discarding most of them. The final images he focused on were computer-aided design (CAD), computer add-ons, and recreational uses.
   He combined and connected these three concepts with his challenge of selling lumber, stirring an idea. The combination of all three with his challenge stirred an idea. The idea: Use CAD to design backyard decks. Provide a computerized system in the lumberyard where salespeople can design decks to customer's specifications. The owner would have a user-friendly kiosk with a large video screen and easy-to-use controls that the salesperson would manipulate. The customer explains the deck's size and the number of stairways needed, and selects railings and spindles. The system could then design it from the ground up and calculate the cost. If the cost is too high, the customer can change the dimensions. Once the price is right, the computer could print out the diagrams

and full instructions. This free service would encourage more building of decks, and the lumberyard would sell more lumber.

The parallel world should be something you know about, and you should use a specific object, situation, event, or example from that world. For instance: "The NFL football team, the San Francisco 49ers" will make a much more fruitful analogy than "football." A specific dance movement is much more fruitful than "ballet." The more details you can record, the better. If you choose "restaurants," choose a specific, familiar restaurant.

Use this list of parallel worlds to get started, but do develop your own unique list that best suits your particular knowledge. You might want to focus on particular disciplines or activities that are of special interest and that are not related to your challenge. When choosing a parallel world, examine four or five possible worlds and then select the one world that best suits the general principles of your challenge.

Parallel Worlds List

Accounting   Acupuncture   Animal Kingdom   Architecture
Art Astrology   Astronomy   Ballet   Baseball   Basketball
Biography   Biology   Birds   Black Power Movement   Bowling
Calculus   Cancer   Cardiology   Caribbean   Cartoons
Chemistry   China   Chiropractic   Civil War   Comics
Composers   Computers   Dance   Dentistry   Desert
Economics   Education   England   Entertainment   Evolution
Farming   Fast-Food Industry   Finance   Fine Cooking   Fishing
Flying   Football   Funeral Homes   Garbage Collecting
Geography   Geology   Germany   Golf   Government
Great Books   Great Depression   Grocery Stores   Hawaii
History   Hunting   Hypnosis   India   IRS   Insects
Interior Decorating   Inventions   Japan   Journalism   Jungle
Korea   Law   Law Enforcement   Literature   Mafia
Manufacturing   Math   Medicine   Meteorology   Military
Mining   Monasteries   Monuments   Moon   Movies   Music
Mythology   Nuclear Power   Physics   Nutrition   Ocean
Old West   Olympics   Pharmacology   Philosophy   Photography
Physical Fitness   Physical Therapy   Physics   Planets
Plumbing   Political Science   Politics   Pornography   Printing
Psychiatry   Psychology   Publishing   Religion   Resorts
Restaurants   Revolutionary War   Russia   Sailing   Sculpture
Seminars   Shakespeare   Skiing   Soap Operas   Sociology
South America   Space   Special Education   Stars   Taverns
Television   TV News   Steel Industry   Sun   Talk Radio
Tennis   Terrorism   Theater   Transportation   Travel   Industry
Unions   Vatican   Vietnam   Wall Street Wholesalers
Wine   World War I   World War II   Yukon

One of the advantages of looking for analogies in parallel worlds is that if one image doesn't work, you can choose another image or another world and still another until you get the inspiration you need. People sometimes make the elementary mistake of thinking that one's first effort at an analogy must be right. But consider the following problem of long division. Does the divisor go into the dividend six, seven or eight times?

$$326{,}574 \div 47$$

Who cares? You don't have to know, if you have any judgment to do long division. You can choose a number, at random if you like, and check out the result. If the number is too small, increase it by one and try again; if too large, decrease it. The good thing about long division is that it always works eventually, even if you make a poor first choice, in which case it just takes a little longer. This is the magic of this technique. You simply generate images from a parallel world and test them out. If you don't get the inspiration you need, you try again.

Groups

Following are "Parallel World" guidelines for small groups. For example, suppose a group wanted ways to show clients the bottom-line benefits of investing in training and personnel development in their R and D department.

1. Ask the group to rephrase the problem as a wish.
    Example: We wish we could get clients to visualize themselves using the new products and skills that would come out of training in this department.

2. Have the group single out the key words in the wish.
    Example: "New products" and "skills."

3. Present the group with a list of ten or so parallel worlds and ask the group to choose two worlds unrelated to the problem.
    Example: "Mining" and "weather."

4. Have the group apply the key words to these worlds to help generate seemingly irrelevant images and associations.

Example: Have the group brainstorm new products and skills in mining and weather. Some possible mining subjects might be "focus-blasting," "new technology to restore the environment," "lights on hats," and so on.

5. Ask the group to improvise connections between their images and associations and the problem.

Example: Focus-blasting inspires one to think about putting a lot of resources into one area of training. You might set up a pilot program small enough so that you could have all the resources you need to do it right–to really get results. Then you would use these results to show clients the payback of investing in training and development.

World of Essences

An enlightening experiment was done by gestalt psychologists with a group of dogs. The dogs were trained to approach something when shown a white square and avoid it when shown a gray square. When the dogs learned this, the experimenters switched to using a gray square and a black square. The dogs immediately shifted to approaching the object in response to the gray square (which had previously triggered avoidance) and avoiding the object when shown the black square (which had not been conditioned to anything). Presumably, rather than perceive the gray as an absolute stimulus, the dogs were responding to the deeper essence of "lighter versus darker" as opposed to gray, white, or black as being things.

As humans, many of us have lost the sensitivity to deeper relationships and essences because we've become educated to focus on the particulars of experience as opposed to the universals. For example, suppose we were asked to design a new can opener. Most of our ideas would be driven by our experience and association with the particulars of existing can openers, and we would likely design something that is only marginally different from existing can openers. If, however, we determined the essence of a can opener to be "opening things" and looked for analogies and cues in other worlds, we increase our chances of discovering a novel idea. One example of "opening things" are pea pods. Ripening weakens the seams on a pea pod and it opens. This inspires the idea of opening a can by pulling a weak seam (like a pea pod). Instead of an idea to improve the can opener, we produced an idea for a new can design.

One of the early design problems in the space program was the problem of reentering the earth's atmosphere without burning up. Scientists were baffled until they determined the essence of the problem. The essence of the problem was to survive frictional heating. They brainstormed and listed every conceivable possibility they could imagine that contained that essence and settled on a meteor. They studied how meteors survived frictional heating. They discovered that the frictional heat generated during entry into the earth's atmosphere was dissipated into the heat of vaporization of the meteor surface. Consequently, an analogy between the space capsule and a meteor led to the use of a sacrificial material on the capsule surface that vaporized and thus dissipated the frictional heating.

Working with principles and essences will break you out of the habit of associating qualities with things and will expand your thinking. For example, the principle of "resonance" lies at the heart of much of Nikola Tesla's work. Resonance describes the way in which large quantities of energy can be exchanged between such systems when their vibrations coincide. An example of "resonance" is a little girl pushing her brother higher and higher on a swing by timing her pushes to coincide with the natural oscillation of the swing. If the pushes are in "resonance," then each impulse adds progressively. Tesla saw this principle at work in all systems in nature, for example, in the swing of the pendulum in a grandfather clock, the notes of a violin, oscillations of an electric current, the waves of a lake, etc., and used this principle as the basis of many of his inventions, including the Tesla coil, a device that turns ordinary household electric current into current at a very high voltage.

To work with the "World of Essences," first decide the major principle represented by your problem. What is the essence of it? For example, the essence of a new marketing strategy might be "attraction," namely, how are things and people attracted. Once you determine its essence, then generate a list of things from other worlds that represent the major principle. Examples of "attracting" are

- Bees attracted to honey
- Magnets attracting metal
- Politicians attracting voters
- People attracted to a Web site on the Internet
- Colleges attracting premier athletes

Select one example and describe it in as much detail as possible. For example, "politicians attracting voters" suggests many things, including the theme of "values," "canvassing voters door to door," and "debates." Use the descriptions to suggest analogies and look for cues to stimulate ideas. For example, both major political parties campaigned on the "values" theme differently in the last presidential election. The Republicans used adjectives–"honesty," "honor," and "reliability"– whereas the Democrats used verbs and specific accomplishments. The campaign using verbs was the more successful with voters who identified it as proactive and action-oriented. This triggers the thought of an action-oriented marketing strategy using action verbs and specific customer benefits.

Sometimes the descriptor itself will provide the cue for an idea as it did for a group of engineers who wanted to improve the telephone. They determined that the essence of a telephone was "a way of communicating." They listed several "different ways of communicating," including

- With sign language
- With nonverbal language
- With hugs and embraces
- Cats, communication by rubbing
- Police codes used to communicate with each other

The descriptor "hugs and embraces" was the cue that inspired them to invent a telephone that could actually reach out and touch you. The telephone incorporates video, audio, and touch. When you press down on a pad of pins (force transducers), the pins come up at the other end of the line. Wherever you touch, or however you move your fingers, that exact same pressure and design will be transmitted to the other pad.

Thomas Edison had a particular talent for identifying the essence of a problem and then finding an appropriate analogy. For example, one of his discoveries was how to send four simultaneous messages along a telegraph wire, two in each direction. This was important at the time–it would quadruple the power of the telegraph without the need of having to build four times the number of wires. The essence of his problem was "flow of current," and he looked to the world of water. He built an "analog" of the electric wire, with pipes and valves and assorted gadgets for affecting the flow of water in the pipe. Using gadgets to force water back and forth in the pattern of wires, he tinkered and ended up separating the separable features of the flow of current, sending one message controlled by one wire and another controlled by another wire.

Worlds of Special Interest

Most of us possess expert knowledge in some hobby, discipline, or special activity. You can create new ideas by transferring relationships and concepts from your area of special interest to your problem. For many years, physiologists could not understand the purpose of the long loops in the kidneys: It was assumed that the loops had no special function and were a relic of the way the kidney had evolved. Then one day, a physiologist with a special interest in engineering looked at the loops and recognized that they could be part of a countercurrent multiplier, a well-known engineering device for increasing the concentration of solutions. His interest in engineering provided the answer to something that had been a medical puzzle for a long time. When you identify an idea in one area, you can then generate other complementary ideas with similar dynamics in other areas. The guidelines are

1. List several concepts from your discipline or area of special interest. For example, if your interest is football, you might list such items as the Super Bowl, player free agency, TV contracts, *Monday Night Football* promotions, expansion franchises, and so on.

2. Select one concept and describe it in as much detail as you can. List the images and thoughts that it inspires. Then use each description to generate ideas. Look for similarities and connections between each description and your problem and draw analogies.

Groups

When brainstorming in a small group, ask each participant to select one discipline or activity of special interest. Each participant then selects a concept from his or her selected discipline and the facilitator lists it on a board or flip chart. After all the concepts are recorded, the group selects one, and the person responsible for it provides a detailed description. For example, suppose a person selected ballet as an area of special interest. He or she would select a particular dance movement as his or her concept. Next, she or he would describe the dance movement in detail, and perhaps, even demonstrate the movement. Now, the group would list descriptions and draw analogies between the dance movement and their problem and use the analogies as stimuli for new ideas. The group would continue to select additional concepts and repeat the process until they are satisfied with the ideas they generated.

A heart surgeon became a fan of Edward Deming, the noted management consultant, and studied his industrial management techniques and attended his seminars. He convinced a group of heart surgeons to apply Deming's techniques to their practice. By applying industrial management techniques to heart surgery, they learned how to share information about how they practiced and stopped functioning as individual craftspeople. They reduced the death rate among their patients by one-fourth.

The World of Nature

Look at the world of nature for analogies with your problem. Artificial intelligence researchers went off on a dead-end track for years by trying to design around a single processing level in neural networks. Eventually it was found that multilayer processing eliminated this fundamental barrier. The AI researchers might have avoided this wasted time and effort by checking first with nature. By asking any biologist, they would have quickly and easily learned that the image-processing cells in the eye exist in three distinct layers.

Consider the story of George de Mestral, a Swiss inventor, who was hunting one day in the late 1940s when he and his dog accidentally brushed up against a bush that left them both covered with burrs. When de Mestral tried to remove the burrs, they clung stubbornly to his clothes. This would be a minor annoyance to most of us, but de Mestral was curious about why the burrs were so hard to remove. After he got home, he studied them under a microscope and discovered that hundreds of tiny hooks on each burr had snagged on the threads of his pants. Thinking analogically, de Mestral imagined comparisons and similarities between the world of "wild burrs" and the world of "fasteners."

There followed several years of work, as de Mestral tried to figure out how to attach tiny hooks to a piece of tape in such a way that they would stay lined up. He also struggled to find a way of producing tiny loops for the hooks to attach to. After testing many methods, he finally succeeded. The result: Velcro fasteners, now used on millions of items, from blood pressure cuffs to tennis shoes.

In the illustration below, the hexagon on the left is contained in the figure on the right, yet it is not perceived as such. Its presence can be verified by tracing its outline with a pencil. No part of its perimeter has been removed or altered.

The pattern on the right is made up of lines that, taken together, make the hexagon invisible, unless you deliberately search for it. Similarly, many of the similarities and similar differences between your subject and objects or events in nature that can help you discover an analogical connection with your subject are well disguised. You have to deliberately search for the appropriate subjects and events in nature.

Take a nature walk (real or imagined) and look around. Underwater construction was made possible by observing how ship-worms tunnel into timber by first constructing tubes. The question to ask is "What objects, events, or patterns in nature can I use to develop my idea?" Suppose you wanted to find a new way to handle home trash. Examples:

- What happens to leaves in the woods?
- How do animals handle their waste?
- How do insects handle waste? Birds? Reptiles?
- How does nature handle volcanic ash?

Then,:

1. Select one example and make an analogy between it and your problem. Describe the analogy in as much detail as possible. List all the similarities and connections that you can. List similar differences.

Example: RCA/Whirlpool engineers wanted to find a new way to handle home trash. They asked what animal handles its own waste most efficiently? Cows were inefficient, but goats were very efficient. Their waste comes out in a dry, well-contained solid form, much like an encapsulated pellet.

2. Try to force a connection between all the items on your list and the problem. Allow yourself to free associate from the items to other ideas as well.

Example: The idea of "encapsulating waste" led to the development of the Trash Masher, the first of a line of trash compactors.

The World of Imagination

Our usual thinking is logical and goal-oriented. Creativity is difficult with this kind of thinking because the conclusion is implicit in the premises. We could think of this kind of thinking as crystalline. It is nicely structured, but the probability of two remotely associated thoughts or concepts bumping into each other is zero. Creative thinking is analogical, fantastical, and associative. We could compare movement toward creative thinking as analogous to heating the crystal. When heated through, it turns into a fluid. In the fluid state, the probability of two remotely associated thoughts or concepts colliding and combining is tremendously increased. If we had a flawed or imperfect crystal (imperfect idea or solution), this is, in fact, just what we would do: heat it so that it turned into a fluid (move toward creative thinking) and then gradually lower the temperature (move back toward logical thinking). The result would be a flawless crystal.

One way to move toward creative thinking (heating the crystal) when your thinking has crystallized is to forget your problem and take an imaginary excursion. You visualize an imaginary excursion into or through some location or time in history that has nothing to do with the problem and look for ways to make analogies between what you imagine and your problem.

For example, a group of Department of Defense weapons specialists were faced with the challenge of modifying missiles. They were stonewalled. Finally, one of the participants suggested that the group take an imaginary excursion into the desert. For ten minutes, they imagined walking through a desert and listed everything they saw and experienced. One of the participants imagined seeing a "sidewinder," a poisonous snake. Someone else remarked that a sidewinder locates its prey by sensing body heat. This inspired the idea of an air-to-air missile that homes in on enemy jets by detecting the planes' heat emissions.

Naturally, it was named the Sidewinder missile.

There are three major steps in the excursion process: the excursion itself, the drawing of analogies between the problem and the events in the excursion, and the analysis of these analogies to see what new ideas or solutions can be created. The guidelines are

1. **Excursion.** Visualize an imaginary excursion into or through some location that has nothing to do with the problem at hand. Close your eyes and imagine a journey through some exotic location, for example, a journey in a submarine to the bottom of the deepest part of the ocean, a visit to a gold miner's camp in 1850, or a safari in Africa. Let go and let your imagination roam. Write down detailed descriptions of everything you see and feel on your imaginary journey.

It's interesting to note that the major nineteenth-century English poet Samuel Taylor Coleridge used imaginary excursions to inspire the exotic imagery in his poetic masterpieces–"The Rime of the Ancient Mariner" and "Kubla Khan." By letting himself go and imagining himself in some remote location or period of time, he was able to see images that he was able to incorporated into his poetry.

2. **Analogies.** Draw analogies between what you saw and the problem. Coleridge once reported that though most people perceive the differences in things, the key to his genius was his eternal pursuit of what is common between things. In addition to analogies, express the connections and relationships between your images and the problem in any way that captures what you see. Try to force a connection between every description of things you saw or experienced on your imaginary journey and the subject.

3. **Analysis.** Look for ways to use the analogies and relationships to solve the problem. Try to figure out what the relationships mean in terms of the subject, that is, how understanding these relationships can be used to solve the problem. This is the really challenging part of the process. It's important to understand that the more you work at figuring out what these connections and relationships are, the greater your chances for a creative breakthrough.

When you relate and make connections between your subject and events or objects from your imaginary excursion, you activate more and different thought patterns. Let us say you make a weak connection between two thoughts. You're unclear as to why they are related or what the significance is. You think about something else and activate a third thought, which is weakly associated to the first two. Since they are already partially activated, all the connections are strengthened. If they are strengthened sufficiently, insight for a new idea or thought occurs.

Suppose you were asked to develop a satisfactory fastener for a firefighter's protective suit. You need something that's protective and something that the firefighter can get in and out of fast. You take an imaginary excursion to another planet in the solar system and imagine finding yourself in a thick jungle. The first thought is "fastener" and the second thought is "thick jungle." You next imagine the planet life to be overlapping and interlaced like a giant, thick, interlaced wall. It's literally impossible to get through. In this example, the connections between the three thoughts might suggest the overlapping and interlacing clutching of a Velcro-like fastener for firefighter's protective suits.

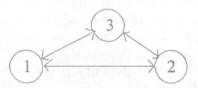

Groups

When using the excursion technique in a group, the facilitator creates the imaginary excursion (we're at the North Pole and trapped in a blizzard, we are scuba diving in the Florida Keys, or we are at the Smithsonian Institute, and so on) and directs the group members to visualize and write down everything they see for ten minutes. Encourage the participants to let go and let their imaginations roam. Then, take ten or fifteen minutes to have the participants draw analogies and express relationships between their visual images and the problem. Each participant should do this silently. Allow them to express relationships in any way they wish. Lastly, the participants share their analogies and other thoughts and determine how the analogies and thoughts can help solve the problem.

One group of interior designers wanted to send videos of their work to potential clients but discovered that it was too expensive. They went on a Wild West excursion and imagined a watering hole where cowboys, frontier people, horses, cattle, and Indians all gathered to drink. This inspired the idea to get fabric manufacturers and other wholesalers and retailers to share the production and distribution costs by paying for minicommercials.

The World of Einstein

Rather than use logic and mathematics to explore possibilities, Einstein would sometimes explore fundamental and abstract principles through his impressions and images by constructing imaginary metaphorical scenarios. He would interact with imaginary beings in imaginary worlds, not with disassociated numbers and facts. For example, he would visualize himself walking alone down a street and "falling in love." Two weeks later, he would imagine meeting the woman he fell in love with for the first time. He would then question and examine the metaphor for ideas and conjectures that he could apply to his real-world problem. How can you fall in love with someone before you meet them? This particular imaginary scenario helped him to think about causality.

On other occasions, Einstein imagined himself as a two-dimensional being living in a two-dimensional world, with a flat measuring rod conducting experiments on infinity; as a man in an elevator being pulled through space by some imaginary creature; or as a blind beetle circling a perfect sphere endlessly. One of his imaginary metaphors was riding on a beam of light, holding a perfect mirror, trying to see his reflection. According to classical physics, you could not, because light leaving your face would have to travel faster than light in order to reach the mirror. Einstein played with these mental pictures and made up different rules for the universe. It was this kind of thinking that led to his famous theory of relativity.

Following are guidelines on how to construct and use imaginary metaphorical scenarios to get ideas and solve problems:

1. Close your eyes, relax, and picture your subject or problem in your mind.
Example: Suppose you are a doctor faced with a patient who has a

malignant tumor in his stomach. It is impossible to operate, but unless the tumor is destroyed, the patient will die. There is a ray that can be used to destroy the tumor. If the rays reach the tumor all at once at sufficiently high intensity, the tumor will be destroyed. Unfortunately, at this intensity the healthy tissue that the rays pass through on the way to the tumor will also be destroyed. At lower intensities, the rays are harmless to healthy tissue, but they will not affect the tumor either. What type of procedure might be used to destroy the tumor with the rays and at the same time avoid destroying the healthy tissue?

2. Identify the "essence" or the principle of the problem. Think of the essence as the fundamental definition and perception of the problem.

Example: The essence of our example problem might be "how to concentrate a force on a target without destroying anything but the target."

3. Forget the problem and concentrate on the "essence" or "principle." Create an imaginary scenario that captures the "essence" of the problem. Use your imagination and write a metaphorical story or fairy tale that presents a similar problem in as much detail as possible. The story must be metaphorical. For instance, in our example, we take the essence of our "medical" problem and write an imaginary metaphorical "military" scenario as follows:

An evil dictator ruled from a strong fortress. The fortress was situated in the middle of the country, surrounded by farms and villages. Many roads radiated outward from the fortress like spokes on a wheel. A good general wanted to destroy the fortress and free the country. The general believed that if his entire army could attack the fortress at once, it could be destroyed. However, the general had reason to believe that the dictator had planted mines on each of the roads. The mines were set so that small bodies of men could pass over them safely, since the dictator needed to be able to move troops and workers to and from the fortress. However, any large force would detonate the mines. Not only would this blow up the road and render it impassable, but the explosions would destroy neighboring property as well. A full-scale direct attack on the fortress, therefore, appeared impossible.

4. Solve the problem as expressed in the imaginary scenario.

Example: One idea would be to divide the army into small groups. Each group charged down a different road in a synchronized fashion. All of the small groups would be able to pass over the mines and then meet simultaneously at the fort and attack it in full strength.

5. Transfer this solution to solve your original problem.

Example: Instead of using a single high-intensity ray (figure A), the doctor (the general) could administer several low-intensity rays at once from different directions (divide the army into small groups). In that way, each ray would be at a low intensity along its path and hence harmless to the healthy tissue (figure B), but the effects of the rays would combine to achieve the effect of a high-intensity ray at their focal point (attacked the fortress in full strength), the site of the tumor (the fortress).

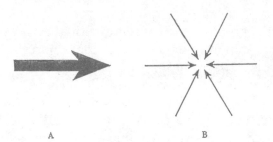

A   B

Think of a river that has cut deep into the land. Water always flows into the most probable places, so when it rains, the water is drained into the deep-cut river. It's drained off so fast it leaves no opportunity for other lakes or other rivers to form. In the same way, your usual way of thinking about a subject determines your focus and directs your thinking into one channel, leaving no opportunity for other approaches or different ways of thinking to form. Your initial focus can be an obstacle to creative thinking. An imaginary scenario helps us to achieve an "out-of-focus" look at the subject or some aspect of it. This out-of-focus experience can trigger new and unexpected ideas and approaches.

Suppose we are in sales and want to convince a hostile prospect to give an honest look at our product. I construct the following imaginary scenario: A Martian spaceship malfunctions and lands near our building. The Martians understand our language somewhat but do not trust us. They are highly suspicious because they have been tricked by the peoples of other planets. We believe we can repair their engine by installing different parts. How can we convince them to let us repair their engine?

One idea would be to introduce the Martians to aliens from other planets that we have helped in the past to demonstrate our trustfulness. If we were to solve our sales problem in the same way we are solving the problem with the Martians, how would we do it? This triggers the idea of putting our prospect in touch with our satisfied customers who speak their language and are familiar with their concerns. Give the satisfied customers a discount on goods and services in return for their time spent talking to prospects.

Sample Scenarios

Following are some sample scenarios to use for some common business problems:

Challenge: How can we reorganize our business?
  Scenario: A comet hits the earth and permanently wipes out everyone's long-term memory, except the people in this room. How do we handle this global situation?

Challenge: How do we improve corporate communications?
  Scenario: Astronauts travel to Mars. While they are visiting Mars, the perception of events becomes different for each astronaut, depending on his or her prior history. They perceive everything differently. A sequence of events can be anything: quick or slow, orderly or random, causal or without cause, salty or sweet, and so on. How can they work together in order to return to earth?

Challenge: How can we create a new marketing promotion?
  Scenario: We discover a group of primitive cave dwellers who live in the mountains and do not understand any language. How do we advance their lives?

Challenge: How can we get upper management to approve our idea?

Scenario: The Later family is immortal. From the beginning of time, no family member has ever died. Each member is alive, and most have married ad infinitum. Joe, the youngest member, desires to marry and wants confirmation of his decision. How does he get his family's approval?

World of Images

Words tend to impose strong, subtle pressures on us to see the world as fixed, fragmented, and static. Yet everything in life is in a state of flux and change. Even the paper on which this book is printed appears to have a stable existence, but we know that it is, at this moment, changing and evolving toward dust. This is one reason why Einstein preferred to use mental images and symbols, instead of words, when he thought. In fact, Einstein rarely thought in words at all when trying to work out a theory.

Did Thomas Jefferson have a beard? Most people have to mentally form an image of Jefferson to answer the question. This is why imagery is useful for recalling details that may not have been initially important and may not have been encoded by our brain. This may explain why creative insights sometimes result when a person forms an image and then notices certain features that were previously overlooked. Perhaps this is why Einstein preferred to work with images instead of with mathematical calculations or words. He was also able to represent the effects, consequences, and possibilities of his subject by visualizing it.

Try to represent the key elements of your challenge in mental images that symbolically represent your subject. Disassociate yourself from labels and words and just make mental pictures of the problem. Close your eyes and picture your challenge or problem in your mind. Block out verbal thoughts. (This can be done by repeating a simple word such as "aum" or "om" over and over.) Try to imagine images that symbolically represent your subject or some aspect of it. Write down or draw the images and associations that you conjure up. Draw analogies between these thoughts and your subject. Look for relationships and connections.

In the following illustration, the challenge is to rearrange the matches to make "nothing." No matchsticks may be bent, broken, or placed over each other. First, try to solve it using your usual way of thinking. Most people cannot solve this problem. Next, close your eyes and imagine the concept of "nothing." What symbolically represents it? Write down the images and associations that you conjure up. See if you can make the connection between your images and the challenge to solve it.

Some 60 percent of people who use this technique solve the problem. Some symbolically represent "nothing" as a zero, and others represent it as "nil" (see following page). Once they make a mental picture of the concept, they work back to the problem and rearrange the matches to correspond to their mental picture.

If you are adept at visualizing, the ideas will emerge spontaneously and effortlessly. If a chain of images emerges, often the first ones are the most significant. If you have trouble conjuring up symbolic images, imagine you meet a Martian who does not understand any earthly language and who communicates with abstract symbols. You want to communicate your problem to the Martian, because you feel it will be able to help you. Write out your problem and then translate it into abstract symbols.

A chemist, who had the task of improving seed corn, imagined images of seeds wearing heavy clothing in the winter and shorts in the summer. The images symbolically represented his problem–how to protect seeds from the elements. The image of clothing inspired him to think of synthetics, including polymers. This led to his idea of intelligent polymer seed coatings, which shift properties as conditions change. The seeds can be planted in any weather or season. They lie protected and dormant when it's cold outside and sprout as soon as the soil reaches the right growing temperature.

A group of engineers used imagery to invent a compact, flexible jacking mechanism that extends some three feet and supports up to five tons. Among the symbolic mental images the group produced were

• A magician who had to create an illusion in which the rope, at first, is coiled and soft, then becomes hard as it extends out into the audience
• The hydraulic principle of the erection of the penis
• A steel tape measure
• A bicycle chain with flexible links that stiffen as they are driven out of the jacking mechanism

These images combined to provide a concept on which the compact jack was ultimately based.

One of the most famous examples of this technique was Friedrich Kekule's discovery that benzene and other organic molecules are closed chains or rings–a result of an image in which he visualized a snake biting its own tail. Thinking analogically, he hypothesized that the carbon atoms in benzene are arranged in a ring.

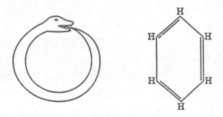

The image of the snake inspired Kekule's analogy that led to his breakthrough discovery. Similarly, Picasso was so intent on seeing the world as pure image that, as a boy, he saw numbers as patterns, not symbols of quantities: 2 became a folded pigeon wing and 0 an eye. It was this interest in seeing the world as pure image and patterns that was a key to the way he saw the world.

Pattern Language

The noted physicist Niels Bohr found language simply inadequate to describe what goes on inside the atom. He worked out his complex atomic models, not with classical mechanical notation, but by visualizing abstract symbols and putting them into different relationships. Later, he translated the visual to the verbal. Even when working with very complex processes, geniuses tend to use graphic, abstract models as the basis for their thinking. These models are often simplifications of reality, focusing only on certain essential elements. Instead of mathematical equations, Einstein often thought in terms of simple pictures of basic shapes (spheres, disks, triangles) and their relationships to each other.

Pattern language is a language of abstract symbols that you create to substitute for words. It's a structured way to translate your problem into symbols and then arrange the symbols into patterns. It was first invented by architects Alexander, Ishikawa, and Silverstein to help create new building designs. The guidelines are

1. Determine and list the major components of your problem. For instance, in marketing a product you might have four components: packaging, distribution, promotion, and selling. Under each component, list as many variations and possibilities as you can (different ways to package, distribute, promote, and sell).

2. Describe each variation by drawing an abstract graphic symbol. Each drawing should be on a separate index card and represent a specific variation. On the back of the card, write the variation. Draw the graphics on different-colored cards or use colored pencils to differentiate the various components. You could draw the appropriate graphics on red cards for packaging, yellow for distribution, blue for marketing, and white for selling.

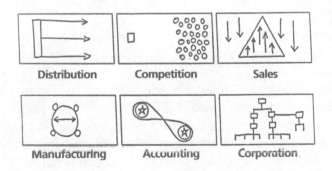

| Distribution | Competition | Sales |
| Manufacturing | Accounting | Corporation |

3. Place all the cards on a table with the graphic symbols facing up. Group and regroup the symbols randomly into various relationships. Try letting the cards arrange themselves without conscious direction, as if they were telling you where they wanted to be. Mix and match the symbols to provoke different sets of interesting relationships, without thinking about what the symbols mean.

4. When you create an interesting arrangement, turn the cards over to see what the written elements are, and then, try to build a new idea from these elements.

5. When stumped, add other components and possibilities or even start an entirely new set.

Sand Tray

Ronald Hoffmann of Cornell University shared the 1981 Nobel Prize in chemistry for a significant breakthrough in theoretical organic chemistry: a way to predict from first principles whether a reaction will occur. He is also a poet. His poetry helped set his imagination in motion using metaphors between chemistry and his poems. Metaphorical thinking shifts your perspective, not gradually, but with a vengeance.

The sand tray technique is an interesting way to think metaphorically by substituting physical objects for mental images. You need a large sand tray. At the start of an encounter with the sand tray, the surface is raked smooth and clean. Surrounding it are literally hundreds of bright objects: tiny dolls, colored marbles, shells, feathers, bits of wood, plastic toy soldiers, a miniature bride and groom, fake dinosaurs, rubber snakes, mean sharks, toy pistols, and so on. Then,

1. Empty your mind of all distractions and concentrate on your subject.
2. Choosing whatever objects you fancy, build a scene in the sand that metaphorically represents your subject or some aspect of your subject.
3. Arrange the objects in any way that you feel is interesting. Keep adding and arranging until the scene "feels right" symbolically.
4. Interpret the scene. The patterns of the scene and each object convey meaning. As you interpret each object, free associate from it. When interpreting the scene, be on the lookout for parts that puzzle you, seem to be missing, or that show up when you change your focus. Ask questions such as
"What is this?"
"What could this mean?"
"What does the frequency of this object mean?"
"Who does this represent?"
"What object comes closest to the essence of my subject?"
"What does this remind me of?"

Among these questions, one may stand out as the key to resolving the problem.

5. Write out your interpretations. Search for clues, new ideas, insights, and new lines of speculation. Combine the interpretations into one all-inclusive narrative. Try writing a story explaining how your sand-tray scene relates to your subject.

The gift of the imagination is more important than a talent for absorbing knowledge. Consider Benoit Mandelbrot, the Euclid of the twentieth century, who invented fractal geometry, which applies to such complicated objects as trees, seacoasts, snowflakes, and crashing waves. Mandelbrot revealed that these objects in nature possess "self-similarity": a twig has the shape of the branch it sprouts from, the branch the shape of the tree. Incredibly, Mandlebrot claims not to know the alphabet or how to use a telephone book. He is untrained in basic mathematics and is unable to do solutions the "straight" way.

When Mandelbrot took the entrance exams at France's prestigious Ecole Polytechnique, he was unable to do algebra but succeeded in getting the top grade by translating the questions mentally into pictures. By thinking visually, he could see things others could not. For example, he couldn't program a computer but developed the skill to debug programs that he could not read, by analyzing the wrong "pictures" these programs produce. He imagined a different way of looking at things and invented a new form of mathematics. The sand-tray technique activates your imagination and allows it to float freely, unrestrained by straight thinking inhibitions.

Groups

In a group, discuss the subject and then ask one participant to build a scene that represents the subject in the sand tray. The group studies the scene and generates as many interpretations as possible. These are listed on a chalkboard and related to the subject one at a time. In this form of expression, undertaken in a protected environment, the answers that emerge often surprise the maker and may reflect everything from an insight about an unarticulated experience to a profound statement about the subject.

Creative Collages

A technique similar in nature to the sand-tray technique is the metaphorical collage. A collage is an assembly of various pictures, either as wholes or fragments put together, in such a way that each element loses its separate identity as it becomes part of the whole. The collage is greater than, and often different from, the sum of it parts.

Max Ernst, one of the leading surrealist artists in the twentieth century, discovered that the chance encounters of two or more dissimilar subjects in a collage stimulated his imagination and encouraged him to think metaphorically. When two or more dissimilar subjects collide in a collage, the imagination transforms them into an altogether new reality transcendent over the separate elements. For example, a picture of seals performing in a marine show next to a picture of a building may become a metaphor for salespeople performing for customers, a user-friendly computer program, a job interview, and so on. The imagination transforms the picture into a symbol for many different things.

Often, the use of metaphors allows one to focus on the more important deeper structures of the subject. Leonardo da Vinci, for instance, used the analogy between the earth and the human body as a way to organize his anatomy; Mozart compared his music to creating a meal to explain his process of composing. Disney's business was that of creating metaphors, and Freud, of course, concentrated heavily on the metaphorical significance of symbols and dreams as a way to understand psychology.

A metaphoric picture allows you to activate your right brain and gives you a view of the problem that might otherwise remain invisible. Years back, a team of Israeli Air Force doctors believed they could improve the bandage. When they protected wounds from germs with bandages, they discovered that the bandages also cut off the body's circulation, which slowed down the healing process. A picture of an electric lamp with cord and a picture of men repairing a bridge were the stimuli for a new idea. They were inspired to think about repairing a broken cord by splicing it. You have to be careful to splice in such a way that the current is not interrupted. One of the elements that conducts electricity is magnesium. This led to the idea of a magnesium-coated bandage that does not interrupt the body's circulation.

Metaphoric images help stimulate your thinking. When you compare your subject with something else and discover the relatedness between them, then your mind can generate other ideas with similar relations. The metaphors you create may provide the clue to some aspect of your subject that otherwise might remain invisible. The guidelines for constructing a creative collage are

1. Cut out several pictures or parts of pictures from magazines, newspapers, catalogs, flyers, and so on.
2. Mix and match the pictures by moving them around into different patterns and associations. Play with the pictures until you get a feeling for possible ways to use these patterns. Form patterns and associations without forcing them. Continue until your collage feels complete. Make one large metaphorical picture by assigning a word or phrase to each picture and then completing the sentence "My subject is a lot like (insert a word or phrase from the montage) because it..."

Think metaphorically and analogically. The R and D staff for a furniture company looked for ways to develop a paint that does not fade, chip, or scratch. They made a collage that included pictures of various trees and plants. The collage triggered a discussion of how trees and plants get their color. Their subsequent research inspired the idea of "everlasting" color. They created the idea of injecting trees with dye additives that would impregnate the plant cells with color, spreading it throughout the tree. The tree is painted before it is cut down.

Another interesting way to collage your subject is to create two separate collages to represent two separate aspects of your subject. Suppose you want to improve corporate communications. You could create one collage to represent upper management and another one to represent employees. With the two sets of visuals, compare the common points and identify the gaps between upper management and the employees.

Groups

This is a fun exercise to do with a small group. Participants enjoy creating collages because they can use the more visual, feeling part of their brains and find an entirely different way of looking at the problem. The guidelines for a small group are

1. Pass out old magazines and scissors.
2. Ask each participant to cut out images and pictures from various magazines that metaphorically represent your subject or some aspect of it.

3. Have each person make a collage. Paste the images and pictures in an arrangement that's aesthetically pleasing.
4. Assign a word or phrase to each picture on the montage.
5. Each person then transforms the subject into one large metaphorical word picture by completing the sentence "Our subject is a lot like (insert a word from the montage) because it..."
6. Hang the collages on a wall and direct the group to compare them, looking for common points, and try to identify any gaps.

Metaphoric images are often the key to genius. Aristotle wrote that whoever is the master of metaphor is the master of thought. In Darwin's case, his most fecund metaphor was the branching tree of evolution, on which he could trace the rise and fall of various species. William James, the American philosopher and psychologist, had a penchant for metaphorically comparing thinking processes to creeks, streams, and rivers; whereas, John Locke, one of the pioneers in modern thinking, would focus on his falconer, whose release of a bird symbolized the quest for human knowledge.

Metaphor Walk

Take a walk around your home or workplace and the surrounding grounds. Look for objects, situations, or events that you can compare with your subject. For example, suppose your problem is how to improve communications in your company. You take a walk and notice potholes in the road. How are "potholes" like your corporate communication problem? For one thing, if potholes are not repaired, they get bigger and more dangerous. Usually road crews are assigned to repair the potholes. Similarly, unless something is done to improve corporate communication, it's likely to deteriorate even further. An idea with a similar relation to "road crews" is to assign someone in the organization to fill the role of "communications coach." The role would entail educating, encouraging, and supporting communication skills in all employees. And just as road crews are rotated, you can rotate the assignment every six months.

The guidelines for taking a metaphor walk are

1. Take a ten-to fifteen-minute walk and look for objects, events, or situations that might make interesting metaphors with your subject. Make a list.

2. When you return, make as many metaphors as you can between your list and your subject. Look for similarities and similar circumstances.

3. Look for ways to transfer principles and similar circumstances from what you observed and your subject. Try to build at least one idea or solution from each metaphor. Ask yourself what new insights the metaphors provide as to how to solve the problem.

Metaphoric thinking helps you look at a problem in a different way. You may be able to solve it or get a different insight by comparing it to something else and looking for similarities or similar circumstances that you can transfer from one subject to the other. For example, if you wanted new ideas or insights for a new product campaign, you might compare the evolution of a new product campaign with the evolution a tree.

Photo Walk

Another way to take a metaphoric walk is take a Polaroid camera and take at least five pictures of visual metaphors of the subject or problem. Then write descriptions of the metaphors. Then, for each metaphor, look for new insights or solutions. For example, suppose you are in charge of improving the new employee training program, and you take a photo of a building under construction. You would first describe what is involved in constructing a building and then transfer similarities or similar circumstances to your training program.

If you're working with a small group, ask each participant to take a walk and come back with at least five photographs of visual metaphors. Then ask each participant to write a description of each metaphor. Post the pictures with the written description of their metaphor posted beneath on a card. Ask the group to tour the photo gallery and then to build ideas or solutions from the visual metaphors.

STRATEGY EIGHT: FINDING WHAT YOU'RE NOT LOOKING FOR

Whenever we attempt to do something and fail, we end up doing something else. As simplistic as this statement may seem, it is the first principle of the creative accident or "serendipity." We may ask ourselves why we have failed to do what we intended, and this is the reasonable, expected thing to do. But the creative accident provokes a different question: What have we done? Answering that question in a novel, unexpected way is the essential creative act. It is not luck but creative insight of the highest order.

The discovery of the electromagnetic laws was a creative accident. The relationship between electricity and magnetism was first observed in 1820 by Hans Øersted in a public lecture at which he was demonstrating the "well-known fact" that electricity and magnetism were completely independent phenomena. This time the experiment failed–an electric current produced a magnetic effect. Øersted was observant enough to notice this effect, honest enough to admit it, and diligent enough to follow up and publish. Maxwell used these experiments to extend Newton's methods of modeling and mathematical analysis in the mechanical and visible world to the invisible world of electricity and magnetism and derived Maxwell's Laws, which opened the doors to our modern age of electricity and electronics.

Even when people set out to do something purposefully and rationally, they wind up doing things they did not intend. John Wesley Hyatt, an Albany printer and mechanic, worked long and hard trying to find a substitute for billiard-ball ivory, then coming into short supply. He invented, instead, celluloid–the first commercially successful plastic.

B. F. Skinner advised people that when they were working on something and found something interesting, they should drop everything else and study it. In fact, he emphasized this as a first principle of scientific methodology. This is what William Shockley and a multidiscipline Bell labs team did. They were formed to invent the MOS transistor and ended up instead with the junction transistor and the new science of semiconductor physics. These developments eventually led to the MOS transistor and then to the integrated circuit and to new breakthroughs in electronics and computers. William Shockley described it as a process of "creative failure methodology."

Richard Feynman had an interesting practical test that he applied when reaching a judgment about a new idea: Did it explain something unrelated to the original problem? That is, "What can you explain that you didn't set out to explain?" and "What did you discover that you didn't set out to discover?" In 1938, twenty-seven-year-old Roy Plunkett set out to invent a new refrigerant. Instead, he created a glob of white waxy material that conducted heat and did not stick to surfaces. Fascinated by this unexpected material, he abandoned his original line of research and experimented with this interesting material, which eventually became known by its trade name, "Teflon."

In principle, the unexpected event that gives rise to a creative invention is not all that different from the unexpected automobile breakdown that forces us to spend a night in a new and interesting town, the book sent to us in error that excites our imagination, or the closed restaurant that forces us to explore a different cuisine. But when looking for ideas or creative solutions, many of us ignore the unexpected, and consequently, lose the opportunity to turn chance into a creative opportunity. You have to give yourself the freedom to see what you are not looking for. In 1839 Charles Goodyear was looking for a way to make rubber easier to work and accidentally spilled a mixture that hardened but was still usable. By allowing himself to go in an unanticipated direction, he invented a practical vulcanization process. By focusing on the "interesting" aspects of the idea, he discovered its potential. Alexander Fleming was not the first physician to notice the mold formed on an exposed culture while studying deadly bacteria. Less gifted physicians would routinely trash this seemingly irrelevant event but Fleming noted it as "interesting" and wondered if it had potential. This interesting observation led to penicillin, which has saved millions of lives. Thomas Edison, while pondering how to make a carbon filament, was mindlessly toying with a piece of putty, turning and twisting in his fingers, when he looked down at his hands and the answer hit him between the eyes: twist the carbon like a rope.

What makes it possible to turn the unlooked-for event into novel fortune? We have to prepare our minds for chance. This is difficult to do when we are looking at a subject, because of our existing emotions and prejudices. Consider the following situation: Susan is twenty-eight years old, single, outspoken and very bright. She majored in sociology and minored in philosophy. As a student, she was deeply concerned with issues of racial discrimination and social justice and also participated in antinuclear demonstrations. Which statement is the most probable?

A. Susan is an office manager.

B. Susan is an office manager and is active
   in the feminist movement.

On any rational account, it is more probable that Susan is an office manager than Susan is both a office manager and active in the feminist movement. The probability of x, after all, is always greater than the probability of independent event x and independent event y. Yet more than 80 percent of subjects, including those who are sophisticated in statistics, assent more readily to the statement that Susan is an office manager and is active in the feminist movement than to the statement that Susan is an office manager.

Asked the abstract question "Which is more probable, x alone or x and y?" subjects readily consent that x alone is more probable. Moreover, when confronted with the apparent contradiction between this abstract response and the Susan question, they readily admit that they have made an error. This seems to reflect a deep-seated bias in human judgment. Given information that Susan is a certain kind of person, subjects readily fit in other events that have, in the past, been representative of such persons, and in the process, intellectually ignore what they otherwise know about probability. People are emotionally prejudiced to the likelihood that someone with certain characteristics will also exhibit other ones (to the extent that someone is a social activist, she is likely to be a feminist).

Generally, we use our intelligence to support and rationalize our emotions and prejudices about a particular subject or idea. Suppose, for example, that you are about to buy a sweater for $125 and a desk organizer for $15. The desk organizer salesman tells you that the organizer you want to buy is on sale at the other branch of the store, twenty minutes away, for $10. Would you make the trip? Most people say they will. Another group is asked a similar question. This time the cost of the sweater is changed to $15, and the cost of the desk organizer is discounted from $125 to $120 at the branch. Of respondents presented with this version, the majority said that they would not make the extra trip. Note that in both cases the total purchases are the same: the choice is always whether to drive twenty minutes to save $5. But apparently respondents evaluate the saving of $5 in relation to the price of the desk organizers. In relative terms, a reduction from $15 to $10 (33 percent) is emotionally less resistible than a reduction from $125 to $120 (less than 5 percent).

Instead of using our intelligence to support our emotions and prejudices, we need to use our intellect to explore our subject before we apply our existing emotions and prejudices. If the above respondents had done that, they would have instantly realized that the choice is the same–whether to drive twenty minutes to save $5. To explore a subject with our intellect, we need to will ourselves to do so.

Exploring

Most people describe the unusual illustration below as a group of ten circles forming a triangle, and the three stars as a separate group. Few people spontaneously would describe the illustration as a six-pointed Star of David, which it represents as well. To see the Star of David, you need to consciously focus on it in a different way.

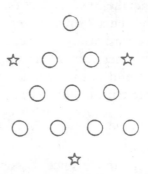

Similarly, to explore a subject with our intellect, we need to "will" ourselves to direct our attention in a different way. A tool to help you achieve this is the PMI (Plus, Minus, Interesting). The PMI is an attention-directing tool that was first introduced by Edward de Bono, an international authority on thinking. It is designed to deliberately direct your attention to all the positive, negative, and interesting aspects about your subject. Carrying out a PMI is simple. What is not simple is to deliberately concentrate your attention in one direction after another when your emotions and prejudices have already decided how you should feel about your subject. In the diagram below, when an idea is emotionally rejected, all creative exploration stops.

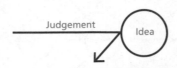

You need to will yourself to look in different directions. Once you have the will to do a PMI, then the natural challenge to your intelligence is to find as many positive, negative, and interesting points as you can. Instead of using intelligence to support your emotions and prejudices, you are now using it to explore the subject matter.

The guidelines for doing a PMI are

1. Make three columns on a sheet of paper. Title the columns "Plus," "Minus," and "Interesting."
2. Under the "Plus" column, list all the positive aspects about the subject that you can.
3. Under the "Minus" column, list all the negative aspects that you can.
4. Under the "Interesting" column, list all those things that are worth noting but do not fit under either "Plus" or "Minus." The "Interesting" items helps us to react to the interest in an idea and not just to judgment feelings and emotions about the idea. "I do not like the idea but there are interesting aspects to it. . . ."

With the PMI, you use your intelligence to explore the subject matter. At the end of the exploration, emotions and feelings can be used to make a decision about the matter. The difference is that the emotions are now applied after the exploration instead of being applied before and so preventing exploration. With a PMI, one of three things can happen:

• You may change your mind about the idea and decide that it is a viable alternative.

• You may still reject the idea as unsound.

• You may move from the idea to another idea. By exploring the "positive" and "interesting" aspects of an idea, you may be able to recycle it into something else.

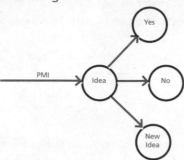

When you put down the P, M, and I points, you react to what you put down and your feelings change. Once a point has been thought and put down under any of the headings, that point cannot be "unthought," and it will influence the final decision.

A while back, a group of designers brainstormed for a new umbrella design. One of the participants suggested a combination umbrella with holster. The holster would be worn on a person's belt. A trigger mechanism in the umbrella handle would release the spring-loaded umbrella when unholstered.

The group thought this was a terrible idea, because everyone would looked armed and dangerous. They decided to do a PMI on the idea, and one of the interesting aspects they focused on was the idea of using the umbrella for protection. This triggered the idea of incorporating a stun gun into the umbrella. If attacked, one touches the attacker with the tip of the umbrella, pulls a trigger, and renders the attacker helpless with a nonlethal shock.

By focusing on the "interesting" aspects of the umbrella idea, they provided themselves with material to look at what they might not have looked for. Just as a carefully designed experiment is an attempt to hurry along the path of logical investigation, so focusing on "interesting" aspects of subjects is an attempt to encourage the chance appearance of ideas that would not have been sought out. Years back, 3M invented a new adhesive for industry. No industry was interested, and management ordered an engineer to burn the samples. The engineer, instead, thought the adhesive had "interesting" aspects and took some samples home. He observed his teenage daughters setting their hair with it and using the adhesive in various other ways. He went to management and convinced them that what they had was a consumer product, not an industrial one, which was manufactured it and marketed it as Scotch tape.

When thinking of creativity, one usually associates it with the generation and evaluation of new, fresh, and original ideas, but there is more to it than that. You can use your intellect to profoundly change the way you perceive any subject or idea through prolonged inspection, thus furthering the creative process. The studies of the Gestalt psychologists concluded that prolonged study of any subject will bring about spontaneous perceptual changes in the subject. The mind, through prolonged inspection of a subject, becomes bored with it and will explore alternative ways of perceiving it by decomposing the whole into parts and looking for the interesting parts. In the early steps of this process, the effects of these changes remain below the level of awareness. After a while, they penetrate consciousness as new ideas and insights. Some great artists, such as Cézanne and Rodin, often spent a long time looking at their subjects before they painted or sculpted them. They were creatively profiting from the disintegration of a subject into something different, brought about by prolonged inspection.

Groups

An interesting exercise is to deliberately present a valueless or dumb idea to a small group. Ask the participants to write a paragraph opinion (yes or no and why) of the idea on a sheet of paper. Discuss the opinions and then ask each participant to do a PMI on the idea. Finally, combine the PMIs into one master PMI. This forces the group to subject the idea to a prolonged inspection. You'll discover that sometimes participants will change their opinion or will discover that an "interesting" aspect will lead to some other idea. This process is not passive but essentially active because the changes are the result of the mind's manipulative operations when exploring the interesting aspects of a subject. This intellectual exploration sometimes makes it possible to turn a valueless idea or some aspect of it into a novel idea.

Latent Potential

Latent potential exists in every subject. We now throw out a large range of objects–from watches to automobile tires–and buy new things, rather than fix them. We rarely rebuild materials for radically different uses. Third World countries, out of necessity, must be more creative and often find a strikingly different purpose for material too worn out to perform its original role. In Nairobi, they recycle worn tires and manufacture sandals. Durability for sandals is a latent potential of auto tires, and the production of sandals defines a functional shift. The Nairobi recycling market is an example of the principle of Darwinian continuous adaptation that led to a quirky shift of function and a new idea.

Evolution works like the Nairobi sandal makers, not like the throwaway society we live in. Species can evolve further only by using what they have in a new and interesting way. Organisms have no equivalent to currency for acquiring something new; they can reconstruct only from their own innards. If organisms could not reuse old material in strikingly new ways, how could evolution ever produce anything novel?

Similarly, every new subject or idea produces a host of creative by-products, initially seen as irrelevant, but available for fashioning in novel new directions. Much of creative genius hinges on the willingness to creatively observe the seemingly irrelevant and find the latent potential.

There are six irregular shapes in the illustration below that can be initially seen as irrelevant. However, you can use your imagination to fashion these irrelevant shapes into meaningful ones. The V-shaped figures can be fashioned by your imagination to form one large triangle, or closed opposite the apex to form three separate white triangles with an apex in each circle, or you can form one large upside-down white triangle. You can also form a six-pointed star by combining the large white upside-down triangle and the one formed by the Vs. Using your imagination, you created a variety of different-sized triangles and stars out of some irrelevant shapes.

In the same way, you can take a seemingly irrelevant subject and use your imagination to find its latent potential and refashion it into something else. Consider the Walkman radio. Sony engineers tried to design a small, portable stereo tape recorder. They failed. They ended up with a small stereo tape player that couldn't record. They gave up on the project and shelved it. One day Masaru Ibuka, honorary chairman of Sony, discovered this failed product and decided to look for its potential. He remembered an entirely different project at Sony where an engineer was working to develop lightweight portable headphones. "What if you combine the headphones with the tape player and leave out the recorder function altogether?"

Ibuka was mixing up functions. The idea that tape players also record was so well established that no one had considered reversing it. Even after Ibuka made his creative association, no one at Sony believed they could market it. Ibuka was not discouraged and plowed ahead with what he called a new concept in entertainment. Ibuka took a failed idea and by combining, eliminating, and reversing found the latent potential and created a brand new product. The Walkman radio became Sony's best-selling electronic product of all time and introduced all of us to "headphone culture."

Ibuka took what existed (a failed product) and recycled it into something new. Similarly, Michelangelo's masterpiece, *David*, was the result of another sculptor's failed attempt. Back in 1463, the authorities of the cathedral of Florence acquired a sixteen-foot-high chunk of white marble to be carved into a sculpture. Two well-known sculptors worked on the piece and gave up, and the badly mangled block was put in storage. Other sculptors were brought in and asked to carve a statue. They refused to work with the mangled block and demanded a new block. They said they couldn't possibly produce art out of the mangled block. Their demands were not economically feasible, so the project was scrapped by the cathedral. Forty years later, Michelangelo took the mangled block of marble from storage and carved it into the youthful, courageous *David* within eighteen months. He took what existed and sculpted it into one of the world's greatest statues.

Recycling

You can recycle any subject or idea into something else by adding to or modifying it in some fashion. During World War II, scientists at the radiation laboratory (the "Rad Lab") at the Massachusetts Institute of Technology worked to improve radar. In the early days of 1944, Rad

Lab scientists were using a new type of radar to detect a tower at a distance of six miles, but by spring when humidity increased, the system did not work. To their frustration, scientists discovered that they had somehow developed a radar that was tuned to the natural frequency of water vapor. Rather than trashing their work, they looked for ways to modify or use this annoyance for some other purpose. Their work developed the technology that eventually led to the microwave oven.

Examine your subject or idea for latent potential to become something different by applying the SCAMPER checklist of questions that were introduced on page 95.

Throughout history, geniuses have demonstrated the ability to recycle an idea and transform it into something else. For example, Francis Bacon transformed Aristotle's inductive thinking method into a new framework important in scientific analysis, and Henry David Thoreau incorporated Hindu and Buddhist ideas into his American transcendental philosophy. The famous architect Frank Lloyd Wright took Japanese temple design principles and modified them to create his spacious, airy Prairie Home.

Fortunes have been made in business by people finding the latent potential in a subject and recycling it into something else. Researchers at 3M developed a temporary glue that was to be used on fixed surfaces, like bulletin boards (you could move the bulletin board from one surface to another). It was not well received on the market, and most of the researchers lost interest in it. Arthur Frye, a 3M chemist, kept looking for ways to recycle it into something else. One day, while he was singing in the choir of the North Presbyterian Church in St. Paul, Minnesota, it hit him. The adhesive would be just the ticket to keep a bookmark in place. The primary use is paper to paper, and thus, the Post-it note was born.

Think of your subject as a living, dynamic organism that is constantly evolving into something different. In the illustration, the pattern in Figure 1 evolves into something that looks like a flower in Figure 2. If you look hard enough at this pattern in Figure 2, you may suddenly see that it could be regarded as a pile of three cubes with the top surface of the top cube marked A. If you continue to look at it, you might see it change to a pile of three cubes with the top surface of the top cube marked B. The thing suddenly re-restructures itself into a completely different pattern without anything being added to it.

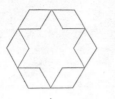
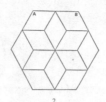

1   2

In much the same way, the latent potential in a subject may suddenly come about through a flash of insight, in a eureka moment. Without information, the whole thing may suddenly restructure itself to give a completely different pattern. The interesting thing is not only that a new pattern emerges quite suddenly, but that it at once becomes obvious. This is a peculiar phenomenon. For example, in 1956 the Jacuzzi brothers invented a whirlpool bath as a treatment for people with arthritis. They sold a few, but essentially did little with their invention. Fifteen years later, Roy Jacuzzi looked for the latent potential in the invention, modified the design, and recycled it into a luxury bath. While the world saw the bath as an arthritic device (pattern A), Roy Jacuzzi consciously looked for the latent potential and suddenly realized it was worth millions as a luxury bath (pattern B), without any new information.

You can find latent potential in any subject if you look hard enough. A company that makes baby wipes changed their package into a product all its own. Once the wipes are gone, the package is recycled into a colorful, Lego-like toy. Containers come in four colors and have interlocking pegs that make them easy to stack. Parents can also use them as stackable storage containers.

Don't Think about It

Take a moment and imagine all the things that the figure might represent. If I asked you to list all the different things that you imagined, I have no doubt that you would come up with several fascinating ideas. However, if I described the figure as the rear view of a housecleaner on hands and knees washing a floor, and then asked you to list alternative explanations, your list would be minimal and much less creative.

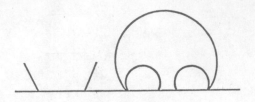

Once the figures are given names and meanings, it is almost impossible to look at them and have the same perception that existed before you knew what it was. The names and meanings fixate you along a certain line of thought.

Expertise in an area can hinder creativity by making us fixated along a certain line of thought. For instance, the capacity to draw in an expert fashion may even be disturbed or undermined by knowledge of the identity of what we are drawing. Betty Edwards, in her book *Drawing on the Right Side of the Brain*, indicates that an individual may be able to draw an object accurately if it is held upside down and the artist cannot recognize what he or she is drawing. At times, we act like homicide detectives hovering around a flattened corpse, discussing our pet theories while ignoring the elephant standing in the same room.

If you want to produce something creative–say a creative design for a new automobile–don't think of an automobile–at least not at first. Much evidence suggests that a more abstract definition of a problem can lead to greater creativity and innovation than the more typical definitions. This is the creative strategy of some of the world's leading creative designers, including Kenton Wiens, architect Arthur Erickson, and Martin Skalski, director of the transportation design sequence at Pratt Institute. Skalski, for example, doesn't tell students to design an automobile or study various automobile designs on the market. Instead he begins the design process by having them create abstract compositions. Then by progressively making the process less abstract, he eventually has them working on the real problem, tying in the connections between the abstract work and the final model.

Restructuring your problem by making it more abstract helps eliminate barriers that result from preconceived notions of what an idea or solution should be. It forces you to test assumptions and explore possibilities. Suppose you want to improve the design of the umbrella. If you work with the more abstract definition "protection from the rain," you are more likely to explore more possibilities, including raincoats or even a new type of town design where there are arcades everywhere and umbrellas are no longer required. Or consider the bookstore owner, for example, who viewed himself as a seller of books, a very specific idea. The trend toward the electronic media put him out of business. On the other hand, if he had viewed himself as a provider of information and entertainment, a more abstract characterization, a switch in the medium would not have been threatening and would have opened up new opportunities.

The mind makes ruts very quickly, and even more so when it stalls and spins its wheels. Making your problem more abstract may suddenly create a space between thoughts sunk in the details of some perception. Instead of getting mired down classifying the mite or fungus, Darwin asked the grand question "What is life?" The guidelines for using the principle of abstraction are

1. Describe an abstract definition of your problem. What is the principle of the problem? What is its essence?
   Example: Our problem is how to protect rural designer mailboxes from theft and vandalism. The principle is protection.

2. Brainstorm for several ideas on protection. Think of ways to protect things.
   - Place in a bank.
   - Rustproof it.
   - Provide good maintenance.
   - Get an insurance policy.
   - Hide it.

3. After you've generated a number of different ideas, restate the problem so that it is slightly less abstract. Again, generate as many solutions as you can.
   Example: Think of ways to protect things that are outside and vulnerable.
   - Hire a guard.
   - Watch it constantly.
   - Drape it with camouflage.
   - Put a fence around it.
   - Keep it well lighted.

4. Finally, consider the real problem. Review the ideas and solutions to the two previous abstractions and use these as stimuli to generate solutions.

Example: The real problem is how to protect rural mailboxes from theft and vandalism. The idea triggered from "get an insurance policy" is to offer an insurance policy to owners of rural mailboxes: $5 a year or $10 for three years to cover the mailbox from theft or destruction.

Alexander Graham Bell was inspired to start development of the telephone when he read an account, written in German, describing an invention that he thought had the function of a telephone. After demonstrating his working telephone, Bell learned that, because of the language barrier, he had misunderstood the report, and the German invention had an entirely different function. The German account was the stimuli that broke his preconceived notion of a telephone and inspired him to think in a different direction. In the same way, ideas and solutions to abstract definitions will provide you the stimuli to break your preconceptions.

Groups

Arthur Erickson, architect and designer, uses an abstraction thinking strategy with his students to help them avoid visual and functional preconceptions and unlock creativity. For example, if he is looking for a new chair design, he will first ask his students to draw a figure in motion. Then he will ask them to build a model (wood, plastic, metal, paper) of a structure that supports that figure in motion. Finally, he will have them use the model as a stimulus for a new chair design.

Following are guidelines for using this thinking strategy in a group situation to reduce their preconceptions about any problem:

1. Describe an abstract definition of the problem. Ask the group to generate and list solutions and ideas.
   Example: Think of ways to store things.
2. Describe a slightly less abstract definition. Again, ask the group to generate solutions and ideas.
   Example: Think of ways to stack things.
3. Describe an even slightly less abstract definition. Again, ask the group for solutions and ideas.
   Example: Think of ways to organize large objects.
4. Introduce the real problem. Ask the group to review all previous ideas and solutions and to use them as stimuli to generate ideas and solutions for the real problem.

Example: Now use these ideas as stimuli to improving a parking garage.

Another way to benefit from abstractions is to start with a specific solution or idea and progressively make it more abstract by asking the provocative question "What really matters?" whereupon the problem is reconsidered at a higher level of abstraction and reformulated. Repeat this kind of questioning ("What really matters?") two or three times in order to see the problem from different angles. For example, you come up with the idea of shredding packing material as a better way of disposing of it. Asking "What really matters?" you decide that what really matters is to reduce the amount of packing material. The idea you come up with is to use thinner packing material. Asking "What really matters?" again, you decide that what really matters is to reduce the number of packages. This level of abstraction leads you to think of alternatives to packages such as refillable, self-serviceable dispensers and standardized containers to be refilled at the point of sale and so on.

Are Your Ideas Crazy Enough?

When people use their imaginations to develop new ideas, those ideas are heavily structured in predictable ways by existing categories and concepts. This is true for scientists, artists, inventors, politicians, and businesspeople. Consider the following accident, which was reported in *The American Railroad Journal* in 1835:

> As a train was approaching the depot at Paterson, an axle of the leading car gave way, which overturned that and the following two cars. None of the passengers were injured, though they felt the shock by the concussion. Mr. Speer, the conductor, a very industrious and sober man, was seated on the car at the break, and unfortunately was crushed to death under the load.

Mr. Speer was the only casualty. What factors contributed to his untimely death? Certainly there was the immediate cause—the breaking of the axle and the overturning of the cars—but there is a subtler cause as well. Note that Mr. Speer was riding on the car, not in it, and that none of the passengers, who were inside, were hurt. Why was he not in the car? What in the world was he doing on top of the car? Speer's death was the result of a design flaw that required conductors to ride on the outside of cars.

This flaw is an example of the phenomenon of structured imagination. Early designs for railway cars were heavily influenced by the properties of the stagecoach, the most common vehicle of the day. The first railway cars were little more than stagecoaches with tracks, with no central aisle and designed so that conductors had to ride outside on running boards. The idea of a central aisle was considered odd and even unsanitary, based on the notion that it would become one long spittoon. Finally, as was true of stagecoaches, the brakes were located on the outside and were operated by the conductor, who was seated on the top front of the car.

We would not consider the developers of the railroads to be unimaginative people. On the contrary, they were visionaries who saw the railroad as the transportation of the future long before other people took the idea seriously. Yet, even after a number of conductors had been killed, there was strong resistance to designing the railway cars so conductors could ride safely inside. As late as 1866, according to the *Railroad and Engineering Journal* (1887), seventy-two trainmen were killed in falls from cars in Massachusetts, New York, and Michigan alone.

What this suggests is that even highly creative individuals and the ideas they develop are susceptible to the constraining influences of structured imagination. The design for a railway car was heavily influenced by what they knew, understood, and were most familiar with—the stagecoach. Even Thomas Edison's idea for an electric lighting distribution system is an example of an idea that was the result of structured imagination. His reliance on the existing gas distribution system at the time led to his stubborn reliance on the problematic procedure of running wires underground, just as gas mains ran underground. More recently, the fact that many modern computer terminals display exactly eighty columns of text is a direct outgrowth from the era when we literally fed data into computers by way of eighty-column punch cards.

The playful openness of creative geniuses is what allows them to explore "interesting" chance events. Once Wolfgang Pauli, the discoverer of electron spin, was presenting a new theory of elementary particles before a professional audience. An extended discussion followed. Niels Bohrs summarized to Pauli that everyone agreed that his theory was crazy. The question that divided them was whether it was crazy enough to have a chance of being correct. Bohrs said his own feeling was that it was not crazy enough.

A logic hides in Bohrs' illogic. In genius, there is a tolerance for unpredictable avenues of thought. The result of unpredictable thinking may be just what is needed to shift the context enough to lead to a new perspective. Paul Cézanne, the father of modern painting, coined a wonderful phrase that captures the whole paradoxical process of mixing unpredictable thinking and intentional tactics. He called the creator's creative activity "making a find."

You can actively seek the accidental discovery by deliberately exploring the odd and unusual. It is this freedom from design or commitment that allows you to juxtapose things that would not otherwise have been arranged in this way, to construct a sequence of events that-would not otherwise have been constructed. A technique to help you deliberately seek the odd and unusual is the following:

1. List several absurd or crazy ideas about your problem. Try to make each one more bizarre than the last.
   Problem: A greeting card company wants new products and new markets.
   Absurd Ideas:
   - Send greeting cards to dead people.
   - Send heavy stones as greeting cards.
   - Send cards COD.
   - Send the person money with the message to "go out and buy your own greeting card."
   - Send a spider.

2. Select one of the absurd ideas.
   Absurd Idea: Send greeting cards to dead people.

3. Extract the principle. What is the principle of the absurd idea?
   Principle: Communicating with the departed.

4. List the features and aspects of the absurd idea.
   Features, Aspects:
   - People communicate with the dead through séances.
   - People leave flowers at cemeteries.
   - People leave poems, letters, and other artifacts.
   - People publish personal poems, messages, etc., in newspapers to the departed.

- People pray for the departed.
- People communicate with Ouija boards, etc.

5. Imagineering. Extract the principle or one of the features and aspects and build it into a practical idea.
　　Example: "Leaving items at the cemetery."
　　Imagineered Idea: The idea the greeting card company created was to publish memoriam cards on sticks so they can be inserted in the ground at the gravesite. The "cards-on-sticks" are sold in florist shops that are located near cemeteries.

What is especially remarkable about a hologram is that if a laser light is shined on just a small part of it, the entire image still appears. Thus, a small portion of the hologram contains information about the entire image. In a similar sense, when you focus on one small "interesting" aspect of a bizarre idea, that one small aspect contains enough information to create a new idea. In our example, the aspect of people "leaving items at the cemetery" contained enough information to create a whole new product line.

More often the danger is not one of overawareness of an idea, but of neglect of ways of looking at things that are blotted out by a dominant idea. The story of the jumping spider illustrates this in a macabre fashion. The schoolboy had an interesting theory: He maintained that spiders could hear with their legs and he said that he could prove this.

He placed the spider in the middle of the table and said, "Jump!" The spider jumped. The boy repeated the demonstration. Then he cut off the spider's legs and put it back in the middle of the table. Again he said, "Jump!" But this time the spider remained quite still. "See," said the boy, "you cut off a spider's legs, and it goes stone deaf."

Many of us can remember instances from our own experience when we were completely oblivious to other ways of looking at our results, so dominated were we by our own theory. It happens all the time in medicine when one doctor, too close to the patient's illness, tries hard to fit things into a certain diagnosis, and then another doctor comes along, and with a fresh look at all the information, offers a better and different diagnosis.

One of the most important early issues facing the scientists in Los Alamos was to find a method to explode the atomic bomb so that it would reach the critical mass necessary for a nuclear chain reaction. The ballistics experts came up with conventional ideas on how to explode the bomb. One of the physicists, Seth Neddermeyer, theorized that an explosion would not drive together the parts of the critical mass in a fission bomb. He felt an explosion would propel the parts apart. His idea was to drive together, to implode. For example, squeeze an orange very evenly and very hard and it implodes, or when you fire bullets against each other, the bullets liquefy on impact. He was ridiculed for this crazy idea when he presented it to his more experienced colleagues. Although Oppenheimer was also dubious about Neddermeyer's idea, he gave him the freedom to explore this unusual theory, which led to the successful triggering of the bomb.

Groups

To use this thinking strategy in a large group, first divide the group into four teams. If you have a small group, especially if you have only four members, you can modify this technique easily. Just have one group member write an idea in each of the cells. If you have more than four people, have them double up to fill in the boxes.

1. Each group gets a sheet that is divided into four boxes: *A* through *D*.

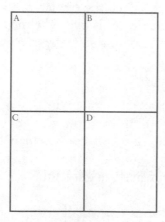

2. Each team fills in cell *A* with an absurd, crazy, or fantastical idea. Encourage the group to come up with the craziest idea possible. When each team has completed cell *A*, the sheets are circulated to a neighboring group.

3. The groups examines the first idea in cell *A* and engineers the idea into something that's more realistic and feasible. The group writes that idea in cell *B* and passes the worksheet to another group.

4. The next group works with the information in both cells *A* and *B* and tries to develop an idea that's even more realistic and feasible. The group writes the idea in cell *C* and then passes the worksheet to the final group.

5. After three passes, the sheets stop with the final team, which has to use the information in all the cells to develop a final idea to be written in cell *D*. The final ideas are then presented to the whole group.

Example: A group of salespeople brainstormed on how to sell more cars. The first team wrote "Marry every potential customer" in cell A. The next team wrote "Send special event cards such as birthday, Christmas, and anniversary cards" in cell B. The third team wrote "Send a flower with a special discount to married couples on their anniversary" in cell C. The idea that was finally presented was to fill the trunk of a newly sold car with flowers and to personally deliver it. When the owner checks out the car and opens the trunk, the owner is overwhelmed and tells his or her friends and relatives about the dealership.

Unrelated Ideas Game

Scientists have discovered that when they presented people with conflicting or incongruous information, the subjects' alertness increased. They concluded that this kind of conflict can be a source of creative drive. The following is a game designed to increase your group's alertness by using unrelated ideas. The guidelines are

1. The facilitator forms two small groups.
2. The problem statement is written down for all participants to see and is read aloud by the facilitator.

Example: How do we increase corporate productivity?
3. The game begins by having a member from the first group suggest an idea that is "unrelated" to the problem.

Example: A member might suggest that the company should give each employee one million dollars.

4. The second group is told that it has three minutes to turn the unrelated idea into a practical solution to the original problem.

Example: A lottery modeled after million-dollar lotteries. Get a roll of numbered tickets. Each time an employee provides a specific suggestion on how to increase productivity, reward him or her with one ticket. At the end of one month, read the ideas and draw a number from a bowl. The winning ticket gets a prize. If there is no winner, double the prize for next month.

5. The facilitator judges the idea. The second group is awarded one point if the solution is judged practical and successful by the facilitator; if the solution is judged unsuccessful, the first group gets the point.

6. The facilitator writes down all the solutions as they are proposed.

7. The groups reverse roles, and the second group proposes an unrelated idea that the first group develops into an idea. The solutions are judged. The groups continue to reverse roles until the game ends.

8. After thirty to forty-five minutes, the game is terminated and the group with the most points is declared the winner.

9. Finally, the facilitator has the group discuss and elaborate on all the proposed solutions to see which ones have the most value.

We have the habit of concentrating on a problem to the exclusion of all other matters. This habit of thinking effectively prevents the formation of new ideas. All outside influences, including chance influences, which could lead to new ways of thinking about the problem, are deliberately excluded. Concentration on the problem only serves to reinforce the rigid way it is being considered at the moment. Bringing in unrelated ideas as an outside influence breaks this concentration and gives you fresh ways of thinking about the problem.

Fantasy

Another way to bring in an outside influence is to fantasize about your subject. The dynamic principle of fantasy is play, which belongs also to the child and appears to be inconsistent with the principle of serious work. Yet, the psychologist Carl Jung noted that without this playing with fantasy, no creative work has ever yet come to birth. It is no coincidence that geniuses take a childlike delight in painting, or composing, or searching for a grand unified theory of the universe. Creative geniuses tend to return to the conceptual world of childhood and are able to wed the most advanced understandings of a field with the sensibilities of a wonder-filled child. Because Einstein could fantasize about space and time, he was able to join his childlike wonder with his scientific expertise in his search for new theories and new ways to understand the universe. While his colleagues kept busy working with what was known, he would wonder why empty space doesn't weigh anything.

A CEO was disappointed in his food-service product line. Playfully, he asked his engineers and chemists to fantasize about products that are impossible to create today, but if they were possible, would change the nature of the food industry forever. One "impossible" idea they imagined was the idea of a food machine, a machine in which you pour universal ingredients (wheat, soy, flour, etc.) and the machine would provide you with any imaginable meal. You simply dial "eggs and bacon" or "turkey dinner with all the trimmings for ten," or whatever you wish, and the machine prepares and serves it. He then asked them to look for practical ideas and ways to come as close to that "impossibility" as possible. The chemists realized there were certain foods, such as breads and pasta, that could be created by machines today. This insight led to the development of the home bread-baking appliance.

Fantasy Envelopes

Following is a game that allows a group to fantasize about impossibilities, resources, and super powers. The guidelines are

1. Divide the group into three teams. Each team gets an envelope with one of the following questions. Team A gets Question 1, team B gets Question 2, and team C gets Question 3.

Question 1: "What is impossible to do today, but if it were possible, would change the nature of the problem forever?"

Question 2: "What would I do if I had all the resources (money, people, time, facilities, etc.) in the world to solve this problem?"

Question 3: "If I were a superhero with supernatural powers and could accomplish anything I wish, how would I handle this problem?"

2. Each team writes an idea or answer on the outside of an envelope. The envelopes are then passed to another team. Their team writes an immediate, specific action that can be taken today to work toward the idea or answer that's written on the outside of the envelope. The idea or suggestion is written on a card and put into the envelope. The envelopes are passed from team to team until each team has had an opportunity to include their ideas and suggestions. Each team generates a specific action for each envelope without looking at what others have written. Discuss and evaluate all the ideas and suggestions at the end.

There is a great value in fantasizing about subjects that do not yet exist. The fantasies take us out of the normal perceptual patterns and place our minds in an unstable position, from which we can "move" to a new idea. We can also fantasize about subjects that could "never" exist in experience.

Crossbreeding Subjects

One way to create subjects that could never exist is to crossbreed two subjects from two different worlds. By actively merging two separate subjects into the same space, you articulate a new identity. This new identity will encourage you to think of connecting links and plausible circumstances to express them. The guidelines are

1. Take your subject or some aspect of it and crossbreed it with a subject from some other world to create a new creature. What happens when you crossbreed X with Y? What happens when you crossbreed your boss with an orange? Or your restaurant with a water buffalo? Suppose you wanted to improve the employee training program. Think about what happens when you crossbreed:

- The trainee with a pickle
- The trainee with a door
- The trainee with a cowboy
- The trainee with a watermelon
- The trainee with a horse
- The trainee with a commuter

2. Draw a picture of your creature.
   Consider the following:
   • How does it relate to its environment?
   • Who is important in its life?
   • What is important in its life?
   • What is the creature's biggest challenge?
   • At what does it excel?
   • If it could have one problem, what would it be?
   • How does if feel about you?

3. Write a two-or three-paragraph story about your creature. If you prefer, just outline it.

4. What are three of its unique strengths?

5. What are three of its unique weaknesses?

6. Create ideas from these crossbreed strengths?

7. Think about the weaknesses. Think about something that can reduce one of the weaknesses. Apply that thought to the problem to create a new idea.

8. Recall your problem.

9. Reread your story.

10. Some images or thoughts from your story will lead to new ideas about your problem.

An owner of a Chinese restaurant crossbred "a restaurant with a cat." One of the strengths of this creature was its ability to go to the customers. This led to the idea of sending his staff to the commuter railroad station, where they passed out menus in the morning to commuters. Each menu had an 800 number and the commuters were advised to place their orders by phone before they left the city. When the commuters arrived back at the station, their meals were ready for pick up.

Chance Favors the Prepared Mind

Alexander Fleming was studying deadly bacteria in 1928 when he removed the cover of the culture plate and noticed that it had become accidentally contaminated. A mold formed on the exposed culture. Fleming noticed that in the area surrounding the mold, the bacteria had disappeared. This was the clue that a lowly mold was a powerful microbe killer that did not harm human tissue. He worked with this mold and tested it on laboratory animals. His work led to the discovery of penicillin, which has saved millions of lives. He attributed his discovery to the "greatest" chance. However, it was his years of diligent research and observation that prepared him to notice the chance event. A less-prepared scientist would have thrown the accidentally contaminated culture away.

In one sense, the creative process starts with all the prior knowledge and experiences that the individual has had that could affect his or her attitude toward creativity and innovation, as well as his or her receptivity to ideas that involve the creative solution. In another example, Ray Kroc, a man in his fifties, spent his adult life preparing himself for the right business opportunity. He constantly looked for it in real estate and sales. He was selling milkshake mixers when he accidentally stumbled into a little hamburger stand owned by Dick and Maurice McDonald. The McDonalds had simplified, economized, and minimized the hamburger stand and had developed a stunning business. Kroc realized immediately that the McDonalds had unwittingly hit upon the concept of fast food–homogenized, predictable items that are quick and easy to prepare. Kroc formed a partnership to franchise the concept, and within a few years, became one of the richest men in America. Consider the thousands of entrepreneurs who had pulled into the hamburger stand and were not prepared to see the staggering potential of the McDonald brothers' fast-food concept.

Louis Pasteur, the French chemist who founded microbiology and invented the process of pasteurization, once warned that chance favors only the prepared mind. Alexander Fleming was intellectually prepared to notice the clue that led to penicillin, and Ray Kroc was experientially prepared to recognize the business concept that would change food service in America. The chance events that inspired their discoveries were seen hundreds of times by others. Fleming was not the first scientist to see a petri dish spoiled by mold, and Kroc was not the first to stumble into the McDonalds' hamburger stand. Yet, because they were prepared,

Fleming saw the far-reaching implications of the mold, and Kroc saw the incredible potential for a new food industry. Their preparation made their serendipitous discoveries highly probable.

Sometimes chance is dramatic and sometimes chance arrives as a faint clue. The more information and data you have, the greater your chance of discovering and exploiting the chance event that may lead to a breakthrough idea. Following are some techniques designed to help you find those clues in some demographic, social, technological, or economic fact or trend that may lead to a new idea:

Opportunity Headlines

Brainstorm for as many interesting demographic, social, technological, or economic facts or trends that you can imagine. Print them on cards–one fact or trend per card. Then string sets of cards together to form headlines that tell a story about something that will, could, or should happen in your own situation. For example, four trends–increased use of credit cards, growing value of brand equity, rising number of Internet users, and ability to use technology to do specific market segmentation–are used to develop the following headline: "It's possible to bypass retailers to sell brand name merchandise on the Web." After developing a set of ten or so headlines, try to figure out the implications of each likely development and take a disciplined look at the capabilities and assets your company has or must get if it's to exploit the opportunities.

Chance Arrangements

Igor Stravinsky, one of the giants in twentieth-century musical composition, in the course of his labors, would deliberately try to draw inspiration from some accidental arrangement. He made profitable use out of accidental arrangements of notes. To contrive an accidental arrangement of facts and trends is to, again, write facts and trends on cards–one fact or trend per card. Create as many cards as you can. Shuffle them and draw three or four at random and place them face down. Turn them over, face up, and build a new idea out of the arrangement. If necessary, fill in the gaps or rearrange the cards until a particular arrangement seems significant or inspiring.

Groups

Give each participant six blank cards and ask him or her to print an interesting fact, trend, or future possibility about your subject (company, market, new markets, etc.) on each card, one per card. After five minutes or so, collect the cards and shuffle them. Then,

1. Randomly distribute three cards to each participant. Make sure no one gets his or her own cards. Ask everyone to study the cards and arrange them in order of personal interest. While participants do this, spread the leftover cards on a large table.
2. Ask participants to exchange the cards they don't like with those on the table. Allow a few minutes for this activity.
3. Ask participants to exchange cards with each other. Every participant must exchange at least one card and may exchange any number.
4. Ask participants to discuss their cards with each other and to form teams. There is no limit to the number of participants who may join the same team, but no team can keep more than three cards.
5. Instruct each team to build an idea from the three cards that your company can exploit.

The physicist, David Bohm, while researching the lives of Einstein, Heisenberg, Pauli, and Bohr, made a remarkable observation. Bohm noticed that their incredible breakthroughs took place through simple, open, and honest conversation. He observed, for instance, that Einstein and his colleagues spent years freely meeting and conversing with each other. During these interactions, they exchanged ideas and talked about ideas that later became the foundations of modern physics. They discussed ideas without trying to change the others' minds and without bitter argument. They felt free to propose whatever was on their minds. They always paid attention to each others' views and established an extraordinary professional fellowship. This freedom to discuss without risk led to the breakthroughs that physicists today take for granted.

Other scientists of the time, in contrast, wasted their careers bickering over petty nuances of opinion and promoting their own ideas at the expense of others. They mistrusted their colleagues, covered up weaknesses, and were reluctant to openly share their work. Many refused to discuss their honest thoughts about physics because of the fear of being labeled controversial by their colleagues. Others were afraid of being called ignorant. The majority of scientists of the time lived in an atmosphere of fear and politics. They produced nothing of significance.

The Spirit of Koinonia

Einstein and his friends illustrate the staggering potential of collaborative thinking. The notion that open and honest collaboration allows thinking to grow as a collective phenomenon can be traced back to Socrates and other thinkers in ancient Greece. Socrates and his friends so revered the concept of group dialogue that they bound themselves by principles of discussion that they established to maintain a sense of collegiality. These principles were known as "Koinonia," which means "spirit of fellowship." The principles they established were

• **Establish Dialogue.** In Greek, the word "dialogue" means a "talking through." The Greeks believed that the key to establishing dialogue is to exchange ideas without trying to change the other person's mind. This is not the same as discussion, which from its Latin root means to "dash to pieces." The basic rules of dialogue for the Greeks were "Don't argue," "Don't interrupt," and "Listen carefully."

• **Clarify Your Thinking.** To clarify your thinking, you must suspend all untested assumptions. Being aware of your assumptions and suspending them allows thought to flow freely. Free thought is blocked if we are unaware of our assumptions or unaware that our thoughts and opinions are based on assumptions. For instance, if you believe that certain people are not creative, you're not likely to give their ideas fair consideration. Check your assumptions about everything and try to maintain an unbiased view.

• **Be Honest.** Say what you think, even if your thoughts are controversial.

The ancient Greeks believed these principles allowed thinking to grow as a collective phenomenon. Koinonia allowed a group to access a larger pool of common thoughts that cannot be accessed individually. A new kind of mind begins to come into being that is based on the development of common thoughts. People are no longer in opposition. They become participants in a pool of common ideas, which are capable of constant development and change.

The notion that the collective intelligence of a group is larger than the intelligence of an individual can be traced back to primitive times when hunter-gather bands would meet to discuss and solve common problems. It is commonly understood and accepted practice. What's difficult is the willingness of a group to discipline itself to brainstorm for ideas openly and productively. Alex Osborn, an advertising executive in Buffalo, New York, recognized this and formalized brainstorming in 1941 as a systematic effort and disciplined practice to produce ideas in a group.

Osborn's idea was to create an uninhibiting environment that would encourage imaginative ideas and thoughts. The usual method is to have a small group discuss a problem. Ideas are offered by participants one at a time. One member records ideas and suggestions on a flip chart or chalkboard. All withhold judgment. After the brainstorming session, the various ideas and suggestions are reviewed and evaluated, and the group agrees on a final resolution.

There are many problems with traditional brainstorming. Sessions can be undercut by group uniformity pressures and perceived threats from managers and bosses. Other sessions fail because people find it difficult to avoid judging and evaluating ideas as they are offered. Personality differences also come into play: Some people are naturally willing to talk; while others tend to be silent.

Illustrated are two circles of equal size. Circle A symbolically represents the creative forces (the black arrows) of a group brainstorming in an uninhibiting environment. Whereas, Circle B represents the creative forces in an inhibiting environment. Circle A is expanding and liberating creative thought, whereas Circle B is contracting and restricting creative thought. The restrictive nature of the forces in Circle B even make the circle appear smaller than it is (they are identical in size). Which brainstorming group would you prefer to join?

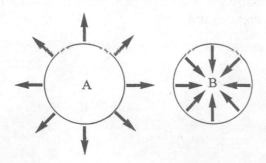

All of us had a taste of good group brainstorming sessions at some time in our lives that provided ideas and thoughts we could never have imagined in advance. But these experiences come rarely and are usually the product of certain conditions. Following are suggested conditions that help overcome these attitudes by enhancing "Koinonia" in your brainstorming sessions:

Participants

Jonas Salk, developer of the vaccine that eradicated polio, made it a standard practice to assemble men and women from very different domains to interact during his group sessions. He felt this practice helped him bring out new ideas that could not arise in the minds of individuals who were from the same domain.

Consider the weaving together of people from different disciplines that led to the discovery of DNA's structure. The successful collaboration included James Watson (microbiologist), Maurice Wilkins (X-ray crystallographer), Francis Crick (physicist), and Linus Pauling (chemist). Their different styles of work were a key aspect to the discovery.

The ideal brainstorming group should be diverse, including experts, nonexperts, and people from different domains within the organization. For example, a marketing group brainstorming for new marketing ideas could invite a customer, someone from manufacturing, an engineer, and a receptionist to the meeting.

Collegiality

All participants must regard one another as equal colleagues, even if they have nothing in common. When you look at the dots in the illustration, your attention is drawn to the lone dot that stands separate and apart from the group of dots.

In the same way, if a participant feels that he or she is not an equal colleague with the rest of a brainstorming group, that participant will become the focus of the session, either consciously or unconsciously, and inhibit the creativity of the group.

Thinking of each other as colleagues is important because thought is participative. Just the willingness to consciously think of each other as colleagues contributes toward interacting as colleagues. We talk differently and more honestly with friends than we do with people who are not friends. Any controlling authority, no matter how carefully presented, will tend to inhibit the free play of thought. If one person is used to having his or her view prevail because he or she is the most senior person present, then that privilege must be surrendered in advance. If one person is used to withholding ideas because he or she is more junior, then the security of "keeping quiet" must also be surrendered.

Suspending All Assumptions

Collegial collaboration is a process we must come to understand and work hard toward. The difficulty of effective collaboration has been demonstrated by several experiments conducted by Howard Gruber and his associates at the University of Geneva. In one experiment, he demonstrates a box that allows two people to peer into it and see the shadow cast by what is to them an unknown object. Because of the angle, each viewer sees a different shape to the shadow. Their task is to share the information about what they see in order to identify the object casting the shadow. For instance, if a cone is placed in the box, one viewer sees a circle, the other a triangle.

The idea was to encourage the viewers to collaborate like two astronomers taking a fix on the heavens from different positions. They see the world in slightly different ways; they take respectful advantage of the fact that one sees it from here and the other from there; and they put together a richer, more soundly based idea of what is really out there than either one could reach alone.

But the opposite happened. Each viewer assumed their view was the correct one and that the other person was apparently confused, blind, or crazy. "How can you see a triangle? I see a circle." This was true of highly intelligent, educated adults. The assumptions made by the viewers made it difficult to collaborate about even a simple object, like a cone.

In order to give fair value to ideas, the group collectively must free themselves of all preconceptions and suspend all assumptions.

Suspending assumptions allows one to look at new ideas in an unbiased way. It is undeniable that by the sheer power of his imagination, Einstein suspended all assumptions that other physicists made about the world and completely reoriented reality. Once one makes assumptions that this is the way it is, all creative thought stops. The group's agreement and discipline of suspending assumptions is key to unblocking the collective imagination.

Suspending Judgment

In an atomic pile, an explosion is prevented by inserting rods of cadmium that mop up the particles that are shooting around. In this way, the energy in the pile is controlled. If there are too many rods, the chain reaction stops, and the pile can no longer produce any energy. People who are unable to appreciate new ideas are like the rods: When a group gets too many of them, it becomes impossible to generate creative energy, and the group will shut down. Require everyone to suspend all criticism and judgment until after the idea generation stage. Whenever someone says, "Yes, but . . .," require the participant to change "Yes, but . . ." to "Yes, and . . ." and continue where the last person left off. This simple change from the negative to the positive will help change the psychology of the group.

Environment

Hold your meetings in a risk-free zone where people can speak their minds without fear of criticism or ridicule. Encourage people to say what they are thinking, even if their thoughts are radical or controversial. Once people realize they can speak freely without being judged or ridiculed, they become comfortable and open. As soon as participants become concerned with "who said what" or "not saying something stupid," creativity is retarded.

Play classical music when people are thinking. Music can be a powerful catalyst in the creative process. It puts participants into a peaceful state of mind, which facilitates reflection. Einstein's son once reflected that whenever Einstein came to a difficult situation in his work, he would take refuge in the music of Beethoven and Mozart, and that the music would exhilarate him and help him resolve his difficulties.

Make the environment visually stimulating by posting pictures and diagrams that are relevant to the subject around the room. For example, suppose you wanted to design a car for upwardly mobile families. You might start by putting together a wall-sized board of photographs and drawings. Use pictures to answer some questions such as "What kinds of houses do these car buyers live in?" "What kind of watches do they buy?" "Where do they go on vacation?" "What kind of art do they hang on their walls?" Mix your own idea sketches in among them. As the swarm of pictures grows, an understanding of who is going to buy this car and what might appeal to them begins to emerge.

Playfulness

One of Walt Disney's greatest secrets was his ability to draw out the inner child in his business associates and combine it with their business acumen. Because he made the work playlike, his associates worked and played together with a missionary zeal. Disney was a true genius who needed to collaborate with other people to express his concepts. Disney got the creative collaboration he needed by consciously creating a humorous and playful environment.

An environment of playfulness and humor is highly conducive to creativity. Playfulness relaxes the tension in a group. In a state of relaxation, individuals show less fixation and rigidity in their thinking. Consequently, a playful group will lose its inhibitions about combining dissimilar concepts and ideas and looking for hidden similarities. These actions are highly conducive to creative thinking, and consequently, a group will generate a much wider range of options than would otherwise be considered.

When we play, we become childlike and begin to behave in spontaneous creative ways. Play and creativity have much in common. In particular, play often involves using objects and actions in new or unusual ways, similar to the imaginative combinations of ideas involved in creative thinking. Picasso once remarked that he became a true artist when he learned how to paint like a child. Einstein has been described as the perennial child and was very much aware of the parallels between creative-thinking thought patterns and those of playful children. Einstein suggested to Piaget that he investigate the way children think of speed and time, thereby inspiring one of the psychologist's most illuminating lines of research.

Facilitator

A skilled facilitator is essential to the process of brainstorming. In the absence of a skilled facilitator, habits of thought will pull the group toward critical, judgmental thinking and away from productive, creative thinking. The skilled facilitator should have strong interpersonal skills, understand the principles of profluent and flexible thinking, and be able to paraphrase and find analogies for suggestions. The facilitator is often a good curator, keeping the group focused, eliminating distractions, and keeping creative thinking alive by liberating the group from trivial and bureaucratic thinking.

The facilitator is not a creator in the same sense that the others are. Rather, the facilitator is the steward, whose job is to liberate the creative thinking of the group. Robert Oppenheimer facilitated the Manhattan Project that developed the atomic bomb during World War II. Oppenheimer couldn't do the individual thinking and tasks required to make the bomb, but he was able to conduct the group of diverse talents and considerable egos, like a great conductor. His facilitation generated the openness and free exchange of information that enabled the group to negotiate a solution. Great facilitators may not be able to compose a Beethoven symphony, but they have an understanding and appreciation of the work and can create the environment needed to realize it.

Stating the Problem

The facilitator should post a common problem statement. It's a good idea at this stage for the facilitator to ask each participant to come up with his or her own personal way of seeing the problem and his or her dream or wishful solution. Engaging participants to look at the problem in a personal way is important for the following reasons:

- Each participant makes the problem his or her own. They can preserve their own individuality and need not to be forced into a shared consensus.
- Engaging participants takes advantage of the diversity of the group.
- Allowing participants to engage in wishful thinking at this point enables the participant to broaden his or her perspective.
- By analyzing wishes as given, they can be broken down into parts of problems that can be dealt with separately.

Idea Production

Quantity breeds quality. The goal is to empty the box. Get every idea from each participant that he or she is capable of imagining. When brainstorming for ideas, suspend all judgment and criticism of ideas and strive for quantity of ideas. Encourage freewheeling and piggybacking. Two ways to increase idea production are

- When you send out an agenda for a brainstorming meeting, ask everyone to bring three new ideas as the ticket of admittance to the meeting.
- Give the group an idea quota. For example, an idea quota of 200 ideas forces the group to put their internal critics on hold and list all ideas, including the obvious and weak. The first third will be the same old ideas they always get. The second third will be more interesting, and the last third will show more imagination and complexity.

Elaboration

Picasso's masterpiece, *Guernica*, demonstrates quite clearly that Picasso was stating a contradiction but a plain fact when he said that a picture remains intact from its first inspiration and yet is not thought out beforehand. He was indicating that the creative process is a holistic one, like the birth and development of a living thing. In nature, the final form of an oak tree or human being is given from the seed at the outset, and yet the form is also shaped as it grows. In the same way, he had an inspiration for *Guernica*, but he explored different expressions and dimensions with sixty-five different sketches before it evolved into its final form.

The longer you work to improve and modify ideas, the more likely it is that the solution will be original and appropriate. Because Picasso kept changing his techniques as he painted *Guernica*, his painting developed into an original masterpiece. Extend the group's thinking by encouraging them to elaborate on the existing ideas in some way. Ask what can be substituted, combined, adapted, magnified, modified, put to some other use, eliminated, rearranged, or reversed in the existing ideas?

Clarifying Thinking

Sigmund Freud believed that you clarify thinking and reasoning not so much by searching for "right" answers, but rather by asking better questions. Good questions widen our understanding of a subject. Often, through questioning, Freud would end up discovering something he didn't set out to discover.

A technique that is helpful for problem solvers in a group to clarify their reasoning is the TQR (Thinker-Questioner-Reflector) technique. Any speaker or listener can call for a TQR session at any time during the session. The person with the idea is designated the Thinker. One person from the group is designated the Questioner. All others become Reflectors. For a specified period of time (five minutes or so), the Thinker thinks out loud, prompted by questions by the Questioner. Then the Reflectors offer any reflections, ideas, or extensions from the interchange. At the least, the idea gets a full hearing and questioners feel they have had a chance to clarify and understand the idea.

Recording

The usual method of recording in a brainstorming session is for the facilitator to list the ideas on a flip chart or chalkboard in a shared display to create a group memory. Shared displays achieve maximal value when the display is more structured than a simple listing of all ideas. Try using generative graphics, such as wall-mounted scrolls of paper. Record the ideas with a cartoon, diagram, or printed phrase, using colored felt markers. The idea is to stimulate full and energetic participation, and to find colorful, stimulating, and graphic ways to portray ideas and illustrate the group's thinking.

Try recording by posting the ideas on a wall or chalkboard in clusters using Post-it notes. Post-it notes make ideas movable and facilitate the "clustering of ideas." When ideas are grouped by common characteristics or themes, an organization or structure begins to arise from the information. More ideas are generated as people begin to see structure and fill in gaps. A sense of priority or dominance is often revealed as one or more of the clusters claim the interest of the group.

Evaluation

At the end of a brainstorming session, make three lists: ideas of immediate usefulness, areas for further exploration, and new approaches to the problem. The facilitator can then categorize the ideas alone, or he or she can have the group evaluate the ideas by voting on the most useful.

A collaborative brainstorming session that reflects Koinonia allows the group to grow a new kind of collective mind based on the development of common thoughts. People are no longer in opposition. They become participants in a pool of common ideas, which are capable of constant development and change.

Group Brainstorming Techniques

Collaboration is one of the best kept secrets in creativity. Even some of the artists that we think of as solitary geniuses were actually entrepreneurial leaders of art teams. Historian William E. Wallace discovered that thirteen people collaborated with Michelangelo on the Sistine Chapel and around two hundred people assisted the master on the Laurentian Library in Florence, Italy. Michelangelo was not only a great artist, he was a CEO of other talent that collaboratively made the art that bore his name. To realize his vision of a full-length animated feature film, Walt Disney assembled a great team of diverse talents to create the breakthrough animated feature film *Snow White and the Seven Dwarfs*. It was Disney's ability to tolerate diversity, allowing his group to retain their individuality while combining their talents that created the cooperative synthesis that made his vision a reality.

Group brainstorming, if done in the right spirit, can generate a rich variety of different perspectives and ideas about any given subject. That's because individuals are magically different and unique from each other and share few common associations. Fill in quickly the first ten thoughts that come into your mind on the lines that emanate from the center when you think of the word "idea." Print single first words and list the first thoughts that come to mind no matter how absurd that may seem. If possible, ask three or four other people to do the exercise at the same time without discussing your associations.

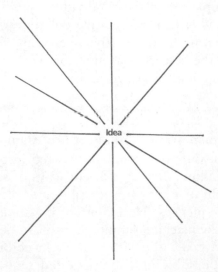

Idea

Your goal is to find those words that are precisely the same. "Thinking," for example, is not the same as "think," and "accident" is not the same as "accidental." When you have finished, compare the words and check to see how many words you have in common. If you are doing this exercise alone, compare your words with mine. (My words are "accident," "fresh," "work," "unconventional," "failure," "think," "predictable," "brainstorm," "time," and "quota.")

Most people assume that there will be many common words and only a few unique to the individual. What this exercise demonstrates is that it is a rarity to find even one word common to all members in a group of three or more. The more people there are in a group, the less chance there is of any one word being common to all members of the group.

If you find one common word, make this the center word and repeat the exercise with the group. You'll likely experience the same result. Even when we find some commonality with others, this commonality is rooted in our fundamental diversity. You'll also discover that when you try this exercise with people who are your closest peers in terms of educational and work experiences, the results are even more uncommon. Most of us assume that the more you educate people, the more clonelike they become. The opposite is true: The more you educate people, the more unique and diverse their networks of associations become. We share few common assumptions with each other. Each of us has the capacity to make an infinite number of uniquely different associations.

The ways people retain their individuality while combining their efforts and talents is critical to creative collaboration. Understanding that is vital to creating a cooperative synthesis. The following techniques are some of the best from around the world that are designed to help groups create a cooperative synthesis:

Brainwriting

Richard Feynman, while working at Los Alamos on the first atomic bomb, noted that only one problem was fed into the computer at a time. Instead of thinking of more efficient ways of solving one problem at a time, he thought of ways of processing multiple problems in parallel, spontaneous sequences. He invented a system for sending three problems through the machine simultaneously. To develop it, he had his team work with colored cards with a different color for each problem. The cards circled the table in a multicolored sequence, small batches occasionally having to pass other batches like impatient golfers playing through. This simple innovation dramatically increased idea production and accelerated the work on the bomb.

Horst Geschka and his associates at the Batelle Institute in Frankfurt, Germany, developed a variety of group creative-thinking techniques called Brainwriting, which, like Feynman's innovative problem-solving approach, are designed to process ideas in parallel, spontaneous sequences. In traditional brainstorming groups, people suggest ideas one at a time. This is serial processing of information. Brainwriting, in contrast, allows multiple ideas to be suggested at the same time. This is parallel processing of information. If a brainwriting group has ten members, up to ten ideas will be generated for every one generated in a typical brainstorming session of ten members. Brainwriting increases idea production dramatically.

The basic guidelines are

1. First, discuss the problem to clarify it. Write the problem in a location visible to all group members.
2. Distribute index cards to each participant and instruct them to silently write their ideas on the cards, one idea per card. Whereas group brainstorming involves participants shouting ideas out loud, brainwriting has people silently writing down ideas.
3. As participants complete their cards, they pass them silently to the person on the right.
4. Tell the group members to read the cards they are passed and to regard them as "stimulation" cards. Write down any new ideas inspired by the "stimulation" cards on blank cards and pass them to the person on their right. Within a few minutes, several idea cards will be rotating around the table.
5. After twenty to thirty minutes, collect all cards and have the group members tape them to a wall. The cards should be arranged into columns according to different categories of ideas, with a title card above each column. Eliminate the duplicates.
6. Evaluate the ideas by giving each participant a packet of self-sticking dots and have them place the dots on their preferred ideas. They can allocate the dots in any manner desired, placing them all on one idea, one each on five different ideas, or any other combination.

Only one person can offer an idea at a time during brainstorming, and despite encouragement to let loose, some people hold back out of inhibition or for fear of ridicule. Brainwriting ensures that the loudest voices don't prevail. Participants feel less pressure from managers and bosses, and ideas can't be shot down as soon as they are offered. You can design your own "brainwriting" format based on two principles:

1. Idea generation is silent.
2. Ideas are created spontaneously in parallel.

Idea Pool

Ask participants to silently generate ideas on index cards and place their cards in the center of the table instead of passing them to the person on their right. Whenever a participant wants or needs a stimulation card, they simply exchange their cards for cards from the pool.

Gallery

This technique reverses the normal process. Instead of moving ideas around for people to examine, the gallery moves people around. Post sheets of flip-chart paper (one per participant) around the room. Participants stand silently and write their ideas on the sheets (one sheet per person) for ten to fifteen minutes. Then the participants are allowed fifteen minutes to walk around the "gallery" and look at the other ideas and take notes. Now, using the other ideas to stimulate further thought, participants return to their sheets and add to or refine their ideas. After about ten minutes of additional writing, the participants examine all the ideas and select the best ones.

Another option for the gallery technique is to ask participants to draw or diagram their ideas instead of listing them. Drawing and diagramming is useful in creative thinking to recover information from memory that would otherwise be unavailable. For example, how many windows are there in your house?

Diagramming your house allows you to inspect and count the windows. Creative insights sometimes occur as a result of drawing or diagramming a problem, because they help us notice certain features that may be overlooked.

Post sheets of flip-chart paper and then ask the participants to draw a sketch or diagram of how the problem might be solved. Then the participants are again allowed to walk around the "gallery" and take notes. Using the notes, they return and refine their own sketches. The group then examines all the sketches and constructs a final solution from parts of different sketches.

Three Plus

Each participant silently writes three ideas on the tops of sheets of paper, one idea per sheet. The sheets are passed to the person on their right. That person is asked to write down an idea that improves on the one listed at the top of the sheet. If participants have difficulty improving on the idea, ask them to list new ones. Do this for all three ideas. After five minutes or so, the idea sheets are again passed to the right. Continue the process until all members receive their original papers.

Airplanes

Have each participant construct a paper airplane. Each participant writes down an idea on the airplane and sends it flying to another participant. Upon reading what's been written on the airplane, he or she writes down a modification or improvement of that idea, or an entirely fresh possibility, and then sends it flying to someone else. Continue the exercise for twenty minutes and then collect and categorize the ideas.

Wall of Ideas

Each participant silently writes ideas on Post-it notes. While the group is writing ideas, the leader collects and pastes them on a wall. Then,

1. When the group is finished generating ideas, the leader reads aloud all the ideas to make sure everyone understands them. If written comments are necessary to clarify the idea, the leader writes it on the note in a different color.
2. The next step is to organize the ideas. Ask the group to come up to the wall and sort the ideas out in some meaningful way. As the ideas are reorganized, the leader will periodically interject questions as to what the topic or criterion is for a partially sorted set of ideas. Eventually, the ideas will be sorted into different sets of ideas.

3. The leader labels each set of ideas with a topic card and pastes it over the idea set. Do this for each separate set of ideas. Some topics can be divided into subtopics for further sorting of ideas.

4. Participants can elaborate on ideas or express concerns by writing their thoughts on additional Post-It notes and pasting them next to the idea or idea set.

5. Prioritize the ideas by giving each participant ten self-sticking dots. The participants prioritize the ideas by placing a dot or dots on the ideas. They can place as many as they wish on an idea.

6. The final step is to capture the end result of the group into a document that is typed and distributed to each of the participants.

Notebooks

In art, there is a group of artists who call themselves futurists. They collaborate on a work, with each artist working on it separately at different times. When the picture is finished, they cannot tell who painted what. The result is usually a remarkable product that reflects several different points of view combined into something different over time. Collaboration over time creates a different dimension and different understanding of a subject in art.

Similarly, a small group can collaborate over time in problem solving to create a deeper understanding and appreciation of the possibilities. The guidelines are

1. Participants are each given a notebook containing problem information and instructions. Each participant writes at least three ideas per day in the notebook for one week.

2. The participants exchange the notebooks with each other every week. Participants can then use the ideas in the new notebooks to trigger, through association, new ideas.

3. The exchange of ideas should stop after four weeks, even if all notebooks haven't made the rounds. The coordinator collects the notebooks, categorizes the ideas, and prepares a summary. The participants gather in a group to discuss the ideas generated.

Two-Week Brainstorming

A variation of the notebook technique is to first brief the group about the problem or subject to be brainstormed and then to ask participants to work on the problem alone for a week and to record their ideas in notebooks. Then,

1. At the end of the week, the individuals bring their notebooks to a group session. Each participant expresses his or her ideas verbally (approximately ten minutes each). The rest of the group is encouraged to discuss the ideas and to develop new ideas around them.
2. Participants are encouraged to record relevant points and ideas in their notebooks.
3. At the end of the group session, participants are then asked to spend another week to do further creative thinking. They can now consider the new concepts and ideas they heard from others or improve their own ideas in light of what they have learned from the group session.
4. At the end of the second week, the group meets again to harvest the ideas, which are then shared, prioritized, and evaluated.

Mixed Sessions

You could also combine individual and group creative thinking in one session. The session starts with a group brainstorming session to define the subject and to develop as many ideas as possible. Then a specific creative-thinking technique is suggested by the facilitator, for example, forcing a connection between the subject and random words as described in "Connecting the Unconnected." The group breaks up and each participant goes off to work on his or her own to use the technique to generate additional ideas, for ten minutes or so. The group is then reassembled and the new ideas are discussed and developed further. If new ideas are desired, a fresh technique is introduced by the facilitator for further individual working. The key is that all individual work is directed by the use of specific techniques. The process is repeated until the group is satisfied with the output.

Clustering

Clustering is a technique that combines the silent generation of ideas with the random clustering of people and ideas. It was inspired by the work of Igor Stravinsky, the genius of modernism in music, who never lost his eagerness to try something new. *The Soldier's Tale* in 1918 was a landmark departure from traditional performance styles by introducing the concept of "clusters" of performers (dancers, narrator, and instrumentalists) who saw themselves uniquely re-creating the composer's work, each performance being a new experiment. The guidelines are

1. Discuss and post a general challenge.
Example: "In what ways might we create a more innovative corporation?"
2. Each participant writes eight responses or ideas on cards, one idea per card.
3. The facilitator collects and shuffles the cards from the entire group.
4. The facilitator randomly distributes three cards to each participant. Make sure that no participant receives his or her original cards. Ask everyone to study the cards and to arrange them in order of personal preference. The facilitator spreads the leftover cards on a table face up.
5. Ask participants to exchange the cards they don't like with those on the table. Allow a couple of minutes for this activity.
6. Next, ask participants to exchange cards with each other. Every participant must exchange at least one card and may exchange any number.
7. Ask participants to form clusters. There is no limit to the number of participants who may join the same cluster, but no cluster may keep more than three cards.
8. Instruct each cluster to prepare a creative way to present their three ideas to the group. They might create a graphic poster, bumper sticker, slogan, logo, T-shirt, television commercial, song, and so on.

A variation of "clustering" is to first ask participants to write as many ideas as they can on index cards for five minutes, one idea per card. Then,

1. Divide the group into teams of three to six members, depending upon the size of the group.

2. The team members pool their cards, which they rank in order of preference.

3. Ask the team to select the top five ideas and to place the rest on a table face up. The other teams are free to review the discarded ideas and use them if they wish.

4. The teams discuss the ideas and are free to replace them with new ideas, if and when they occur (but the team can only retain five at any one time). They are encouraged to refine or improve upon the ideas they have selected.

5. All the teams, meeting together, share the ideas verbally.

6. The group prioritizes the ideas and shortens the list to the five most promising.

7. The group elaborates on these ideas and then assesses and evaluates them.

Open Meetings

Open brainstorming meetings give all employees–from janitors to CEOs–the opportunity and the motivation to suggest ideas. The purpose behind the formlessness of an open meeting is to let ideas take their own shape, undistorted by status or personal politics. Open meetings are governed by a few simple guidelines, a general theme, and very loose time limits.

There is no agenda for the meeting. Someone reads the meeting's general theme aloud and invites everyone to identify a related issue for which they assume responsibility. When someone suggests an issue, that person writes it on a large sheet of paper, reads it aloud, and posts it on one of the walls. This process continues until all the issues have been posted.

The next phase is known as the "idea marketplace." During it, everyone is invited to sign up on one of the large "issue" sheets to discuss the issue. Participants can sign up for as many groups as they wish. Sponsors of each issue convene their groups to side rooms, discuss the issue, and record any ideas or other information suggested. Ideally, several smaller rooms near the larger meeting room should be available where the small groups can convene and pursue their issue. Each small group should honor the "law of two feet." The law is if any participant becomes bored or has nothing to contribute to the group, honor the group and walk away.

Another way to conduct an open meeting is to do it over a computer network by designing a computer linkup to give everyone in the company access to open group discussions. Employees can send and receive real-time messages and tap into a central database where a general theme is posted, for example, "How can we reduce expenses?" People post issues that relate to the general theme and others get in touch with each other to interact about the issues that interest them. They can call up the results of their discussions, at their convenience, and send each other e-mail messages until they generate the ideas they want.

KJ Brainstorming

A leading creativity researcher, psychologist Howard Gruber of the University of Geneva, indicates that in the creative process, slight shifts of perspective go on all the time, at various scales, before the creative solution is reached. These shifts occur when one identifies a nuance. A nuance is a shade of meaning or subtlety of perception. Many, many small shifts couple together over time, eventually producing a major shift of perception. Gruber also noted that creative geniuses are keenly sensitive to nuances, and particularly, nuances having to do with certain themes.

Potentially, a group brainstorming session generates quantities of ideas, with each idea full of potential nuances. Each idea is saturated with shades of meaning. Yet, our usual pattern of organizing a group session is to take a reductionist approach rather than let ideas evolve out of the dimensions of nuances, as a creator would.

Jiro Kawakita, professor at the Tokyo Institute of Technology, developed a brainstorming technique that allows an idea to shape its course according to the neutral facts and nuances of the situation. In Japan it's known as the *kami-kire ho*, which means "scrap-paper technique." It's called "scrap paper," because originally Kawakita had participants write thoughts and ideas on scrap paper. The technique is commonly referred to in the West as simply KJ.

The technique synthesizes different individual perspectives and experiences into a problem definition and solution that is acceptable to the group. There are two types of activity in KJ: understanding the problem and solving the problem. Understanding the problem is getting each member of the group to get a sense of the essence of the problem definition; solving the problem means encouraging all members to participate in suggesting solutions.

For example, a problem might be disposing of cooking-oil waste. Understanding the problem is to be sensitive to the relevant facts, subtleties, and nuances of disposing of it in its liquid form. What are the neutral facts? How is it disposed? What damage does it cause? What facts are relevant? What facts are verifiable?

Once facts are collected, solutions are proposed. One suggested solution would be some sort of inexpensive vegetable additive, which contains no chemicals, that you mix into the hot oil so that when the mixture cools, it becomes a solid for disposal with regular garbage. Or another suggestion might be to add a chemical additive to the cooking oil that could transform the oil into fertilizer for gardens. And so on.

The procedures for KJ are

1. **Problem Definition**. The group leader cites a general area of concern (e.g., sales, costs, distribution, competition).

   A. Each person writes facts on index cards that are related to this one concern, writing one fact per card, on as many cards as they wish. The idea is to get people to think of everything they can that may be pertinent to the problem.

   B. The group leader collects and distributes the cards so no person receives his or her own cards.

   C. The group leader then reads one card aloud.

   D. Participants find cards in their stacks that contain related facts and read these aloud, building a set. A set is a collection of cards with related facts.

   E. The group gives the set a name that they all agree reflects the essence of the set and puts it on a name-set card. The name must meet the following conditions:

   • It can be verified by using the facts from which it was generated.
   • It should not be too general.
   • It should not be a simple aggregation of the subset facts.

Naming the set means boiling down the key facts of a problem and then extracting the essence or essentials of the problem.

F. The group continues until all the facts are in name sets, and then the group combines the name sets until there is one all-inclusive group that they name, agreeing that the name reflects the essence of the all-inclusive problem definition set. The final set should include all the facts and name-essences previously formulated in the subsets.

This final all-inclusive name set should end up being the closest approximation of the definition and essence of the problem. It should represent a consensus definition and understanding of the problem. The purpose of sorting facts into sets is to bring about new ways of thinking about old categories and files of facts.

Kawakita believed that when the group has a common understanding of the problem, it comes into alignment. Alignment means that each person in the group affirms the problem definition and shares in a communion, a feeling of personal support with each member of the group.

2. **Problem Solution**. Each member writes suggested solutions and ideas on cards, one solution per card. Each writes as many solutions as one wishes. The goal is to produce 100 cards or more.

A. The group leader collects the cards and distributes the cards so that no person receives his or her own cards.

B. The leader reads one proposed idea out loud.

C. Members select solutions on their cards that relate to the one that was read aloud. Continue until all related solutions are read. This builds a solution set.

D. The set is named and a name-set card is written for it. Continue until all the solutions are placed in sets and until an all-inclusive solution set is obtained. The final solution set's essence should encompass all the previously suggested solutions.

The title for the final solution set should capture the essence of all the suggestions. Ask the group, "What is the essence of the properties and characteristics that are indispensable to these ideas?" This question should inspire a number of ideas and thoughts. Finally, the facilitator should ask participants for additional ideas that come to mind. These ideas may be related or unrelated or they may be different perspectives on the problem. The facilitator should graphically depict these to make it easier to understand their meaning and relationship to one another. The idea is to build a visual conceptual picture.

When participants produce cards, the problem definition expands; and when they compress the cards into name-sets, the problem definition contracts. The expanding and contracting of sets squeezes the information out of its usual categories into its many subtleties and nuances. It is the group's awareness of the subtleties and nuances of the problem that changes the context in which the problem is seen. This change in context may lead to the sudden solution or the sudden idea.

NHK

Another technique designed to squeeze out nuances is NHK, which was developed by Hiroshi Takahashi at the Japan Broadcasting Company (NHK). This method works like an eggbeater, churning ideas again and again to produce new ideas. The guidelines are

1. In response to a problem statement, participants write down five ideas on separate cards.
2. Participants form into teams of five. Each person explains his or her ideas to the other members of the team. Other members write down any new ideas that come to mind on separate cards.
3. The cards are collected and sorted into groups of related themes.
4. New teams of two or three people are formed. Each group takes one or more of the sorted groups of cards and brainstorms for ideas that are related to those on the cards. This lasts up to half an hour. The new ideas are also written on cards.
5. At the end of this session, each group organizes its cards by theme and presents the ideas to the rest of the group. All ideas are written on a chalkboard or flip chart by the facilitator for all to see.
6. Participants are formed into new groups of ten people each, and they brainstorm improvements regarding the ideas on the chalkboard or flip chart, one idea at a time.

Storyboarding

Leonardo da Vinci used to pin his ideas up on a wall and examine them over time. This visual display of ideas enabled him to see how one idea related to another and how all the pieces came together. A popular American technique of displaying information on a wall is the storyboard.

In 1928 Walt Disney and his artists were working on his first talking cartoon *Steamboat Willie*. Disney wanted full animation. To animate everything required thousands of drawings. They were piled in stacks all over the place. It was hard to know what had been finished and what still needed to be done. They had to have meetings all the time, just to find out what was going on.

Walt Disney came up with the idea of having his artists pin their drawings on the walls of the studio in sequence so he could see in a glance how far along the project was. Each scene was then used as a point around which a complete story could be told. The story was told on a wall covered with a special kind of board, hence the term "storyboard."

Storyboarding quickly became a routine part of Disney's planning procedure for both animated and live-action films. He could walk in at any time of the day or night and see progress on any given project at a glance. Storyboards kept branching out into many uses. Disneyland and Walt Disney World were both "operationally" planned using storyboards.

Mike Vance recognized the problem-solving potential for this technique and was the first to refine it into a brainstorming technique. A variety of related procedures for generating ideas has evolved since then. Although there are some significant differences among the procedures, all of them share the common feature begun by Walt Disney: laying out key concepts that are linked together to form a complete whole.

Storyboarding can be likened to taking your thoughts and the thoughts of others and making them visible, by spreading them on a wall as you work on your problem. Following are basic guidelines used by many storyboarding methods:

1. **Topic**. Tape or pin the topic card on the wall. In our example, the topic is to "create a new restaurant."

2. **Purpose**. Normally, most people start with a "purpose" header, which helps the group brainstorm the purposes for pursuing a par-

ticular topic. Each brainstormed purpose is written on a card and posted beneath the "purpose" card. For example, among the possible purposes for starting an new restaurant are making money, fulfilling a need, and serving the customer.

3. **Headers.** Identify and list "headers," which are primarily the major issues, attributes, or solution categories of the process. Each one is written on a card and posted. Our example has these headers: "purpose," "name," "location," "theme," "architecture," "atmosphere," "seating," "menu," "employees," "entertainment," and "miscellaneous." Arrange and rearrange the headers until you come up with the sequence that best tells the story.

4. **Miscellaneous.** It's a good idea to include a "miscellaneous" header to contain all those items that don't fit within the other categories. Place thoughts in this column as the rest of the columns are brainstormed. Some of these may become separate headers themselves if enough similar items appear in the miscellaneous column. In our example, suppose participants listed several advertising and marketing suggestions and ideas. These ideas would create additional headers, or if significant enough, might merit separate storyboards.

5. **Brainstorm.** Group members use each category as a stimulus for problem solutions and write these ideas, solutions, and thoughts on cards. Each card is posted beneath the appropriate header card. For example, all the brainstormed names for the new restaurant would be posted underneath the "Name" header, all the suggested menu items would be listed under the "Menu" header, and so on.

During a storyboard session, consider all ideas relevant, no matter how impractical they appear. Encourage the group to think positively and defer judgment until a later time. Once the ideas start flowing, those working with the storyboard will become immersed in the problem and will "hitchhike" onto other ideas to create additional ideas. Encourage participants to examine the solutions and try to generate additional ideas from them or combine solutions across categories and use them as stimuli for new ideas.

6. **Flexibility**. Keep the storyboard flexible and dynamic. As ideas and suggestions accumulate, you may find it necessary to add more headers. For example, in our restaurant example, "environment" could be split into "physical environment" and "atmosphere." Think of the board as a living, dynamic thing that is constantly evolving toward the ideal solution.

7. **Incubate**. The process continues until the group generates a sufficient number of ideas or time is called. It's usually a good idea to brainstorm for ideas using a storyboard over a time period of a few days or weeks to allow the ideas to incubate and cross-fertilize.

8. **Materials**. You can use a wide variety of materials to create your storyboard: cork boards, white boards, chalkboards, or walls, anything that provides a surface where you can add, delete, or move things around. You can use different colors to distinguish headers and columns. Depending on which system you use, you'll need push pins, scissors, wide marking pens, chalk, and a supply of cards, Post-it notes, or Jotz notes. Take a photograph of the completed board so it can be reconstructed and reworked in the future, if necessary.

The beauty of storyboarding is in its flexibility and adaptability to your needs. You can modify the guidelines to meet your requirements. It's a good idea to keep the process simple at first. After you've become comfortable with it, you can expand it at will.

Purpose
- Idea
- Idea
- Idea

Location
- Idea
- Idea
- Idea
- Idea

Name
- Idea
- Idea
- Idea
- Idea
- Idea
- Idea
- Idea

Theme
- Idea
- Idea
- Idea
- Idea

Environment
- Idea
- Idea
- Idea

Menu
- Idea
- Idea
- Idea
- Idea

Entertainment
- Idea
- Idea

Marketing
- Idea
- Idea
- Idea

Misc.
- Idea

AFTERWORD

In the introduction, I wrote about my fascination with Charles Darwin's theory of biological evolution and the attempts of scholars to apply Darwinian ideas to creativity and genius. I first became interested in Darwin in college when I read about Darwin's experience with John Gould. When Darwin returned to England after he visited the Galapagos, he distributed his finch specimens to professional zoologists to be properly identified. One of the most distinguished experts was John Gould. *What was the most revealing was not what happened to Darwin, but what had not happened to Gould.*

Darwin's notes show Gould taking him through all the birds he had named. Gould kept flip-flopping back and forth about the number of different species of finches: The information was there, but he didn't quite know what to make of it. He assumed that since God made one set of birds when he created the world, the specimens from different locations would be identical. It didn't occur to him to look for differences by location. Gould thought that the birds were so different that they might be distinct species.

What was remarkable to me about the encounter is the completely different impact it had on the two men. Gould thought the way he had been taught to think, like an expert taxonomist, and didn't see, in the finches, the textbook example of evolution unfolding right before him. Darwin didn't even know they were finches. So the guy who had the intelligence, knowledge, and the expertise didn't see the differences, and the guy with far less knowledge and expertise came up with an idea that shaped the way we think about the world.

Darwin came up with the idea because he was a productive thinker. He generated a multiplicity of perspectives and theories. Gould would compare new ideas and theories with his existing patterns of experience. He thought reproductively. If the ideas didn't fit with what he had been taught, he rejected them as worthless. On the other hand, Darwin was willing to disregard what past thinkers thought and was willing to entertain different perspectives and different theories to see where they would lead.

Most us are educated to think like John Gould. We were all born as spontaneous, creative thinkers. Yet a great deal of our education may be regarded as the inculcation of mind-sets. We were taught how to handle problems and new phenomena with fixed mental attitudes (based on what past thinkers thought) that predetermine our response to problems or situations. In short, we were taught "what" to think instead of "how" to think. We entered school as a question mark and graduated as a period.

Consequently, we tend to process information the same way over and over again instead of searching for alternatives. Once we think we know what works or can be done, it becomes hard for us to consider alternative ideas. We tend to develop narrow ideas and stick with them until proven wrong. Let's say that to advertise our product, we use television commercials during a popular prime-time sitcom. We are fairly happy with the results, and the television campaign seems to work. Are we going to check out other ideas that we don't think will be as good or better? Are we likely to explore alternative ways to advertise our product? Probably not.

Even when we actively seek information to test our ideas to see if we are right, we usually ignore paths that might lead us to discover alternatives. Following is an interesting experiment, which was originally conducted by the British psychologist Peter Watson, that demonstrates this attitude. Watson would present subjects with the following three numbers in sequence.

$$2 \quad 4 \quad 6$$

He would then ask subjects to explain the number rule for the sequence and to give other examples of the rule. The subjects could ask as many questions as they wished without penalty.

He found that almost invariably most people will initially say, "Four, Six, Eight" or some similar sequence. And Watson would say,

"Yes, that is an example of a number rule." Then they will say, "twenty, twenty-two, twenty-four" or "fifty, fifty-two, fifty-four" and so on—all numbers increasing by two. After a few tries, and getting affirmative answers each time, they are confident, without exploring alternative possibilities, that the rule is that the numbers increase by two.

Actually, the rule Watson was looking for is much simpler; it's simply that the numbers increase. They could be 1, 2, 3 or 10, 20, 40 or 400, 678, 10,944. And testing such an alternative would be easy. All the subjects had to say was "one, two, three" to Watson to test it and it would be affirmed. Or for example, a subject could throw out any series of numbers–for example, 5, 4, 3–to see if they got a positive or negative answer. And that information would tell them a lot about whether their guess about the rule is true.

The profound discovery Watson made was that most people process the same information over and over until proven wrong, without searching for alternatives, even when there is no penalty for asking questions that give them a negative answer. In his hundreds of experiments, he, incredibly, never had an instance in which someone spontaneously offered an alternative hypotheses to find out if it were true. In short, his subjects didn't even try to find out if there is a simpler–or even another–rule.

Creative geniuses don't think this way. The creative genius will always look for alternative ways to think about a subject. Even when the old ways are well established, the geniuses will invent new ways of thinking. If something doesn't work, they look at it several different ways until they find a new line of thought. It is this willingness to entertain different perspectives and alternative ideas that broadens their thinking and opens them up to new information and the new possibilities that the rest of us don't see.

In summary, creative geniuses are productive thinkers. To change the way you think and become a more productive thinker, you need to learn how to think like a genius. When you need original ideas or creative solutions for your business and personal problems, you need to

- Generate a multiplicity of different perspectives about your subject until you find the perspective you want. Genius often comes from finding a new perspective that no one else has taken.
- Generate a large quantity of alternatives and conjectures. From this quantity, retain the best ideas for further development and elaboration.

• Produce variation in your ideas by incorporating random, chance, or unrelated factors.

As I wrote these final words, I was reminded of an ancient Chinese story about a rainmaker who was hired to bring rain to a parched part of China. The rainmaker, a small, wizened, old man, upon arriving, sniffed the air with obvious disgust as he got out of his cart and asked to be left alone in a cottage outside the village; even his meals were to be left outside the door.

Nothing was heard from him for three days. Then it not only rained, but there was also a big downfall of snow, unknown at that time of the year. Very much impressed, the villagers sought him out and asked him how he could make it rain and even snow. The rainmaker replied, "I have not made the rain or the snow; I am not responsible for it." The villagers insisted that they had been in the midst of a terrible drought until he came, and then after three days they even had quantities of snow.

"Oh, I can explain that. You see, the rain and snow were always here. But as soon as I got here, I saw that your minds were out of order and that you had forgotten how to see. So I remained here until once more you could see what was always right before your eyes."

It is my hope that the strategies in this book will show you how to look for different ways to think about your problems. When you do that, you will rethink the way you see things, and you, like the Chinese villagers, will see what is right before your eyes.

BIBLIOGRAPHY

Albert, Robert S. "Genius: Present-Day Status of the Concept and Its Implications for the Study of Creativity and Giftedness." *American Psychologist*, 24: 743 – 753.

——, ed. *Genius and Eminence*. Woburn, MA: Butterworth-Heinemann, Pergamom Press, 1992.

Andersen, P. and D. Cadbury. *Imagined Worlds: Stories of Scientific Discovery*. London: Ariel Books, 1985 (out of print).

Anderson, Emily. *The Letters of Mozart and His Family*, second ed. New York: W. W. Norton, 1986.

Arieti, S. (1976). *Creativity: The Magic Synthesis*. New York: Basic Books, 1976 (out of print).

Arnheim, R. *Picasso's* Guernica: *The Genesis of a Painting*. New York: Oxford University Press, 1962 (out of print).

Ashton, Dore. *Picasso on Art: A Selection of Views*. New York: Da Capo Press, 1988.

Barnes, Jonathan, cd. *The Complete Works of Aristotle*. Princeton: Princeton University Press, 1983.

Barron, F. *Creative Person and the Creative Process*. New York: Holt, Rinehart and Winston, 1969 (out of print).

——, and D. M. Harrington. "Creativity, Intelligence, and Personality."*Annual Review of Psychology* 32 (1981): 439–476.

Bell, Eric. *Men of Mathematics*. New York: Simon & Schuster, 1986.

Bellak, L. "Creativity: Some Random Notes to a Systematic Consideration." *Journal of Projective Thinking* 22 (1984): 363–380.

Bennis, Warren, and Patricia Biederman. *Organizing Genius: The Secrets of Creative Collaboration*. Reading, MA: Addison-Wesley, 1996.

Bernadac, Marie-Laure, and P. Dubouchet. *Picasso: Master of the New Idea*. Trans. by Carey Lovelace. New York: Harry N. Abrams, 1993.

Boden, M. *The Creative Mind: Myths and Mechanisms*. New York: Basic Books, 1991 (out of print).

Bohm, D., and F. P. Peat. *Science, Order, and Creativity*. New York: Bantam Books, 1987 (out of print).

Bohr, Niels. *Atomic Theory and the Description of Nature*. Woodbridge, CT: Ox Bow Press, 1987.

Bouchard, Thomas J., and M. Hare. "Size, Performance, and Potential in Brainstorming Groups." *Journal of Applied Psychology* 54 (1970): 51–55.

Bramly, S. *Leonardo: Discovering the Life of Leonardo da Vinci*. New York: HarperCollins, 1991 (out of print).

Brian, Denis. *Genius Talk: Conversations with Nobel Scientists and Other Luminaries*. New York: Plenum Press, 1995.

Briggs, J. *Fire in the Crucible*. New York: St. Martin's Press, 1990 (out of print).

Briskman, L. "Creative Product and Creative Process in Science and Art." *Inquiry* 23 (1991): 83–106.

Burke, James. *The Pinball Effect*. New York: Little, Brown and Company, 1997.

Callow, Philip. *From Noon to Starry Night: A Life of Walt Whitman*. New York: Ivan R. Dee, 1992.

Campbell, D. T. "Blind Variation and Selective Retention in Creative Thought as in Other Thought Processes" *Psychological Review* 67 (1960): 380–400.

——. "Unjustified Variation and Selective Retention in Scientific Discovery." In *Studies in the Philosophy of Biology*, edited by F.J. Ayala and T. Dobzhansky, pp. 139–161. London: Macmillan, 1974 (out of print).

Cannon, W. B. "The Role of Chance in Discovery." *Scientific Monthly* 50 (1940): 204–209.

Chastel, A. *The Genius of Leonardo da Vinci*. New York: Orion Press, 1961 (out of print).

Chomsky, Noam. *Language and Mind*. New York: Harcourt Brace College Pubs., 1972.

Clark, D. *Great Inventors and Discoveries*. London: Marshall Cavendish Books, 1978 (out of print).

Clark, R.W. *Einstein: The Life and Times*. New York: World, 1971 (out of print).

Conot, Robert. *Thomas A. Edison: A Streak of Luck*. New York: Da Capo Press, 1986.

Cox, Catharine. *Early Mental Traits of Three Hundred Geniuses*. Stanford, CA: Stanford University Press, 1926.

Crandall, R. "The Relationship Between Quantity and Quality of Publications." *Personality and Social Psychology Bulletin* 4 (1978): 379–380.

Cropper, A. J. *The Quantum Physicists*. New York: Oxford University Press, 1970 (out of print).

Csikszentmihalyi, Mihaly. *Flow: The Psychology of Optimal Experience*. New York: HarperCollins, 1991.

Culhane, John. *Walt Disney's Fantasia*. New York: Harry N. Abrams, 1987.

Darwin, Charles. *The Autobiography of Charles Darwin (1809–1882)*. New York: W.W. Norton, 1993.

Darwin, Francis, ed. *The Life and Letters of Charles Darwin*. New York: Appleton, 1911 (out of print).

——, ed. *The Autobiography of Charles Darwin and Selected Letters*. New York: Dover, 1958.

De Mille, Agnes. *Martha: The Life and Work of Martha Graham*. New York: Random House, 1992.

Dennett, Daniel. *Kinds of Minds*. New York: Basic Books, 1997.

Detolnay, C. *Michelangelo: Sculptor, Painter, Architect*. Princeton, NJ: Princeton University Press, 1975 (out of print).

Eiseley, L. *Darwin's Century: Evolution and the Men Who Discovered It*. New York: Anchor Books, 1961.

Everdell, William. *The First Moderns*. Chicago: University of Chicago Press, 1997.

Feynman, Richard. *Surely You're Joking, Mr. Feynman: Adventures of a Curious Character*. New York: W.W. Norton, 1997.

Finch, Christoper. *The Art of Walt Disney*. New York: Harry N. Abrams, 1995.

Findlay, C., and C. Lumsden. "The Creative Mind: Toward an Evolutionary Theory of Discovery and Invention." *Journal of Social and Biological Structures* 11 (1988): 3–55.

Finke, Ronald, ed. *Creative Imagery: Discoveries and Inventions in Visualization*. Hillsdale, NJ: Erlbaum, 1990.

Freud, Sigmund. *A General Introduction to Psychoanalysis*, reprint ed. New York: W. W. Norton, Liveright, 1989.

——. *An Autobiographical Study*, reprint ed. New York: W. W. Norton, 1989.

Garcia, Emanuel. *Understanding Freud: The Man and His Ideas*. New York: New York University Press, 1992.

Gardner, Howard. *Arts and Human Development: A Psychological Study of the Artistic Process*. New York: Wiley, 1973 (out of print).

——. *Frames of Mind*, reprint ed. New York: Basic Books, 1993.

——. *The Mind's New Science*. New York: Basic Books, 1987.

——. *Art, Mind, and Brain: A Cognitive Approach to Creativity*. New York: Basic Books, 1984.

——. *Creating Minds*. New York: Basic Books, 1994.

Gedo, John. *Portraits of the Artist*. Hillsdale, NJ: Analytic Press, 1989.

Gentner, D. "Structure-Mapping: A Theoretical Framework for Analogy." *Cognitive Science* 7 (1983): 155–170.

Getzels, J., and Mihaly Csikszentmihalyi. *The Creative Vision: A Longitudinal Study of Problem Finding in Art*. New York: Wiley-Interscience, 1976 (out of print).

Gilbert, D. T. "How Mental Systems Believe." *American Psychologist* 46 (1991): 107–119.

Gilot, Francoise, and Carlton Lake. *Life with Picasso*. New York: Doubleday, 1989.

Gleick, James. *Genius: The Life and Science of Richard Feynman*. New York: Pantheon, 1992.

Goldsmith, D. *The Ultimate Einstein*. New York: Simon and Schuster, 1997.

Gordon, W. *Synectics: The Development of Creative Capacity*. New York: Dutton, 1961 (out of print).

Grosvenor, Edwin, and Morgan Wesson. *Alexander Graham Bell*. New York: Harry N. Abrams, 1997.

Gruber, H. E. *Darwin on Man*, second ed. Chicago: University of Chicago Press, 1982 (out of print).

——, and S. N. Davis. "Inching Our Way to Mount Olympus: The Evolving Systems Approach to Creative Thinking." In *The Nature of Creativity*, edited by R. J. Sternberg, pp. 243–70. New York: Cambridge University Press, 1988.

——, M. Terrell, and M. Wertheimer, eds. *Contemporary Approaches to Creative Thinking*. New York: Atherton Press, 1962 (out of print).

Guilford, J. P. *Intelligence, Creativity, and Their Educational Implications*. San Diego: EDITS Pubs., 1968.

——. "Intellectual Resources and Their Values As Seen by Scientists." In *Scientific Creativity*, ed. by C.W. Taylor and F. Barron, pp. 101–118. New York: Wiley, 1963 (out of print).

——. *The Nature of Human Intelligence*. New York: McGraw-Hill, 1967 (out of print).

Hadamard, J. *An Essay on the Psychology of Invention in the Mathematical Field*. Princeton, NJ: Princeton University Press, 1945 (out of print).

Hoffmann, Banesh, and Helen Dukas. *Albert Einstein: Creator and Rebel*. New York: NAL-Dutton, 1973.

Holton, G., and Y. Elkana, eds. *Albert Einstein: Historical and Cultural Perspectives*. Princeton, NJ: Princeton University Press, 1982.

——. "On Trying to Understand Scientific Genius." *The American Scholar* 41 (1971): 98–99.

——. *Thematic Origins of Scientific Thought: Kepler to Einstein*, reprint ed. Cambridge, MA: Harvard University Press, 1988.

Homer, Willliam. *Seurat and the Science of Painting*, reprint ed. New York: Hacker Art Books, 1985.

Horgan, Paul. *Encounters with Stravinsky*, reprint ed. Middletown, CT: Wesleyan University Press, 1989.

Horn, J. "Human Abilities: A Review of Research and Theory in the Early 1970s." *Annual Review of Psychology* 27 (1976): 437–485.

Infeld, Leopold. *Albert Einstein: His Work and Its Influence on Our World*. New York: Scribner's, 1950 (out of print).

Jackson, Douglas, and J. Rushton, eds. *Scientific Excellence*. Beverly Hills, CA: Sage Publications, 1987.

James, William. "Great Men, Great Thoughts, and the Environment. *Atlantic Monthly* 46 (1880): 441–459.

Jansson, D. G., and S. M. Smith. "Design Fixation." *Design Studies* 12 (1) (1987): 3–11.

Jenkins, R. "Elements of Style: Continuities in Edison's Thinking." *Annals of the New York Academy of Sciences* 424 (1983): 149–162.

Jones, E. *The Life and Work of Sigmund Freud*. New York: Basic Books, 1961 (out of print).

Judson, Horace. *The Eighth Day of Creation: Makers of the Revolution in Biology*. Plainview, NY: Cold Spring Harbor, 1996.

Koestler, Arthur. *The Act of Creation*. New York: Viking Penguin, 1990.

Kohler, Wolfgang. *The Task of Gestalt Psychology*. Ann Arbor, MI: Books on Demand.

Landrum, Gene. *Profiles of Genius*. New York: Prometheus Books, 1993.

Lorenz, Konrad. "The Role of Gestalt Perception in Animal and Human Behavior." In *Aspects of Form*, edited by L. Whyte, pp. 157–178. Bloomington, IN: Midland Books, 1966.

Macfarlane, Gwen. *Alexander Fleming: The Man and the Myth*. Cambridge, MA: Harvard University Press, 1984.

Mednick, S. "The Associative Basis of the Creative Process." *Psychological Review* 69 (1962): 220–232.

Miller, Arthur I. *Insights of Genius*. New York: Springer-Verlag New York, 1996.

Mumford, M. D., and S. B. Gustafson. "Creativity Syndrome: Integration, Application, and Innovation." *Psychological Bulletin* 103 (1) (1988): 27–43.

Murphy, G. L. "Comprehending Complex Concepts." *Cognitive Science* 12 (1988): 529–562.

Ochse, R. *Before the Gates of Excellence: The Determinants of Creative Genius*. New York: Cambridge University Press, 1990.

Ortony, Andrew, ed. *Metaphor and Thought*, second ed. New York: Cambridge University Press, 1993.

Osborn, A. *Applied Imagination*. New York: Charles Scribner's Sons, 1953 (out of print).

Peat, David. *In Search of Nikola Tesla*. Bath: Ashgrove UK, 1997.

Perkins, David N. *The Mind's Best Work*. Cambridge, MA: Cambridge University Press, 1981 (out of print).

——. "The Possibility of Invention." In *The Nature of Creativity: Contemporary Psychological Perspectives*, edited by R. J. Sternberg. Cambridge, MA: Cambridge University Press, 1988 (out of print).

Piaget, Jean. *The Child's Conception of the World*, reprint ed. Totowa, NJ: Littlefield, Adams, 1983.

Poe, Richard. *The Einstein Factor*. Rocklin, CA: Prima Publishing, 1995.

Popper, Karl. *The Logic of Scientific Discovery,* fourteenth ed. New York: Routledge, 1996.

Pyenson, Lewis. *The Young Einstein*. Philadelphia: IOP Pub., 1995.

Reed, S., G. Ernst, and R. Banerjii. "The Role of Transfer Between Similar Problem States." *Cognitive Psychology* 6 (1974): 436–450.

Richards, Robert J. *The Meaning of Evolution*. Chicago: University of Chicago Press, 1992.

Rothenberg, Albert. "Artistic Creation As Stimulated by Superimposed Versus Combined-Opposite Visual Images." *Journal of Personality and Social Psychology* 50 (1986): 370–381.

——, and Carl Hausman, eds. *The Creativity Question*. Durham, NC: Duke University Press, 1976.

——. *The Emerging Goddess: The Creative Process in Art, Science and Other Fields*. Chicago: University of Chicago Press, 1989.

Runes, Dagobert, ed. *The Diary and Sundry Observations of Thomas Alva Edison*, reprint ed. New York: Greenwood Press, 1968.

Russell, Bertrand. *Basic Writings of Bertrand Russell*. New York: Simon & Schuster, 1961 (out of print).

Schapiro, Meyer. *Paul Cézanne*. New York: Harry N. Abrams, 1983.

Senge, Peter. *The Fifth Discipline*. New York: Doubleday, 1990.

Seward, A. C. *Darwin and Modern Science*. Cambridge, MA: Cambridge University Press, 1909 (out of print).

Shrady, Maria. *Moments of Insight*. New York: Harper & Row, 1972 (out of print).

Simonton, Dean K. "Genius and Chance: A Darwinian Perspective." In *Creativity*, edited by J. Brockman.

——. *Scientific Genius*. New York: Cambridge University Press, 1988.

——. "Emergence and Realization of Genius: The Lives and Works of 120 Classical Composers." *Journal of Personality and Social Psychology* 60 (1991): 607–619.

——. "Foresight in Insight? A Darwinian Answer." In *The Nature of Insight*, edited by R. J. Sternberg and J. E. Davidson. Cambridge, MA: MIT Press, 1992.

——. *Greatness, Who Makes History and Why*. New York: The Guilford Press, 1994.

——. *Genius, Creativity and Leadership*. Cambridge, MA: Harvard University Press, 1984.

Skinner, B. F. *The Science of Behavior*. New York: Macmillan, 1953 (out of print).

Sloboda, John. *The Musical Mind*. New York: Oxford University Press, 1986.

Smith, S. M., and S. E. Blenkenship. "Incubation Effects." *Bulletin of the Psychonomic Society* 2 (1994): 31–49.

Stager, R. *A History of Psychological Theories*. New York: Macmillan, 1988 (out of print).

Stein, M. *Stimulating Creativity*, vols I and II. New York: Academic Press, 1974 (out of print).

Sternberg, R. J., and J. Davidson, eds. *The Nature of Insight*. Cambridge, MA: MIT Press, 1994 (out of print).

——. *Beyond I.Q.* New York: Cambridge University Press, 1984.

——. "Implicit Theories of Intelligence, Creativity and Wisdom." *Journal of Personality and Social Psychology* 49 (1985): 607–677.

—, ed. *The Nature of Creativity*. New York: Cambridge University Press, 1988.

Suler, J. R., and J. Rizziello. "Imagery and Verbal Processes in Creativity." *Journal of Creative Behavior* 21 (1987): 1–6.

Tax, S. *Evolution After Darwin*. Chicago: University of Chicago Press, 1960 (out of print).

Taylor, C., and F. Barron, eds. *Scientific Creativity*. New York: Wiley (out of print).

Thagard, Paul. *Mental Leaps: Analogy in Creative Thought*, reprint ed. Cambridge, MA: MIT Press, 1996.

Treffinger, J., S. K. Isakesen, and R. L. Firestien. *Handbook of Creative Learning*. New York: Center for Creative Learning, 1982 (out of print).

Tsanoff, Radoslav. *The Ways of Genius*. New York: Harper & Row, 1949 (out of print).

Tufte, Edward. *The Visual Display of Quantitative Information*. Cheshire, CT: Graphics Press, 1983.

Vesari, Giorgio. *Lives of the Artists*. New York: Viking Penguin, 1988.

Vosniadou, Stella, and A. Ortony, eds. *Similarity and Analogical Reasoning*. New York: Cambridge University Press, 1989 (out of print).

Wallace, Doris B., and H. E. Gruber, eds. *Creative People at Work*. New York: Oxford University Press, 1992.

Wallach, Michael. *The Intelligence-Creativity Distinction*. Morristown, NJ: General Learning Corporation, 1971 (out of print).

Wallas, G. *The Art of Thought*. New York: Harcourt, Brace, 1926 (out of print).

Watson, P. "Reasoning." *New Horizons in Psychology*, vol. 1. Harmondsworth, Middlesex: Penguin, 1966 (out of print).

Watson, James. *The Double Helix*. New York: NAL-Dutton, 1969.

Wechsler, J., ed. *On Aesthetics in Science*. Cambridge, MA: Birkhauser, 1987.

Weisberg, Robert. *Creativity, Genius and Other Myths*. New York: Freeman, 1986.

——; M. DiCamillo, and D. Phillips. "Transferring Old Associations to New Problems." *Journal of Verbal Learning and Verbal Behavior* 17 (1978): 219–228.

Wertheimer, Max. *Productive Thinking*, reprint ed. Westport, CT: Greenwood Press, 1978.

Westfall, Richard S. *Never at Rest: A Biography of Isaac Newton*. New York: University of Cambridge Press, 1983.

White, John H. *The Amerian Railroad Passenger Car*. Baltimore: John Hopkins University Press, 1985.

White, R. K. "The Versatility of Genius." *Journal of Social Psychology* 2 (1931): 460–489.

Williams, George. *Adaptation and Natural Selection*. Princeton, NJ: Princeton University Press, 1974.

Williams, L. *Michael Faraday: A Biography*. New York: Basic Books, 1965 (out of print).

Wilson, Edward O. *On Human Nature*. Cambridge, MA: Harvard University Press, 1978.

——. *The Diversity of Life*. Cambridge, MA: Harvard University Press, 1992.

Winner, Ellen. *Invented Worlds*. Cambridge, MA: Harvard University Press, 1982.

Zubo, V. P. *Leonardo da Vinci*. Ann Arbor, MI: Books on Demand (out of print).

Zuckerman, H. *Sensation Seeking*. Hillsdale, NJ: Erlbaum, 1979 (out of print).

Contact the Author

The author welcomes your comments about the material in this book or his other works, which include *Thinkertoys (A Handbook of Business Creativity)* and *ThinkPak (A Brainstorming Card Set)*. Both are published by Ten Speed Press (800-841-BOOK).

Michael Michalko
165 Percy Road
Churchville, NY 14428
Email: michalko@frontiernet.net

Also by Michael Michalko:

Thinkertoys
This idea-generating sourcebook presents dozens of field-tested, immediately useable tools for generating ideas and stimulating creativity.
7 3/8 x 9 1/4 inches, 352 pages, ISBN 0-89815-408-1

ThinkPak
An unusual creativity tool, this deck of 56 idea-stimulating cards can
help anyone come up with ideas for inventing or improving products,
services, systems, and companies.
4 3/8 x 7 inch box w/ booklet, 56 cards, ISBN 0-89815-607-6

For more information, or to order, call the publisher at the number
below. We accept VISA, Mastercard, and American Express. You may
also wish to write for our free catalog of over 500 books, posters, and
audiotapes.

Ten Speed Press   800-841-BOOK
P.O. Box 7123   order@tenspeed.com
Berkeley, CA 94707   www.tenspeedpress.com

INDEX